The Politics
of Writing
in Iran

The Politics of Writing in Iran

A History of Modern Persian Literature

Kamran Talattof

Syracuse University Press

The paper used in this publication meets the minimum requirements of American National Standard for Information Sciences—Permanence of Paper for Printed Library Materials, ANSI Z39.48'1984. ∞™

Library of Congress Cataloging-in-Publication Data

Talattof, Kamran.
    The politics of writing in Iran : a history of modern Persian literature / Kamran Talattof. — 1st ed.
        p. cm.
    Originally presented as the author's thesis (Ph. D.)—University of Michigan, 1996.
    Includes bibliographical references (p.) and index.
    ISBN 0-8156-2818-8 (cloth : alk. paper). — ISBN 0-8156-2819-6 (pbk. : alk. paper)
    1. Persian literature—20th century—History and criticism.
    2. Politics and literature—Iran—History—20th century.
    3. Literature and society—Iran—History—20th century. 4. Literary movements—Iran. I. Title.
    PK6415.5.T35 1999
    891'.5509358—dc21 99-37867

To the courageous women of Iran
and the Middle East

Kamran Talattof teaches Persian language and literature and Iranian culture at the University of Arizona and has taught at Princeton University, the University of Michigan, and Ohio State University. He is coeditor of *Contemporary Debates in Islam: An Anthology of Modernist and Fundamentalist Thought* (with Mansoor Moaddel) and *The Poetry of Nizami Ganjavi: Knowledge, Love, and Rhetoric* (with Jerome Clinton), and he has completed an English translation with Jocelyn Sharlet of *Women Without Men* by Shahrnush Parsipur for Syracuse University Press.

Contents

Preface

IN THIS BOOK I EXPLAIN THE PATTERN of literary change in Iran and provide an understanding of the formation of modern Persian literary history. I focus on the relationship between the constructive elements of literary creativity, literary movement, ideology, and the metaphors that modern Persian authors have used to express their ideological concerns. I complicate conventional situations of structuralism by analyzing the effects of historicism on the production and reception of literary texts in Iran. I suggest that Persian literary history is not an integrated continuum but a series of distinct episodic movements shaped by shifting ideologies of representation. Emerging in the late nineteenth and early twentieth centuries as a secular activity, Persian literature grasped its own modernity by reencoding past aesthetic practices in terms of new conceptions of identity and historicity. Since then—drawing, in part, on concepts of ideology derived from Western paradigms—modern Persian literature responds to changing social and political conditions through developing complex strategies of metaphorical and allegorical representations capable of both constructing and denouncing cultural continuities.

Thus, I have several objectives: (1) to offer an analytical model for understanding literary change by defining literary movement, ideology, and metaphor; (2) to illustrate the connection between literature and ideology; (3) to analyze the themes and symbolic configurations of Persian literature and their formative influence on social movements, such as the 1979 Iranian Revolution; (4) to identify the ideological differences between literary products before and after the Revolution; and (5) to explore how literary changes are due to the impact of social movements. I address these issues through the analysis of selected works of major pre- and postrevolutionary literary figures. I survey their works according to the author's gender, the date of publication, and their popularity as reflected in the number of printings.

By pointing out the limitations of structuralism, which has dominated Persian literary criticism, I hope that this theory-driven analysis of the historical development of contemporary literature will better illustrate that factors such as class struggle, state politics, and economic dependency cannot fully explain the complexity of Iranian historical experience. A thorough historiography must take into account the seriousness of literary activity in this society.

This book is the revised version of my dissertation which I submitted in partial fulfillment of the requirements of the degree of Doctor of Philosophy (Near Eastern Studies) at the University of Michigan in 1996. I am grateful to Ahmad Karimi Hakkak, Mansoor Moaddel, Michael Beard, Farzaneh Milani, Mary Muller, James Stewart-Robinson, Nasrin Rahimieh, and Caryl Emerson, who provided me with timely comments. I have benefited from the works of these and many other scholars who have written on different aspects of Iranian and Middle Eastern studies especially gender and literature. I am also grateful to Bettie McDavid Mason and Mary Murrell for their intellectual seriousness and dedication through the editorial stage of this book. I am most thankful to my mother who first planted the seed of love for education and scholarship within me. Without the help, support, and encouragement provided by my family, Christine and Arjang, this book would not have been possible. I would also like to thank the University of Michigan and Princeton University for the grants that supported my research.

A Note on Translation and Transliteration

EXCEPT FOR A FEW MODIFICATIONS, I have kept within the bounds of literal translation, trying to remain as faithful as possible to the original. The title of every nonprimary source (Persian, Arabic, Turkish, etc.) is accompanied by a literal English translation of the title the first time it appears and is only referred to by the translated title thereafter. If an English translation of any of the works cited exists, a footnote provides its bibliographical information. I have developed this practice solely to maintain an easy flow within the English text, and it should not be assumed that an entire English translation of every text exists. In the few cases where I have benefited from previous translations, the footnotes also indicate those sources.

In transliterating the names of authors and individuals and the titles of books, short stories, poems, and other writings, I have adopted the Library of Congress system of transliteration (without the diacritical marks) to provide a more accessible bibliography. Exceptions include names and titles that are directly quoted from other sources and those terms that have entered common usage, such as Reza Shah and Tehran. I have used the ending ih instead of ah (for example Jamalzadih instead of Jamalzadah that is used by the Library of Congress System of Transliteration) because most modern works have been transliterated with this spelling in recent years. I have used ' for hamza and ' for ayn. Also, in transliterating selected poems and passages, I have modified this system in order to reproduce as closely as possible the sound of the Persian original.

The Politics
of Writing
in Iran

1

Introduction: Episodic Literary Movement—A Model for Understanding Literary History

> "I hear voices in everything and the dialogic
> relationship between them."
> —Bakhtin

THIS BOOK CONTRIBUTES to ongoing theoretical projects that uncover the ideological presuppositions behind literary practices. A considerable number of literary critics have emphasized the importance of ideology in literary creativities by challenging nonideological or at least nonpolitical approaches toward literature.[1] According to Spivak, for example, ideology is unavoidable and one cannot "step out of" it.[2] Likewise, Sinfield explains that "ideology produces, makes plausible, concepts and systems to explain who we are, who the others are, how the world works."[3] And Eagleton believes that the category of the aesthetic is in direct relation to the dominant forms of ideology in class and society and that "the construction of the modern notion of the aesthetic artifact is thus inseparable from the construction of the dominant ideological forms of class-society, and indeed from a whole new form of human subjectivity appropriate to the social order."[4] These keen observers provide insight into the question of ideology and its influence on literature, but they do not explain the factors that determine an ideology of representation (an ideology as the impetus for the act of representation) and how it is produced. They do not explain why authors write what they write and when they write. Thus their perspectives have little practical application in the study of literatures, such as Persian, that have been highly ideological in their representation.

1

Because of repressive political conditions, authoritarian regimes, and censorship in Iran, conscientious Persian authors have tended to encode their political ideas in order to avoid persecution. Consequently, they use metaphors to describe social problems and criticize the political system.[5] Such subtle means of conveying ideological stances become a constitutive feature of literary works. By communicating their ideas, modern authors participate in a collective action to promote a certain type of ideology. At times the ideologies they promote are Western, and their adoption by Iranian intellectuals requires understanding the problematic of ideology and its role in the formation of the history of modern Persian literature.

The few scholars who have focused to some extent on the ideological or political aspects of modern Persian literature adopt one of two limited approaches. A few, such as Kritzeck, Hakimi, Field, Browne, Jafari, Hairi, and Mudaris, see literature as the product of Islamic culture and indiscriminately read diverse literary texts of different eras expecting to find some Islamic elements. For these scholars Islam, as a system of symbols, represents the most significant factor in the explanation of the cultural, intellectual, and literary history of Iran, and thus they understand Persian literature only as an Islamic ideological presentation. Kritzeck, for example, classifies the literary works written during the modern period as "modern Islamic literature," and Hakimi recommends the study of literature as a "means of increasing and protecting Islamic culture."[6] For other scholars, such as Sipanlu, Gulsurkhi, Sultanpur, Dawlatabadi, and Huquqi, the key concept in determining what they consider "true literature" has been the text's contribution to the revolutionary movement against the Iranian authoritarian states and the role it may play in the struggle against the ruling powers. They value modern Persian literature only on the basis of the authors' commitment to the people's cause and thus disdain literary texts that are not committed to such social issues. To evaluate a literary text, these scholars adhere to Marxist literary criticism and its classification of literary works according to their degree of commitment to social causes.[7] Sipanlu, for example, believes the criterion for distinguishing a true literary work" is that it contain "the essential elements of social justice and general aspects of the peoples' poor social condition."[8]

Although these approaches illuminate some nuances of Persian literature from particular periods, they are utterly incapable of explaining the broader issues of problematics of ideology of representation, literary change, and the history of modern Persian literature. They generalize extensively and they overlook the ideological interaction between a literary work and the discursive context within which the work was produced and ignore the fact that such interactions have given rise to diverse literary and social movements over time. Further, such approaches limit the reading and, ironically, serve views such as structuralism that disregard the role of ideology and politics in the study of literature.

The impact of ideology on the formation of modern Persian literature is more complex. Persian literary history is not an integrated continuum but a series of distinct episodes distinguishable by their ideology of representation. The study of this literary history therefore requires perspectives cognizant of such a pattern of literary change. This book, which approaches the analysis of modern literature in terms of ideology of representation, literary movements, and metaphor, offers an analytical model that views modern Persian literature as a set of episodic literary movements. This concept forces attention upon the constructive role of ideology in the production of modern Persian literature and explains its history as a combination of several distinctive episodic literary movements. It also leads to a redefinition of ideology in terms of metaphor, which both ideological and literary utterances share.

Literary Movements in Modern Persian Literature

Modern Persian literature emerged during the late nineteenth and early twentieth centuries as a secular activity and has since demonstrated close affinity to such diverse ideological paradigms as nationalism, Marxism, feminism, and Islamism. Each ideological paradigm has, in its own way, influenced the form, characterization, and figurative language of literary texts. It has set the criteria for indigenous literary criticism and has determined which issues related to politics, religion, or culture are to be the focus of literary journals.[9] And these ideological features have changed in an episodic fashion according to the prevailing social and political conditions. The contact between literary and ideological paradigms has determined the politics of writing.

Persianism: A Literary Revolution

I venture the term *Persianism* to describe the earliest modern literary movement, which has been referred to as "modernist" or "nationalist" by other scholars. It emerged during the late nineteenth century and early twentieth century, when traditional forms of poetry came under attack by a new wave of writers who, mostly through their contact with the West, approached literature in a radically different way. The constitutional movement (1906–1911) and later Reza Shah's project to modernize Iran provided further encouragement for the development of this movement.[10] This literary episode was characterized by modernist ideas such as the use of Western literary forms, new styles, and the promotion of nontraditional culture. Such ideas shaped the thematic and figurative features of literary works in this period, but the authors exceeded the simple expression of these aspirations. These authors sought, on the one hand, to modernize society through the reform of the Persian language and, on the other, regarded traditional culture of the Qajar period and religion as barriers to the evolution of Persian literature. "Persianism" therefore refers to an ideology that not only inspired authors to write in a new style with the hope of modernizing literature but also made that ideology the theme of literary works. Muhammad Ali Jamalzadih's "Farsi Shikar Ast" (Persian Is Sugar), Sadiq Hidayat's *Buf-i Kur* (Blind Owl), Jalal Al-i Ahmad's *Sih Tar* (Seh Tar), Khusraw Shahani's "Murdih Kishi" (Pallbearing), and Nima Yushij's "Manili" all exemplify this literary episode in Iran, which is the focus of chapter 2.

Committed Literature: A Revolutionary Literature

The term *Committed Literature* generally refers to the works of writers who dedicate themselves to the advocacy of certain beliefs and agendas, especially those related to political and ideological efforts in bringing about social reform.[11] Marxist and leftist authors are a prime example of this trend, as they show a strong commitment toward the people's cause, social change, and social welfare.[12] The terms *Marxist, resistance,* and *leftist literature* have been used interchangeably in Iran to describe the pervasive literary movement of the 1940s to the 1970s, which I consider the second episode of modern Persian literature.

The ideological presuppositions of this episode began to appear after the abdication of Reza Shah in 1941 and during a period of what was, relatively speaking, political freedom when the growth of socialist activities provided a stimulus for the spread of Marxist ideas into literature. Committed Literature gained dominance in the 1950s—after the monarchy was reestablished through a coup d'état in 1953 and after Muhammad Reza Shah began authoritarian rule. This literary movement subsequently played a central role in the rise of the revolutionary movement and then promptly declined after the 1979 Revolution.

During this period Marxist ideology shaped the works of the majority of writers, whose themes revolved around issues of equality, justice, and freedom, colored by Iran's own cultural particularities. These authors, holding the monarchy responsible for the violation of human rights and for social injustice, committed themselves to the struggle against the Shah's rule. Hushang Gulshiri's "Arusak-i Chini-i Man" (My China Doll), Samad Bihrangi's *Mahi Siyah-i Kuchulu* (The Little Black Fish), and the poetry of Ahmad Shamlu and Khusraw Gulsurkhi are among the prominent examples of works produced by this literary movement in Iran.

As I have argued elsewhere, in this episode Iranian women writers, like the men, emphasized social and political issues such as social justice and political freedom more than specific gender issues.[13] Although they presented themes related to women, they offered them in the context of male-dominated leftist literature. The themes, style, form, and figurative language of Committed Literature remained dominant in this women's literature until the 1979 Revolution. Simin Danishvar's *Savushun* (Savushun) and the poetry of Furugh Farrukhzad and Simin Bihbahani supported Committed Literature. This episode will be covered in chapter 3.

Islamic Literature

The 1979 Revolution replaced a secular authoritarian regime with a religious state. The state immediately began to suppress Marxist and other leftist activities that had increased during the course of the revolution (1976–79), causing literary communities to decentralize. Without the hegemony of Committed Literature, other social and literary discourses, such as Islamic literature, emerged. This episode took shape as authors began to write fiction and poetry wholly inspired by the events of the Islamic movements, contemporary Islamic politics, and religious concepts. The decline of the Marxist literary movement and the simultaneous rise of political Islam to state ideology after the 1979 Iranian Revolution provided the context for the rise of this episode, which I refer to as *modern Islamic literature* or the *literature of the Islamic Revolution*. After the Revolution, Islamic political ideas, for the first time, became substantial themes in the works of a great number of Iranian Muslim writers. The Islamic government and religious leaders frequently emphasized that art and literature are important for advancing the Islamization of society, and they have helped to create a wide readership for Muslim writers through their oratory. Moreover, religious critics attempted to define and regulate this Islamic literary movement by determining their own aesthetic criteria in harmony with state ideology. Muhammad Nurizad's "Mard va Karbala" (The Man and Karbala), Nusrat Allah Mahmudzadih's *Marsiah Halabchih* (The Elegy of Halabja), and Muhsin Makhmalbaf's "Mara Bibus" (Kiss Me) and *Bagh-i Bulur* (The Crystal Garden) exemplify more established Islamic fiction. The works of Musavi Garmarudi and Tahirih Saffarzadah represent contemporary Islamic poetry in Iran. Chapter 4 will study this episode.

Feminist Literary Movement

The 1979 Revolution, ironically, created a new context for innovative ways of culture production and provided grounds for exploring the connection between ideology and literature. One prominent example of the impact of the Revolution is the change in the themes of women's writing from prerevolutionary social issues to a postrevolutionary feminist consciousness. In the postrevolutionary period, feminist themes and gender issues have gained central significance. Women's demonstrations against mandatory veiling immediately after the Revolution initiated this shift and then provided a context not only for the articulation but also for the expansion of feminist discourse. Shahrnush Parsipur's *Zanan Bidun-i Mardan* (Women Without Men), and Muniru Ravanipur's *Sangha-yi Shaytan* (Satan's Stones) exemplify this new literary movement. The postrevolutionary works of Simin Bihbahani and Simin Danishvar, when compared with their earlier works, demonstrate that a shift in women's literary discourse has indeed occurred. Chapter 5 explores this episode of modern Persian literature, in which postrevolutionary Iranian women's writings turn to feminism.

An analysis of all of these movements supports the contention that because of changes in the social context, literary shifts occur in an episodic fashion and that state ideology and political opposition play a determinative role in shaping literary movements. Moreover, it attests that each literary episode chronicles the change in relationship between authors and readers. By canonizing words, metaphors, and genres, through their individual creativity, and by creating a loyal readership, literary activists in each episode create a consensus within the opposition (and sometimes in support of the state), reflecting the political culture of the ruling elites. Thus a full understanding of canons is possible only through a full understanding of gender, culture, and ideology and when the ideological paradigms come into contact with each other. By defusing conflicting views and inviting all readers to participate in the dominant movement, a univocal practice influences individual responses to culture production. This is the fundamental function of each episodic literary movement.

This is not to say that there is absolutely no continuity in the process of literary production. Some of the tropes and metaphors from the classical period (such as those portraying gardens and old men), some Sufi concepts (such as *pir* "wise mentor") and some Islamic references (such as the incidents of Karbala) appear in modern episodes of Persian literature. *Shab* (night) continued to be used in all episodes as a powerful image. Islamic literature continued to use the Committed Literature's forms. However, the implementation of these persistent metaphors and forms is quite different in each period and in each episode. *Shab*, for example, meant "religious tradition" in Persianism, "Shah's dictatorial rule" in Committed Literature, "the past" in Islamic literature, and "patriarchy" in many women's writings in the postrevolutionary period. And Islamic authors employed committed forms for a truly subversive purpose. Moreover, although there is one dominant trend in each episode, works can be found that either represent an earlier episode or that can be considered early antecedents of a future episode. In each period there are, of course, works that not only reflect their time but also carry some of the great aspects of classical Persian literature or carry an idea that even can be appealing to future generations. *Blind Owl* has in it a resonance the *Ruba'iyat* of *Khayyam* (d. 1122) and *Kalidar* resonate *the Book of Kings* of Firdawsi (932–1020). These kinds of works can be more easily analyzed over and over for their literary values. But they too reflect their time. For each episode, I have selected important works of the most prominent writers (well published, well discussed, often emulated by other writers) for my analyses. However, I believe that once the scope and definition of each episode is set, it will be easy to detect the dominant discourse of the time in other writers' works.

Episodic Literary Movement

How can one explain the overriding significance of a particular ideological issue in literary works of each episode? What factors explain the
shifts in literary creativity? Why is the literature of each episode
marked by a certain set of themes and a specific figurative language?
And, in particular, what are the themes, types of characters, forms,
metaphors, and discursive contexts that characterize the nature of literary production in each episode?

To answer these questions, I put forward the concept of episodic literary movement. Using this model, I argue that literary production, as
a cultural phenomenon, is a discontinuous process that evolves within
movements and in an episodic fashion. Although broader social and
personal factors are important in the formation of literary works, the
actual process of producing literary meanings can be most successfully
analyzed within the dynamic of the discursive context of the movements within which the meanings are produced. In fact, in each literary movement, literary meanings conveyed through theme (the
substance, the idea), characterization (the dialogue, the strategy of
behavior), form (the shape, the structure), and style (the mode of
expression, the figurative language) always force a reflection upon
their changing social and historical conditions and their discursive
context. From this perspective and by locating the text in the context of
its movement, a thorough understanding of the encoded meaning is
more possible. Such a point of view also makes an explanation of literary history more plausible.

To explain this model and my argument, I will first define the constitutive elements of the concept of episodic literary movement one by
one: literary episode, ideology of representation, the metaphors that
convey the ideology, literary movement, and discursive interpretation.
In doing so, I also intend to offer an alternative definition of ideology
in terms of metaphor.

Literary Episode

A literary episode is a cluster of interrelated, aesthetically significant
literary texts that form a discursive movement in a particular historical period. Each cluster demonstrates a harmony within itself and a difference from others. A literary episode is thematic and temporal, a
convergence of meanings at a particular time. It contains a collection

of provisional, debated meanings. In an episode, as in Foucault's notion of the historical "episteme," the emphasis is on discontinuity rather than smooth progression or continuity.[14] By episode, therefore, I refer to a segment of literary history, a segment that is integral to, yet separable from, a history of literature. Literary history, in this view, consists of various discontinuous literary episodes.

By "episodic," then, I refer to the quality attributed to a succession of loosely connected events within a literary history. Episodes occur in succession and may overlap with insignificant interrelationship. Because no direct connections exist between episodes, any one of them could be studied alone without serious damage to the perception of the whole. The concept of episodic literary movement helps not only to discern the shifting ideologies of representation and the pattern of literary change in Iran, but also to explain this discontinuous process of literary production by reflecting upon its changing discursive context and the predominant social movement.

In conceptualizing the idea of literary episode, I have benefited from Moaddel's notion of episode in his works on ideological production, Saussure's concept of binary opposition, and Bakhtin's theoretical contentions on ideological sign systems. Moaddel describes the production of ideology as a discontinuous process that proceeds in an episodic fashion.[15] He also argues that the state's discourse plays a decisive role in the construction of the opposition's ideology, forcing it to construct an agenda of its own and to define its identity.[16] This sociological model has a close affinity to the works of Saussure, for whom the production of signs and their meanings should be understood in relation to other signs, not in terms of the actual object (i.e., the signified).[17] Identities, for Saussure, are the result of difference, although, as Derrida reveals, difference itself results in meanings that are unstable and undecidable.[18]

Bakhtin, yet more relevant, perceives language as plural and multiple, a socioideological sign system laden with "evaluative accents" and closely bound up with material contexts of its production.[19] Bakhtin's theory of narrative helps clarify the process of literary discourse. He states that each literary enunciation is a form of literary discourse that should be seen as shaping both the speech and consciousness of the hero.[20] He also insists, as Emerson notes, that the world of each concrete text has a voice and a character that demand constant rethinking and reinterpretation and that are designed to encourage a response.[21] Finally, Bakhtin's theory of "the dialogic" explains the relationship between the author and social and literary conventions. Herrmann explains: "In its most general terms, the dialogic views language as social practice, as the struggle between language systems within a particular sociohistorical context. When that struggle ends, the word becomes monologic, limited to a monolithic symbolic system characterized by arbitrary political power and literary convention." This struggle engages the subjects in dialogue and thus informs their ideological utterances and, consequently, their position within a social system. Herrmann concludes that, based on the theory of the dialogic, the relationship between the female writer and her themes and characters is similar to the relationship between the female writer and the dominant literary discourse.[22] However, as Emerson aptly notices, "utterance" for Bakhtin does not mean simply the "outer struggle" between ideologies, but also implies that any utterance reflects numerous internal struggles through the unforgettable nature of the uttered words, layered intonations, time, and context. As a consequence, their full power or meaning cannot be realized until uttered within a certain context. Indeed, the fact that words convey "potential struggle" concerns Bakhtin more than other struggles waged, won, or lost at any given moment. Therefore, "utterance," as he employs it, lacks the stability and abstract versatility of a metaphor.[23]

Ideology of Representation

By the phrase "ideology of representation," I refer to any ideology that leads to literary representation and may cause a particular literary practice to prevail in a particular period once the ideology is advocated by literary communities. It also refers to the attributes of literary creativity through which any text becomes ideologically engaged. Ideology, in general, whether that of the state or of the opposition, is a characteristic aspect of life, and representation in literary or nonliterary forms provides insight into politics and history.[24] According to many, ideology is in close relationship with discourse. Moaddel conceptualizes ideology as "a discourse consisting of a set of general principles, concepts, symbols, and rituals used by actors to address problems in a particular historical episode."[25] For Eagleton, ideology "can also denote any significant conjuncture between discourse and political interests."[26] And it is true that ideologies are matters of "discourse" and exist only in relation to other ideologies and that the conceptualization of ideology as discourse provides an understanding of the way in which ideology functions in social processes, especially in culture production. However, the empirical facts about the discontinuous nature of cultural activities and historical developments in Iran force another approach to the definition of ideology and the concept of discourse.

I believe ideology guides the conceptual and perceptual system within which its advocate thinks, communicates, and acts. It has a similar constructive impact on the advocates of a literary movement and on the metaphors they use in the representation of certain social and literary issues. Ideology is not therefore simply a set of ideas associated with certain social classes or a hierarchy of values used to justify human actions, but rather a movemental element determined according to the syntagmatic and paradigmatic rules of expression. Once established in forms of social, religious, or literary discourses, ideologies motivate political movements and create new semantic systems. Ideology has a constructive impact on literary representations, and, because it is based on the ever-changing social context, it makes literary production a discontinuous process. This impact is not always immediately obvious but it does always problematize reading, and the result is different modes of interpretation. More specifically, reading is problematic because ideological representations contain unstable ideological metaphors. Thus ideology can be best defined in terms of metaphor.

It is indeed through metaphors that ideologies are often imported. The dominant ideology of the opposition and even the state's general discourse are frequently related to imported ideologies, be it from Europe or promoted by socialist or other international movements. Each episode shows readiness to adhere to a broader international trend. The rise of Persianism, Marxism, Islamic fundamentalism, and feminism did not occur in Iran in isolation; as will be discussed in the conclusion, the Arab countries and Turkey have experienced similar changes. In each of these places, internal conflicts create an oppositional force which, inspired by international and regional sociocultural trends, freely borrows ideas from them in the form of metaphors and other tropes. That is, the intellectual opposition constructs its ideology in relation to a host of sources: the state's ideology, universal ideologies that are available to the members, the class from which the majority of the opposition hails, and miscellaneous resources acquired.

Metaphor

Metaphor is more than a linguistic feature. It is a mode in which things and signs are perceived in terms of other things and signs and thus belongs to the realm of cultural episodes.[27] It functions as a means of communication between literary systems, language systems, and systems of thought, which are inevitably related to each other. Yet how are these systems interrelated? How is a sign carried from one systemic unit, such as a political entity, to another, such as literature? Which figures of language actually convey the ideological signs? Among literary devices, metaphor serves as a means through which ideology and other paradigms, including literature, converse with one another. Moreover, metaphors, as they function on behalf of ideology in literary texts, act as agents in social movement. Because they convey ideology, metaphors are more often than not determined by the dominant literary movement of their time. Thus the connection between ideology and literature is best understood as the locus where metaphors convey social realities.[28]

In prerevolutionary Iran, the notion of revolution heavily influenced and in fact shaped social and literary discourses. From the mid fifties until the late seventies, literary works were intended primarily to express the authors' feelings about oppression, deprivation, personal and collective unfulfillment, and other social and personal problems. However, because ideological premises could not be expressed openly— say, as a party manifesto—they were conveyed implicitly in works of literature. Hence the importance of metaphor transcended the realm of literary creativity. Through metaphorical language authors expressed these concerns and offered a utopia attainable only through social change. These metaphors not only shaped the ideology of both writers and their audiences but also influenced readers' lives. Metaphors directed writers' inspiration, shaped their language, and, like ideology, guided the conceptual and perceptual system through which their readers thought, communicated, and acted.[29] Metaphors established an implicit and sometimes explicit parallel with ideology. They helped the reader understand the meaning of the text and assist in defining the hidden ideological message.

Thus ideology may be best conceptualized as a set of more or less structured metaphors that express people's ideals and direct their activities in a movement. As Geertz states, "In metaphor one has, of course, a stratification of meaning, in which an incongruity of sense on one level produces an influx of significance on another." The power of metaphor is inextricably dependent on the ideology that lies in those "deeper discordant layers" of meaning.[30]

Metaphors vary from episode to episode accordingly. They change because they are not only linguistic and rhetorical devices but also parts of speech that explain new conditions. They are arbitrary but, as signs, exist in relation to other signs, activities, and cultural experiences. As a result, each episodic literary movement can be said to transcend literary language not only because it has a thematic relation with real life but also because the literary metaphor plays a vital role in shaping the conceptual system of the advocates of that movement. Indeed, this changing ideological function of metaphor as the representational aspect of language helps elucidate the change in literary enunciations.

The production and use of metaphor is, like ideology, a discontinuous process that proceeds in an episodic fashion. As they make the transition from the classical period of Persian literature, some images, lexical elements, and signs undergo a lexical and metaphorical metamorphosis in which they are emptied of their conventional meanings. Others do not. These metaphors change both syntagmatically and paradigmatically in order to express hope and define activities. Let us consider the example of the word "night" (shab), which illustrates these points. The definition of "night" in modern Persian literature is a departure from that of the classical period. In classical literature, as Karimi-Hakkak, explains, night is "an absolute entity much like the spring."[31] Night for the advocate of literary modernism, on the contrary, serves as a metaphor for a personal state of mind: loneliness, desperation, or hopelessness. These feelings may belong to the protagonist's mood and state of mind, but they also reflect cultural problems. When the committed authors in a later episode express the consequences of a despotic regime in terms of the darkness (siyahi) of the night (shab) and praise the result of a revolution in terms of brightness (rushanaʾi) of the day (ruz), they establish a coherent metaphorical and/or ideological system in relation to the ideology of the ruling elite.

Accordingly, Iranian readers tend not to take the word "night" for night, "day" for day, or "spring" for spring. Instead, readers take these words as metaphors that stand for other things, interpreting them as life under dictatorship, being free to live in a free society, or being able to look forward to a bright future respectively. Iranian writers assign multiple levels of meanings to words and expect the readers to decipher them.[32] In Committed Literature, the metaphor of night is of a political nature, in postrevolutionary feminist discourse, night indicates patriarchy, and in Islamic discourse it signifies the era of anti-Islamic kings. Under such conditions the texts become so deeply coded that the message can be uncovered neither at the literal level nor through a structural analysis of the text but rather through understanding the author's ideology of representation; the authors' metaphors.

Let us consider another example. In Persian literature themes have frequently appeared that are related to the historical events of the Battle of Karbala in 680 C.E., when Husayn ibn Ali ibn Abi Talib, the third Shiite imam, and his small group of supporters and family (seventy-two armed men plus women and children) were murdered by Yazid (of the Umayyad dynasty). Karbala, however, has held various meanings in the modern period. For the pioneer modernist fiction writer, Hidayat, it has signified traditionalism and backwardness. For authors of Committed Literature such as Danishvar and Dawlatabadi, Karbala symbolizes resistance and rebellion. For recent Muslim authors under the Islamic states, it holds religious significance. Even the absence of Karbala metaphors in the postrevolutionary feminist movement is not accidental; Iranian women writers have no use for them nor can they afford the consequences at the hands of the state that are sure to follow upon any feminist approach to that event. Therefore, the treatment of Karbala metaphors in every episode has been entirely ideological.

Another example of the production and use of metaphor in modern Persian literature specifically involves the postrevolutionary feminist movement. Iranian feminists, frustrated by persistent male domination and sexism and hoping for a society in which gender discrimination is abolished, use metaphors that are not sexually objective. They subvert the male-dominated literature, especially when they deal with cultural and sexual oppression. They sabotage forms of imagery produced by men and transgress the boundaries between these forms. Their language, as Bakhtin's dialogic suggests, becomes social practice.[33] Their metaphors then refer to the body, which is often the object of control. Their metaphors subvert the established language as they bring to the foreground that which has traditionally been absent. New feminine style and thought (subversive thought) expressed through their metaphors may well bring about change and, to use Hélène Cixous' words, "be the precursory movement of a transformation of social and cultural standards."[34] In other words, the advent of modern ideologies in Iran, including Marxism, nationalism, feminism, and the recent Islamic discourse, attests to this affinity between ideology and metaphor.

When people compose metaphors in a system or when the people who use the metaphors organize themselves in a system in order to deal with common frustrations, their literary and nonliterary representations become highly ideological. Their metaphors stretch beyond the limits of the organizational boundary and thus turn into a discourse. I thus suggest here that discourse is the language of a certain ideological climate in which a section or a cross-section of society uses a common set of metaphors to communicate and consider social or aesthetic issues.

Literary Movement

These processes of ideological production are not totally disconnected and/or structured in the way that discourse is. They are at least connected through the language they use. The causal relationship between discourse (especially literary discourse) and ideology may therefore be better understood in terms of the relationship between metaphor and movement. The relationship between metaphor and movement can also explain the emergence of a new ideology of representation. And because the concept of movement is not as structured as discourse, it can explain some of the continuities that exist between episodes.

The term *movement*, as applied to a trend or development in literature, has a leftist, oppositional, and revolutionary connotation in Iranian contexts. The functions of a movement include the disclosure of social problems as well as the criticism—and, ultimately, the subversion—of the cultural or political system. One may think of a literary movement in terms of its ideology of representation. In that regard literary movements demonstrate a close affinity with other social movements, all inevitably displaying a "discursive" quality. However, as I have pointed out, a movement is different from a discourse in that the movement is not completely structured; its beginning and end are blurred. The product of one movement and its declining energy serve to create a new one. In a spiral pattern, a movement brings things from the past and transfers things into the future, and it gains energy in contact with other paradigms. A movement is at times quite organized and at other times detectable only through the presence of certain literary ideas and meanings that together advocate a certain ideology of representation.

Literary movements promote ideas and meanings through a specific language that has the characteristics of its own time and conditions.[35] The texts that carry these ideas and promote this literary language become significant. In this regard a literary movement shapes a literary episode and is related to the broader sociopolitical and oppositional movements of its time.

Discursive Interpretation

Literary movements also shape the way communities interpret literature. The dominant mode of reading in Iranian literary communities changes every time a new episode appears. Each movement has forced its own way of reading. These communities (which consist of authors and readers as well as literary critics, journalists, satirists, and film critics: all those who produce the country's high culture) show strong sensitivity to diverse social problems and try to solve them through writing and reading, using the dominant metaphors of their own time. They have existed since the rise of modernist literature, but in each episode their concerns transcend the realm of literary creativity. Their members, variously Persianist, Marxist, liberal, Muslim, and feminist, were sometimes organized in small groups and associations such as Anjoman-i Danishkadih (Association of Colleges), Kanun-i Navisandigan-i Iran (The Writers' Association of Iran) and sometimes gathered around a specific publication such as *Sukhan* (Speech), *Majallah Musiqi* (Journal of Music), and *Kaveh* (the name of a mythical hero). These communities have since been effective both inside and outside organized political groups and have been affected by the specific ideology in each episode. Their activities, such as writing, reading, and conversation, created and reflected changes in the role of the reader: from that of a passive reader who simply memorized the beautiful classical verses to that of an active reader who vigorously responds to politically significant texts.

By encouraging such a mode of reading, authors promote a subjectivity in their readers, teach them the desired way of interpreting a text, and establish a set of criteria for evaluating literature. Such an enterprise shapes the readers' literary tastes and teaches them to value political meaning more than literary form. This enterprise influenced the new generation of writers, who studied the established authors' works and then followed a mimetic pattern every time a movement arose.

Each episodic movement therefore affects the process of reading. Readers scrutinize tropes, figures, and metaphors to interpret the full range of syntactical and grammatical features in search of the implicit or explicit ideological message. Ideology correlates with literature not only because one is often embedded in the other or because they both share a certain set of metaphors, but also because ideology plays a role in the interpretation of literature. The dominant movement often influences such a reading and involves the reader in what can be conceptualized as discursive interpretation. Here again, the ideology is condensed into a set of metaphors that the author then uses to propagate ideas. For instance, through metaphors leftist literary activists wrote literary works to promote the cause of the people's struggle against the political system and dedicated poetry and short stories to the memory of those who lost their lives in this struggle. The readers received these messages through a figurative language in which metaphors and other tropes communicated the author's frustration with social problems.

Authors assume that the reader will interpret the text "positively," and readers often do react positively. For example, readers eagerly read the works of such authors as Bihrangi, Sultanpur, and Shamlu as protests against the shah's rule. Indeed, as I have noted above, literature in the prerevolutionary period served as a medium through which the advocates of leftist politics encouraged readers to comment on the ills of society and to act against injustice, inequality, and the lack of freedom. Many readers joined the revolutionary movement by reading the ideologically loaded works of the writers of Committed Literature. Dawlatabadi, a prominent Persian fiction writer, explains that when he was arrested by the secret police, he was told that one reason for his arrest was that every time police arrested oppositional political activists, they found his books in their houses.[36] Another example of the responsive contribution of readers to the writers' struggle was readers' active participation in the Ten Poetry Nights held by the Writers' Association of Iran in October 1977 in Tehran. On these nights writers recited poetry and gave lectures and indirectly addressed the question of freedom and justice.[37] Thousands of intellectuals, mostly students, participated in these meetings each night and commended the ideological messages that were enunciated through these literary works. Night by night, the gatherings grew increasingly aggressive until they finally turned into violent riots and demonstrations—which, in fact, marked the beginning of the popular uprising that precipitated the 1979 Revolution.

This sequence of events shows clearly that readers respond to authors' literary struggles by becoming involved in ideological interpretations of literary texts and acting upon them. One may conclude that, through reading, the movement functions within the text and, simultaneously, the literary text functions within the movement.

In brief, literary meanings are conveyed through the language of the text, its figures, and its textuality. However, no matter how unstable, these meanings refer to a transcendental signified outside the texts. Each episode in literary history represents specific literary meanings and semantic fields that are controlled, redefined, and expanded by the authors' ideology of representation. In other words, semantic and figurative aspects of language vary from episode to episode insofar as authors advocate a different ideology in different social and political conditions.

The concept of episodic literary movement as a means of analyzing literary history helps us understand the role of ideology in literature and the role of literature in social movements. It explains how literature in a certain time and space becomes a method for defining both what and how to read and how to act upon what is read. It provides an explanation of how literary production changes in an episodic fashion and how in each episode a new set of metaphors promotes a new ideology.

I should, however, mention that the concept of Episodic Literary Movement has no quarrel with the issue as to whether a particular text can exist outside ideology or not. Nor does it concern itself with whether an ideology is contained in every single text or not. Moreover, it denies neither the imaginary aspect nor the creativity that are associated with literature or its autonomy but rather points out literature's power when it points out literature's role in social change. The concept of Episodic Literary Movement is concerned with ideology insofar as it determines the figurative language and develops metaphors in a preponderance of literary production in diverse episodes.

2

Persianism: The Ideology Of Literary Revolution in the Early Twentieth Century

ALTHOUGH THE HISTORY OF THE QAJAR DYNASTY (1779–1925) was marked by disastrous defeats to Russia, loss of territory, assassinations, European diplomatic competition for control of the polity, and cultural backwardness, traditional writers were preoccupied with the imitation of the great poets of the classical period and failed to address the urgent questions of their time. Qajar literary elites advocated traditionalist Islam and opposed modernity. Accordingly, Persian literature, which during the course of a millennium had reached a high level of excellence in the creation of epics, panegyrics, and ghazals as well as in historical, mystical, and didactic writings through a sophisticated system of prosody and rhyme patterns, form, and imagery, declined enormously under the Qajars. During the last decades under the Qajars, poets such as Qa'ani Shirazi (d. 1853) wrote socially and aesthetically irrelevant panegyrics or religious elegies while remaining faithful to the restrictive rules of classical prosody and rhyme patterns.[1]

Progressive ideas and secular social activities proliferated toward the end of this dynasty and were further encouraged throughout the reign of Mozaffar ad-Din Shah (1896–1907), especially during the Constitutional Revolution of 1906.[2] The revolution brought a variety of different forces with different goals together. Intellectuals were thereby immensely inspired by liberal nationalistic tendencies and Western ideas.[3] Full-scale modernization became an urgent issue under Reza Shah (1925 to 1941), who through a coup d'état against the incompetent Ahmad Shah (1909–25) in February 1921 came to power and terminated the rule of the Qajar dynasty in 1925. Reza Shah encouraged secular social and literary activities and boldly attempted to eliminate what he considered to be obstacles to progress and modernization. He sponsored social reforms and promoted a Western lifestyle.[4] His government's reforms included ridding his country of British and Russian occupation, taking control of banks and other financial institutions, developing industry, creating a modern educational system, and supporting women's social activities and equal rights. He limited the influence of the clergy, glorified Iran's pre-Islamic history, praised the Aryan race as the origin of Iranians, gave great recognition to the Zoroastrian religion, and took actions to purify the Persian language of Arabic words. His government even attempted to romanize the Persian alphabet.[5] Reza Shah's reforms met with opposition, which varied greatly from group to group, although most were merely suspicious of his government. Literary activists managed to keep their distance from the state but could not strongly oppose the reforms because they had already engaged in promoting modernization themselves. Since the Constitutional Revolution (1906), when the first signs of literary reform began to appear in reaction to the literary decadence of the Qajar period, new writers such as Taqi Rafʿat (d. 1920) campaigned against the artificiality and arbitrariness of the old prose.[6] These writers were in contact with the West and thereby promoted new styles and ideas.

At this juncture, literary journals also emphasized the necessity of the use of simple Persian and indeed encouraged their contributors to write in a language that could be understood by ordinary people. Journals such as *Sur-i Israfil* (Israfil's Trumpet) and the authors associated with them helped to create a more modern, flexible language.[7] They believed that the process of modernization depended in large part upon simplifying the Persian language and releasing it from the influence of Arab-Islamic culture. These journals invented words such as *bakhsnameh* (bylaws), *parleman* (parliament), *sabte ahval* (office of identity registration), *burs* (stock), and *roshanfikr* (intellectual), which they thought were necessary for the presentation of modern ideas and Western concepts. These new ideas, in turn, increased the number of journals published after the Constitutional Revolution. In 1909 alone, ninety-nine new journals were published.[8] They actually competed over presenting new concepts and meanings. At times they failed to create the terminology they needed and therefore used Western words directly in their writings. These journals also frequently published the works of poets such as Arif, Ishqi, and Yazdi, whose poems were marked with simplicity and clarity.[9] As Afshar points out, these journals had indeed a great effect on general writing style.[10]

Over time, new writers confronted the traditionalists in a more organized way. The traditionalists, of course, already had their own organizations—e.g., Maktab-e Saʿdi (Saʿdi's School) and Anjuman-i Nizami (Nizami's Society)—and they published articles in journals such as *Naw Bahar* (New Spring) and *Azadistan* (The Free Land). The modernists created comparable formal organizations, such as Danishkadih (The Place of Knowledge), and informal groups such as Rabʿ (The Four), led by Sadiq Hidayat. They also organized themselves around journals such as *Namih-i Parsi* (Persian Letters), *Farangistan* (Europe), *ʿIlm va Hunar* (Science and Art), and *Kaveh* (Kaveh).[11]

The two sides confronted each other by writing for and against the necessity of literary change. *Persian Letters* published an article by A. Azad Maraghiʾi stating that the traditionalists "mixed up the fluent sweet Persian language with the bitter foreign Arabic and in doing so they have cut their own roots. Worse than that, they are still sleeping and do not see how others are sacrificing themselves for the fluency and progress of this language."[12] *Farangistan* went as far as to suggest to "use Latin instead of Arabic if a need for new words exists."[13] *Science and Art*, in order to "strengthen the nationhood," published the translation of the pre-Islamic Zoroastrian text *Gathas* by Ibrahim Purdavud, hoping to preserve and promote "Persian literary treasures."[14] *Kaveh*, named after a mythical blacksmith who once saved an Iranian kingdom, published the first short stories of Muhammad Ali Jamalzadih, who also advocated a reform in the language. In the first issues of *Kaveh*'s second period, Taqizadih wrote, "the journal's ideology and goal is to promote Western life style and to struggle for the preservation and purity of Persian language and literature and its [writing system]."[15]

As the debate persisted, the traditionalists argued that any innovation in the language would be to its detriment. The modernists argued that such fears were groundless. *Kaveh*, whose writers strongly supported the change of Persian script from Arabic to either Latin or one of the ancient Iranian alphabets, published an article in which two pieces of writing were compared. The author illustrated how awkward and repulsive the old prose looked in comparison to the new. Later the journal published another article that compared old and new poetry and came to the same conclusion about the necessity for change in the language. The traditionalists responded harshly to these claims in a series of articles in *The Free Land*. The debate raged in this way until the publication of the essay "Modernist Manifesto," a call for a literary revolution. In it, the journalist and literary activist Taqi Rafʿat wrote, "We are in the most critical time. What we want is modernity in literature, no less than the modernity we want in the world of ideas and technology."[16]

Given these circumstances and the extensive modernization program of the government of Reza Shah, early grassroots activities evolved into a literary movement. With the publication of a new style of poetry by Nima Yushij and short stories by M. A. Jamalzadih and Sadiq Hidayat, this literary movement became dominant.[17] Nima's so-called New Poetry, which violated strict rules about the division of syllables into short and long and overlong syllables and ignored prefabricated patterns and styles, led to the development of Persian free verse. Ahmad Karimi-Hakkak points to several major differences between modern and classical Persian poetry. New or modern poetry is generally more serious, the classical more leisurely. The modern is socially conscious, while the classical is more personal. "The formal differences between classical and modern Persian poetry are even more profound. Classical Persian poets strove not so much for structural unity as for formal unity. An ode, for example, consists of a certain number of lines of equal length, following an unchangeable meter and a precise, rigid rhyme pattern established by convention and the practice of former poets. All of this has disappeared from modern poetry."[18]

Clashes over Persian poetry culminated in the question of whether rhyme and meter should remain essential elements in poetry. Fazlullah Parvin on this issue wrote, "while these modernists reject the signficant past literary tradition and consider it meaningless, they are not capable of replacing it with anything of their own."[19] Modernists argued that classical forms were no longer capable of answering contemporary needs and that meter and other elements of classical poems had become barriers to poetic expression. This current of modern poetry culminated in the works of Nima Yushij (1897–1960), who established New Poetry and formulated free verse systematically. He replaced the religious themes with social issues through the use of non-religious imagery.

Fiction also began to benefit from a simple and comprehensible language using new styles and forms. It too experienced a complete break with the earlier inflated, ornamental style. Like poets, the fiction writers did not praise any Muslim personalities; they blamed society's problems on Islam and admired the West. They too promoted proper and correct writing according to a new standard system closer to the spoken language.

These literary changes gave rise to the first episode of modern Persian literature. Its pioneering writers claimed to understand modernity and to know their readers' tastes and expectations for social change. Perceiving the traditional literary elite as a barrier to modernity, they mercilessly attacked the rigid forms of traditional literary presentation and, in doing so, approached literature in a radically different way. Writers not only wrote in a new style but also made new ideas and precepts intrinsic components and themes of their work. It was not accidental that the critic and social reformer Ahmad Kasravi (1888–1945) criticized, in what he considered pure Persian, all the classical works except Firdawsi's *Shahnamah* (The Book of Kings). This tenth-century book was spared because its author wrote it in an effort to revive Persian, which after the Islamic conquest was on the verge of extinction.[20] Perhaps as a direct consequence of stances such as this and his antireligious writings, Kasravi was assassinated by a minor Islamic group in 1945. Similarly, Jalal al-Din Mirza wrote a voluminous history of Iran in what he called "purified Persian."[21] And A. H. Zarrinkub openly portrayed the two centuries after the Islamic conquest of Iran as a period of regression and "silence" because this period did not witness major literary creativity.[22] It was not accidental either that Hidayat, in an effort to reinterpret the classical literature, chose to write on Umar Khayam, for he had expressed an aversion to Islamic philosophy and a predisposition for the pre-Islamic period. Miskub, in his belated Persianist book *Huviyat-e Irani va Zaban-i Farsi* (The National Iranian Identity and the Persian Language) (1994), reminds his readers that "Because of their religious education, Taqizadih's Persian and even worse, Mirza Muhammad Khan Qazvini's Persian never completely freed themselves from the influence of the Arabic language and its vocabulary. They were both quite knowledgeable in their own fields but they both wrote in an ugly Persian."[23] The new writers, quite purposefully, mocked religious titles. *Haji*, a title given to one who has completed the pilgrimage to Mecca, often appears in early modern short stories in ways conveying negative impressions of Islamic cul-

ture. A Haji is portrayed as fanatical, conservative, and stingy. Jamalzadih's "Haj Qurban Ali," Hidayat's "Haji Aqa," and Sadiq Chuback's
"Qalpaq Duzd" (The Hubcap Thief) all portray Hajis as the guardians
of tradition and the perpetrators of depravity. A Haji in these works is
not solely a particular individual who may have certain flaws, certain
diseases, or specific problems, but also represents a social force inhibit-
ing progress.[24]

Because such an affinity existed between this early literary movement and Reza Shah's state ideology, some scholars have labeled the
writers of this period nationalists. Yarshater, for example, believes that
nationalism was the leading force behind Hidayat's "mocking flip-
pancy" in his outstanding works of fiction.[25] And Saad, in analyzing
the works of Jamalzadih and Hidayat, among others, argues that the
intention was nation building.[26] It is true that nationalism influenced
the literary activists in this period (as liberalism during the Constitutional period influenced activists in their advocacy of democracy), but
overall the literature did not acquire a specifically nationalistic character. The most important writers of this period—M. A. Jamalzadih,
Sadiq Hidayat, and Nima Yushij—did not pursue nationalism. They
are not known to have ever actively participated in any nationalist
movement. They did not support their nation-state, native soil, culture,
traditions, or territorial authorities but instead left Iran to live in
Europe or in isolation. Moreover, their writings contain much antistate
and antinational sentiments as well as, much anti-Iranian rhetoric.[27]

Neither can one consider this literary discourse to be a mere imitation of Western genres, as suggested by literary critics such as Azarakhshi or Mohandessi. Azarakhshi, one of Nima [Yushij]'s opponents,
stated, "following World War I, several revolutionary leaders went to
France, Turkey, and Germany, where they learned about some of the
intellectual and artistic trends, which ultimately created chaos in Persian language and literature and caused a discontinuity between the
contemporary and original Iranian cultures."[28] Mohandessi believes
that as a result of the introduction of print in 1812, European literature
affected Persian literature irreparably and eventually generated the
modern literary movement.[29] It is true that modernist authors used
some Western models, but their works were not limited to the exigencies of Westernization or rote imitation of Western forms.[30] Rather, in
many respects, they are rooted quite purposefully in the literary traditions of Iran. Even referring to them as modernists should be done

with caution, not because modernism is too broad and too vague, but because, as history has proved, their movement did not lead to an overall modernity similar to that of Western modernists.[31]

The term *Persianism* (Parsigera'i) best captures the nature of the literary movement that resulted in the emergence of modern Persian literature. Again, its advocates had several immediate objectives: to denounce the use of Arabic terminology; to work toward the purification of the Persian language through poetry; to promote a fictional language closer to common parlance instead of the conventional style; to link ancient Iran to the present time and expunge centuries of Islamic dominance from the memory; and, finally, to promote modernity by creating new literary forms. They especially believed that the old traditional literature could not adequately address the new social issues, such as modernization, democracy, and progress. By "Persianism," therefore, I refer to this literary episode that reflected upon and deeply criticized many aspects of Iranian national characteristics, including social life and traditional culture but excluding the Persian language. The Persian language was considered the most truthful and admirable index of the Iranian heritage. The task was, therefore, to purify and secularize this language and, at times, to show how damaging the seventh-century Islamic conquest of Persia had been to Iranian culture and society.

Persianism surfaced in the work of the pioneers of modern Persian literature at both ideological and linguistic levels. The old ideas, symbols, stories, fables, mores, and Quranic metaphors—all intrinsic elements of classical Persian literature—were used in new genres, often in a satirical manner, to criticize traditional forms. Thus there was some continuity in the use of classical metaphors, but only for the purpose of conveying totally different meanings. Nima's work established not only New Poetry and a new approach to Persian prosody, but also a whole new mode of thinking. His approach, which met with harsh criticism, he defended on theoretical grounds. He often portrayed himself as a literary revolutionary who suffered for being the originator of New Poetry. Enunciations of Persianism were even bolder and more seditious in the works of other major writers of this period; Muhammad Ali Jamalzadih (1892–1997) and Sadiq Hidayat (1903–1951) and the younger writers they influenced, such as Jalal Al-i Ahmad (1923–1969), in his early writings, and Khusraw Shahani (1929–).

Ideology and Self-Portrayal in the Poetry of Nima Yushij

Although Nima's poetry may seem to revolve around somewhat per-sonal and at times political themes, it helped Persianism remarkably. A quiet and rather unassuming young author from the Caspian Sea region, Nima Yushij (Ali Esfandiyari) became the most celebrated poet of this period, and the most emulated. He so influenced the next gen-eration of Iranian poets that he has been deemed the father of New Per-sian Poetry. At the nexus of the new and old culture, Nima's ideology called for relinquishing traditional poetic style in favor of literary modernity.

In Nima Yushij's poetry, night, darkness, and the seashore often symbolize an undesirable situation whereas day, light, and the vast-ness of the sea stand for progress and better circumstances. His pro-tagonists—sometimes a man, sometimes a bird—are repeatedly trapped in these situations and "suffering" in darkness and gloom before the matter is resolved. These sorts of metaphorical allusions and references to suffering appear not only in his poems but also in his speeches and theoretical writings, such as *Arzish-i Ihsasat va Panj Maqalih-i Digar* ("The Value of Feelings" and Five Other Articles) (1939). Nima's critics believe that these references to suffering derive from the pain felt by the poet in his struggle against injustice and his anguish at observing his people's misfortune. Dastghayb, Kasravi, Tah-baz, and others take Nima's portrayals of suffering as evidence of Nima's commitment to the revolution and leftist literature, ascribing to him a sort of leftist and socialist ideology.[32] It is true that such por-trayals in Nima's work address social concerns through the lexical, rhetorical, and symbolic manipulation of language. However, I argue that Nima's allusions to suffering and struggle are often connected to his own experience in advancing New Persian Poetry and to his role in the movement against traditionalist Qajar poetry, a role that caused him to suffer tremendously. The source of his suffering, in other words, is related to the obstacles continually placed in his way as he attempted to express his ideological concerns about literary modernity and poetic form.

Nima's longest poem, "Manali" (also pronounced Maneli) (1947), best demonstrates his ideological and literary project even though it may not represent his best poetic creativity. Indeed, some critics con-sider "Manali" Nima's worst poem.[33] However, this poem is long enough (approximately one thousand verses) to include a variety of examples of Nima's approaches to poetry. I am particularly interested in his use of the metaphors of shore and sea to depict his opposition to what he perceived as the complacent nature of nineteenth-century Persian literature, which seemed to limit itself to the imitation of the great masters of the classical period. The poem's central theme revolves around the poet's struggle for a new poetic language, a central topic for Persianism.

Nima wrote the poem in response to the 1944 Persian translation by Sadiq Hidayat of a Japanese legend, "Urashima."[34] Nima, of course, is not the only poet writing in response to, or under the effect of, a foreign literature in this period. In his analysis of literary hybridization in Persian literary texts, Karimi-Hakkak states that "although they owe their existence to their author's contact with certain identifiable texts of foreign origin, they have been classified in their own linguistic culture neither as verse translations of those foreign texts, nor as imitations in any sense."[35] Even though it demonstrates a significant maturity in its narration, plot, and symbolism, I consider "Manali" an example of literary hybridization because it features a main idea that remains similar to that of "Urashima." In an introduction to the poem, Nima even admits that "this story, with some differences, can be found in other literatures. I am not the first one to speak about a mermaid."[36] A comparative reading of "Manali" and "Urashima" may bring about a better understanding of Nima's motive in creating the complex and symbolically rich versified story of "Manali" based on the simple plot of "Urashima." It may also help to understand the role of metaphor in Nima's advocacy of Persianism.

Different versions of the tale "Urashima" are found all over Japan and other East Asian countries. The story frequently appears in Japanese children's books. Labeled as a narrative of a Japanese Rip Van Winkle, "Urashima" even found its way to the United States in the late nineteenth century. The oldest version of the tale is found in the eighth-century quasi-historical record, the *Nihongi*. It relates a story that supposedly occurred in A.D. 477 in a southwestern province of Japan, involving a fisherman named Urashima.[37] Hidayat translated one of the shorter renditions and subsequently published it in the literary journal *Sukhan* in late 1944.[38] According to this version, Urashima sets out to sea every night to make his living by catching fish. One night, haunted by the moon and in a state of between sleep and wakefulness,

Urashima is distracted from his surroundings and his boat gets lost in a dark area of the sea. Suddenly, a mermaid grabs him in her arms and takes him to her place at the bottom of the sea. There, singing her sea songs, she casts a sea spell upon him. Eventually she tells him: "You, the fisherman of the middle sea, you are beautiful. Your long hair is enchained around my heart. Do not leave me." Urashima refuses and asks her to release him, imploring "for the dear gods' sake, let me go—I want to go home." She insists that if he stays he will be the king of the deep sea. He replies, "Let me go—my little children await my return." Finally, when the daughter of the deep sea, the mermaid, begins to weep, Urashima agrees to stay, but only for one night.

The next morning the mermaid carries him to the shore, where she gives him a box and asks him never to open it. As he joyfully runs through the sweet-scented pine trees toward his dear home, Urashima calls his children's names the way he had taught them to do, imitating the sea bird's note. But when he finally arrives home, he finds only ruins covered with grass where his house once stood. He shouts, "What is this? Have I lost my mind? Have I left my eyes in the sea?" He sits down on the grass and cries out, "Help me, gods. Where is my wife? What about my children?" He desperately seeks an explanation for what has happened from other people, but no one recognizes him, and everybody treats him as a stranger. He knows the places, houses, and even the stones of the roads but cannot identify anyone. At sunset he goes back to the town gate, where he asks passersby if they know of a fisherman called Urashima in this town. They all answer that they have never heard of such a person. Eventually a very old man passes by. When asked whether he knows anything about Urashima, the old man replies, "There once was one by that name, but, sir, that person drowned years ago when I was still a little child. Occasionally, my grandfather spoke of him. This happened long, long ago." When Urashima asks, "What became of that man?" the old man responds that not only Urashima but many of his descendants, including his sons and even his grandsons, have all passed away. Urashima begins to walk toward the graveyard in the green valley where the dead of his village are laid to rest. On his way he listens to the trees twisting in the cold night wind. He salutes the moonlight that has remained unchanged and helps him find the tombs of his sons. When he finds the tombs, there is nothing else for him to do. Lost in reverie, Urashima returns to the seashore and opens the box. A puff of white smoke comes from it, and in a moment he ages, grows feeble, and finally lies down to die on the very spot.[39]

Nima's "Manali" begins with the narrator pondering why he remembers the story of a fisherman who unsuccessfully combs the sea for fish every night. On one particular journey, Manali, the fisherman, finds the night beautiful and the moon shiny and playful amid the clouds. The gentle breeze stops blowing now and then, adding to the beauty of the night. Although such a beautiful natural scene should sooth him, Manali remains so disturbed that his anxieties even seem to affect the night. As he begins to reflect on his problems and worries, a strong wind rises and the sea becomes stormy. A wave crashes against his boat, and his fear increases. Now nature too is disturbed. Manali suddenly hears someone calling his name. A mermaid beckons him, and soon thereafter the condition of the sea improves. The mermaid asks the fisherman what business has brought him to the sea. Surprised and afraid, Manali hesitates but eventually explains that he is a fisherman troubled by an undesirable situation.

> Bi gonah hastam man,
> kar-e man sayd dar ab.
> v-andar omid-e cheh rezqi na-chiz,
> hameh omram rafteh bar ab!
> Tang-ruzi-tar az man kas nist,
> dar jahani keh beh khun-i del-e khod bayad zist.
> ranjam ar chand faravantar az ranj-e kasan dar meqdar,
> Man mardi am bi tab o tavan kaz harkas,
> kamtaram bar khordar. (355)

> [I am innocent,
> Fishing in water is my business.
> In the hope of finding my daily bread,
> my whole life is gone with the wind.
> No one is more distressed than I,
> in a world where I live miserably.
> My suffering, however, is the greatest
> Poor and powerless,
> I am a man who has the least.]

Manali complains that he works hard yet earns little, and this not only wearies him but also makes him reluctant to continuing to work on the sea. The mermaid sits on a rock to console him.

Zahreh benma-y ay mard,
v-az rah-e khish magard.
Andar in dayereh-e tang gozar,
bim kam avar o andisheh mabar! (356)

[Be brave, oh man.
Do not turn away from your path.
Pass through this tight circle,
have no fear and no concern.]

She then poses several basic questions: "Where do you come from? Where are you going? What do you do?" Knowing Manali better through her conversation with him, she sympathizes with him about his problems and, telling him to come closer, states that the whole world is cruel.

The mermaid soon makes it clear that she is very kind and tells Manali how fortunate he is to have found a helpful mermaid in this sea. She then begins to speculate on social life, work, success, and fame. Interested, Manali informs her that each of her words evokes an emotional memory in him. He appreciates all he hears from her but asks, "What is the use of prestige and a good name in such a chaotic world?" This is where we see that Manali suffers overwork but gains no tangible reward. "I have become ugly," he says, "and it is good that you cannot see me, thanks to the weather, which is still overcast" (359). The mermaid responds:

Nah. To zibai o behtar bashar asti. Cheh ghami.
Andar in rah beh kari keh torast.
Kar-e to niz chenan chun to beh jay-e khod naghz o zibast,
vaz pay-e sud-e to hast o degeran.
Taʿn o tahqir-e kas az arzesh-e kar-e kas natavanad kast.
Har kasi ra rahi-st.
Ankeh rah-e degaran beshnasad,
Del be ghal o ghash-e agahist.
Cheshm-e del mibayad,
keh ze har rang beh maʿni ayad.
Az cheh pay bar pay-e in fekr ravi,
keh cheh keshti o cheh bayad deravi? (359)

[No, you are a beautiful, decent person, don't worry.
On this path, on which you tarry,
your work, too, in turn is eloquent and graceful,
And it will benefit you and others.
Taunt and contempt do not decrease the value of one's work.
Everyone has a way.
He who knows the ways of other folk
is well informed and not deceived.
It takes the insight of a heart
to give meaning to each hue.
Why do you think about
what you have cultivated and what you will harvest?]

Their discussion moves far beyond fishing, labor, and tedious endeavors. It revolves around creative activities such as how to give colors meaning. It focuses on an entity that the mermaid defines as beautiful and fluent. Speaking about the truth of beauty and fluency, Manali asks, "How can I earn what I wish?" The mermaid tells him that although he is poor, he already has something precious:

Agarat rizq na be andazah-ast,
dar avaz hast to ra chiz-e degar
rah-e dur amadeh'i
bordeh-'i az nazdik,
be suy-e dur nazar kon
. . . .
Ta nabashad kesheshi,
Tan-e jandar nagardad pabast. (361)

[If you don't have enough livelihood,
you have something else instead.
You have come a long way.
Do not look here—
Look to the horizon.
Cry less, we all have a load to carry
. . . .
Unless there is an attraction
Don't give your heart to distraction.]

She continues with this view, saying that one who seeks perfection must eventually become perfect and that despite its frustrations, such a search makes one appreciate life even more.

Little by little, it becomes evident that the poem discusses some of the issues that concern the poet himself. Issues related to life and attitude, in conjunction with allusions to poetic devices, elegance, eloquence, and meaningfulness of work, leave little doubt about the self-portrayal in the poem. To be sure, as the conversation between the mermaid and the fisherman progresses, the many uncertainties and deep-seated problems that surface in Manali's soul are also similar to the poet's. A monologue in which the mermaid, acting as Manali's mouthpiece, lists the underlying concerns of the protagonist, marks a turning point in the poem:

> Ah! Danestam-at az chist be in khuy shodeh.
> Bas ke na yafteh'i,
> dar bad o khub-e jahan ba gham mipayvandi.
> . . . .
> Va to-'i az hamegan dir-pasand avar tar.
> To bar ani ke fara avari az ja-ye boland,
> gar fara namadehat chizi bar vefq-e morad.
> Cheh beh az in ke jahani digar,
> ba to juyad ma'ni
> v-az to girad bonyad?
> Sukhteh z-atash-e digar ze nakhost.
> . . . .
> To'i az atashe digar dar dud.
> In to ra bas bashad,
> Kashena-ye ranj-at,
> na hameh kas bashad.(364–65)

> [Ah! I know why you have acquired his outlook.
> Since you have not found anything,
> you join sorrow with the good and bad of the world
> You are immensely hard to please
> one who has decided to rise up to the summit.
> Even if you have not gained anything yet,
> what better than a new world
> that will gain meaning from you,
> that will be established by you?

Touched by another flame since the beginning,
You are in the smoke of different fire.

. . . .

This alone will be sufficient for you,
even though not everyone
knows of your suffering.]

This passage also reconfirms that the conversation is not about the fisherman's poverty but, rather, about his attempts to overcome the obstacles that hinder him from breaking through to a successful, fulfilling life. Deeply concerned about his work, the protagonist is still incapable of producing as much as he desires because his work is not rewarding enough. Yet this problem loses its importance when he receives his real reward, the opportunity to give a new meaning to the world. Although Manali occasionally complains, from this point on he is more energetic after reflecting on the mermaid's words. An internal voice now urges him to try harder rather than give up: not only will people appreciate his work but also he will create a whole new world.

This climactic monologue also reveals the symbolic significance of the mermaid. She admonishes Manali to open his eyes and to realize that he will have a good life, provided that he goes with her. Manali is stunned. The mermaid assures him that she can give him all he seeks from the deep sea. As Manali considers the mermaid's offer, he berates himself for listening so readily to a woman who may—for all he knows—be Satan. However, he soon pushes these thoughts aside and decides to go with her. He now finds himself at the mouth of a river, where he sees a few boats resting on shore and a ruined cottage in the distance. He also hears a shepherd who sings, plays a reed, and recites a poem. Manali hears a voice in his head telling him to go to the sea because he had stayed in that stagnant state (lajan) too long and it is now time to do something new. The voice urges him to free himself from his chains (pay afzar) and reach for a higher goal.

Manali now declares that he loves the mermaid, yet he worries about the outcome, fearing that his love, which represents a "new meaning," might seem laughable to others. The mermaid reminds him that he should not hesitate because he has a superior goal and that on such a path there are friends who will support him. Manali continues to worry about his solitude, aware that his lack of anyone with whom he might discuss his goals remains a problem for him in evaluating his quest. The mermaid contends that she, in fact, has learned from Manali that "life will begin with what is known to make a path to the unknown" (364–65). The mermaid delivers a long speech, complimenting Manali on his sweet lips and expressing her love for him. She also informs him that she suffers from a sickness that can be cured only by human food. After receiving some food from him, she asks for Manali's shirt, which he surrenders—a present that brings them closer together. The mermaid appreciates his generosity and says she will never forget this favor. Manali, becoming more and more attached to the mermaid, brings her to the boat, where they sleep together before disappearing into the water.

The next day we see Manali, he is moving back to the village, which he finds deserted. Worried he remembers the mermaid telling him that his home now is in the sea with her. He realizes that, in fact, he has no reason to return to the village. He cannot remember the path anymore. His mind, his heart, and his feelings draw him to the sea and the mermaid; and he finds himself lonely on land. As he makes his way, he appeals to animals and flowers, who give him varying and at times contradictory advice. Once he reaches his home, he discovers that he does not belong there anymore, even though everyone has been waiting for him. He remarks:

> Kas nakard-ast be qadr-e man dar kar derang
> nakeshideh ast bar andazeh-ye man ranj kasi
> cheqadar ranj-e man o lazzat-e man bud nehan!
> beh dar andakht cheh andisheh-ʾi duram az rah. (383)

> [No one has been delayed as long as I,
> no one has suffered as much as I
> How I kept my suffering and my joy hidden!
> what made me take the wrong path?]

He realizes that his returning home has only amounted to a test of his decisiveness for continuation of his new path. He meditates on just what he needs to confront: self-consciousness.

> Cheh parishan shodeh am.
> akher-e omr cheh heyran shodeham!
> In sokhanha ze koja miayad,
> man-e viran shudeh ra kist keh u mipayad?
> Che fosuni ke be ab,

dar fekandand o be karam kardand!
ke be chashmam hameh chiz degarguneh shod o biganeh. (383)

[I am so disheveled now.
At the end of my life, I am so perplexed.
Where are these words coming from?
Who is it that watches over wretched me?
What magic is in the water
that it affects me so?
And makes me see things differently. . . .]

Manali concludes at last that, though there will be some criticism about the way he sees things, it does not matter. "I have to speak of the beauty even as I must endure the ugly responses I hear." He walks faster. Every natural thing—the water, the stone, even the dust—assists him in his journey by serving as a bridge from one point to the next. He realizes that nothing seems clear on the land and that he is incapable of navigating there any longer. He concludes that he must return to the open sea, and that is the end of the story.

"Manali": The Convergence of Nima's Ideology and "Urashima"

Nima gives the Urashima story multi-level significance through the question of language and meaning. Moreover, his characters are more complex than those in the Japanese legend and have completely different fates. As the plot, characterization, and the symbols in "Manali" indicate, the poem is an attempt at self-portrayal. What results is a complicated legend overladen by Nima's symbolic language. Through a process of codification, Nima uses symbols to point to his two concerns: ideology and suffering. The important symbols include the two characters as well as physical objects such as the sea, the village, the oar, the clothes, and the bridge.

Like Nima, Manali is an intellectual using a metaphorical language to portray his struggle in gaining acceptance. He uses a philosophical vocabulary to communicate his innermost feelings, impressions, sensibilities, and, most importantly, his suffering. His impressions flow out of a deep contemplation; his sensibilities reverberate with the condition of his environment; and his sufferings reflect his inability to gain acceptance. Manali's mood changes often, but he is always bold, unafraid, and yet concerned. He has high goals and ambitions as he faces challenges in his quest for change. In all this he evokes the way that Nima saw himself. To be sure, Manali at one point "slows down and seeks little," just as in Nima's life, there came a time when he slowed down by seeking refuge in the mountains from the urban crowd.[40] Manali and Nima have some common physical marks too. Due to hard work, both are thin and have lost their hair.[41]

The title of this poem indicates another connection between Nima and his protagonist. Pointing to himself as poet, he may have devised the title, "Manali," by playing with the verb *mandan* (to remain, to stay, to last, to survive) and his given name *Ali: man* (remain, stay [imperative]) plus *Ali* (Ali Nuri, his official name) equals *Manali* to mean the enduring Ali. In fact, *Ali* and a derivative of the verb *mandan* make other similar sounding names, such as Mandehali or Bemunalli or Mandali, all meaning "the son" *(Ali)* left to a parent after the death of all his siblings. Nima may also have come up with the title by inverting the syllables of his pen name and then adding the result to his official first name. Thus, Nima becomes Mani; which, combined with Ali, gives us Maniali or Manali.[42]

The presentation of the mermaid in "Manali" is well thought out. Manali goes to sea with his ordinary goal of catching fish but ends up finding a mermaid who appears at the right moment to rejuvenate him and counsel him about life. The mermaid is naked, delicate, cold, and in need of love; yet she can cure, heal, help, and warm him like a fire. She is magical and mighty, yet cries for Manali's food and clothing. This mix of attributes makes her especially complex. The mermaid personifies the persistent craving for advancement, progress, and cultural change. She encourages Manali to go further into the sea, to venture into the unknown. She also empowers him through her love to make a decision, to choose between the sea and the shore. She teaches Manali a secret language with which he can describe nature. The mermaid, thus symbolizing creativity or the imaginative mind, is a truth-seeking character who eventually unites with Manali. Characterization of the mermaid's enabling powers symbolize the value of New Poetry. The mermaid also provides the key to the poem: the sea (the future, New Poetry) is clearly to be preferred to the land (the old past and vanishing present, the old poetry).

The changing sea and its disparate attributes likewise transcend the natural features of a normal sea. Crazy, heavy, silent, huge, calm, noisy, rebellious, cooperative, frequent, and chanting, it can become angry or become victorious.[43] It can prevail over the shore, making Manali see everything in terms of the colors of the sea. The stormy sea is a metaphor for a chaotic society. The poet forces such an interpretation when he occasionally describes the seagulls and the windy sea in a tense different from the tense of the rest of the poem. Eventually, this differentiation makes the fictional sea of the poem a metaphor for the turbulent life in that historical period. The village, on the contrary, is quiet, dark, stagnant, and unattractive—an image reinforced by the descriptions of a "groggy dog" and a "half-dead fire" there (369). Given the depressing nature of the place, it is not surprising that Manali, unlike Urashima, shows no excitement upon returning home and does not stay for long.

To describe the situations on the sea or on land, Nima uses terms such as "criticism," "articulation," "eloquence," and "rhetoric" (359). These words are not related to the physical characteristics of a village or a sea. They directly refer to the poet's concerns about the nature of poetry. The village brings to mind the old ideas and the old poetry, whereas the mermaid and the sea represent what a new kind of poetry may be able to achieve. While the village is always decrepit and silent, the sea and the mermaid are always actively changing or speaking.

The description of the fisherman's oar also resembles that of a pen or quill. The mermaid describes it as a "small piece of wood," a "tool," saying "Agarat az kaf birun shodeh bashad paru,/ inat abzar ay mard."[If you have lost your oar / Here is your tool, oh man] (355), to which Manili reacts; "na paru-ye man aramam mighaltad dar qaleb-e dast" [no, my oar is rolling gently in the palm of my hand (373). In the cultural debate of the 1940s, the pen (*qalam,* a generic term) was sometimes referred to as a tool for achieving cultural change but more often as a useful weapon in the struggle for modernity. The oar (pen), although a small piece of wood, can nonetheless battle the heavy waves of the turbulent sea (change). Manali is told on the shore to pick up another oar if he loses his first. If taken literally, this line seems frivolous at first. Anyone familiar with the sea, especially a fisherman like Manali, would know that additional oars are not conveniently at hand in the middle of the sea, unless the person came prepared for just such an emergency and had a spare—or, more unlikely, just happened to find one floating in the water. But the oar is meant to be taken not literally but figuratively. The terminology—such as eloquence, creative work, temptation, rhythm, and rhyme—that Nima uses to describe the sea, the village, and Manali's state of mind also confirms that his oar symbolizes the poet's pen.

Clothes are another important symbol in the poem. On two occasions the dialogue between the mermaid and Manali revolves around clothes. Soon after their encounter, the mermaid offers to make shirts for Manali if he decides to stay with her:

> Ta to ra sazam tanpush
> andar andazam az jerm-e takandadeh-e abari keh beh sobh-e
> roshan,
> bar sarir-e daryast,
> mayeh-i ra keh barazad beh tanant pirahan. (366)

> [I will make you a garment
> from the transparent morning cloud,
> that crown of the sea,
> a shirt that will become you.]

This passage indicates that she, as a mermaid, does not need a shirt but is capable of making him one that will somehow change him. Later, at one significant moment before they make love; she tells him:

> Ba hava-ʾi keh beh ru-ye daryast
> darad az nazukiham pust be tan mikhoshkad.
> agar az lotf-e to pirahan-e to
> tan-i man mipushid." (377)

> [To the bottom of the sea I belong.
> Your love brought me to the surface.
> Here my skin has started to get dry,
> And, if only out of kindness, your shirt would cover my body.]

Manali "takes his shabby (zhendeh) garment off" and gives it to her. The surrendering of the shirt to the mermaid represents for Manali a shedding of his former worldview, attitude, and lifestyle. That is, the clothes symbolize the old forms; Persian words like Rakht, Lebas, or Pushesh (all mean "clothes") also refer to a person's general appearance or the outer form of an object or an idea. Thus, Nima is metaphorically recounting his own shedding of the old forms and style of poetry in order to create a union with the new. As Janati Ataʿi notices, Nima emphasizes that "clothes and makeup (Lebas and Arayesh) can obviously add to the beauty of people, and therefore I believe that rhythm is necessary for both classical and modernist verse." Moreover, he believes "rhythm must be the proper garment *(Pushesh)* for our meanings and feelings."[44]

These and other signs and symbols in the poem make it evident that the actual concern of the poet is self-portrayal. Pertinent to the development of the story of "Manali" is the symbol of the bridge. Manali manages to return to the sea only after the stones and the water cooperate to form a bridge for him.

> Dar takapuy o shetab
> gasht har poshteh-i khakash hamun
> pol biyafkand beh payash rud ab
> rah chamaz o lam dadandash kasan guzarad.
> sang bar sang shekastand az ham
> ku beh manzelgah-e khod rah barad. (386)

> [Struggling and in a hurry,
> Every pile of dust became a steep hill,
> Every river laid a bridge in his way.
> They all helped him to pass easily,
> Putting stone on stone
> Until he arrived at home.]

Similarly, Nima describes in a letter to his friend Shin Partaw, another Persianist poet, that he wants his poetry to act as "a bridge on which all will be able to pass over the water."[45] Thus, according to him, only through a deliberate and laborious effort can one bridge the gap between the past and the future or the old and new poetry. He writes that "every stone was placed through research and precise calculation to make a bridge on the water, and this required spending tedious days and nights at work." This was done, he continues, for "others to pass easily, only the fools will go through the water thinking that there is no need for a bridge."[46] The images of the bridge in the poem and the letter are therefore analogous. They reveal the significance of Nima's discourse of self-portrayal—significance derived, as he frequently mentions, from the fact that the construction of such a bridge is wrought with much pain.

"Manali" also represents Nima's insistence that a poet of New Poetry should describe nature in a novel yet always direct way—in the way that the poet himself sees, feels, and experiences it. The later part of the poem, which includes Manali's thoughts about the mermaid, the sea, the near future, and consequently New Poetry, has clearer verse and style than the earlier part. As Manali moves towards a new state of mind, his language changes accordingly and becomes more concise. In some of the early sections where Nima alludes to old poetry, on the contrary, rhymes—at times meaningless and at times grammatically awkward—seem to have been imposed on the poem: "paymud" with "keh bud"; "valaʾi kon" with "balaʾi kon"; "dayereh-ye zendani" with "sargardani"; "pay afzar" with "dast bar ar"; "boland nazar" with "inguneh mabar" (371).

"Manali" is similar in some of its symbolic significance to and yet profoundly different from "Urashima" both in obvious and subtle ways. Although the Japanese fisherman is poor, he refrains from complaining and returns regularly to the sea. He seems content with his life. Manali, on the other hand, is an unhappy, unsatisfied, and rebellious character who welcomes any change to the status quo. He is "modern." Urashima's encounter with the mermaid does not open a new perspective for him; he immediately asserts his unwillingness to stay with her and must, in fact, be brought to the bottom of the sea against his will.[47] He happily returns home only to be disappointed when he realizes the great length of his absence. Never, even as he walks back toward the shore at the end of the story, does he pursue any particular purpose or declare a goal in life. Urashima lacks sociopolitical initiative. Manali, on the other hand, initiates his own actions. His occasional ambivalence is only the result of the importance of the questions that require his deeper consideration. He frequently thinks out loud and then acts thoughtfully. He returns to his village to discern how he feels about the past and decides to return to the sea only after he has weighed his emotions and thoughts.

The two works portray the mermaid and the time she spends interacting with the protagonists in different ways. Urashima is afraid of the mermaid and does not have a dialogue with her. He sleeps with her against his will and pays for it with the rest of his life, which seems to have been spent in that one night, making Time a central theme in this story. Manali, on the other hand, discusses many issues with the mermaid at length and eventually falls in love with her. The mermaid in "Urashima" destroys the man; the one in "Manali" improves him. The mermaid in "Urashima" is mysterious, witch-like, and tyrannical. The mermaid in "Manali," in contrast, is caring, nurturing, and in need of human love, thereby presenting a positive image of women.

Allegory in Nima's Work

Every stanza of "Manali," as well as its plot, is part of an allegory of Nima's life story, his role in the advent of New Poetry, and the difficulties he underwent while confronting those who ridiculed him for his innovations. When Nima's opponents criticized him for his inaccurate use of Persian words and his grammatical mistakes, Nima labeled the practitioners of traditional poetry reactionaries.[48] In "Manali" terms such as "mud" *(lajan)* and "prison" *(dayereh-ye zendani)* are meaningful when they are taken as metaphors for the old poetry. Similarly the expression "something higher" *(valatar)* is comprehensible only if taken to mean New Poetry. Fisherman or poet, Manali decides to leave behind the past, the old ways, the uncertainties. He rebels against stagnant and unchanging forms. He prefers the adventures of the sea to the safety of the shore. He chooses to move forward and face new challenges. As a fisherman and a poet, he is someone who can converse with the sea:

> Heybat-e tireh-ye darya-yash mikhand khamush sorudi dar gush.
> ba navahayash manand-e navaha-ye delash.
> Midavidandash jan yafteh, az pish-e nazar,
> chizha kuh pasand-e del-e khod dasht beh yad. (353–54)

> [The dark enormity of the sea was singing a silent song in his ear.
> And its tune, like that in his heart,
> was everything that he liked to remember,
> running alive in front of his eyes.]

As he listens to the sea, he visualizes nature being rejuvenated in front of him. Nima Yushij in his writings on poetics states that the vivid depiction of life is possible only in New Poetry—when nature is no longer bound by limiting classical prosody. The vividness of nature and the sensation conveyed in this stanza is in part due to the remarkable empathy that Nima shares with his protagonist.

Nima develops similar themes in "Qayiq" (The Boat) (1952). Here Nima uses a set of symbols to portray a downhearted man with a beached boat, shouting for help from friends. The man finds his friends laughing at him because his "boat does not move rhythmically" and because his language and tone are not traditional. What he hears from these people causes him much suffering. Nevertheless, he needs their help because he has no way to cross the water alone. The symbols of seashore, sea, boat, and the boatman all combine to present the situation that Nima actually faced as he attempted to convince a large audience to acknowledge his notion of New Poetry and to aid its realization. In order to cross the sea, in order to make his "shout" heard and be effective, he needs his friends' cooperation and understanding:

> Man chehreham gerefteh
> man qayeqam neshasteh beh khoshki.
> Ba qayeqam neshasteh beh khoshki
> faryad mizanam.
> . . . .
> Maqsud-e man ze harfam ma'lum bar shomast
> yek dast bi sedast.
> Man, dast-e man ze dast-e shuoma mikuonad talab.
> Faryad-e man shekasteh agar dar galu, va-gar
> faryad-e man resa
> man az baray-e khalas-e khod va shom a
> faryad mizanam.
> Faryad mizanam. (499–500)

> [My face is downcast,
> my boat is beached.
> With my boat beached, I shout. . . .
> . . . .
> You know what I mean,
> One hand is voiceless.
> I and my hand both seek help from you.
> My shout, whether broken in my throat,
> my shout, whether loud,
> is to free you and myself.
> I shout,
> I shout.]

As was the case in "Manali," the divide between the boatman and the intellectual is so narrow that the voice of the poet defending his ideological presentation of form and Persianist ideas is easily detected. The shout, is not, as some scholars of Nima imply, a shout against injustice and in support of the poor. Nor is it a call to join hands in a leftist revolution.[49] It is rather an invitation to participate in the modernization of Persian language and poetry.

In several other poems, diverse beings represent the poet's struggle. In "Quqnus" (The Phoenix) (1936), the mythical bird somehow manages to perch on a bamboo tree. Surrounded by other birds, the phoenix begins to groan. From these sounds, it constructs an imaginary structure comprehensible to all the other birds. Eventually the phoenix shouts from the bottom of its heart, making a sound that is not easy for the other birds to understand, and then throws itself into the fire. From its ashes, instead of the phoenix itself, other fledglings arise.[50] The phoenix is, of course, Nima himself, the structure represents the building of his New Poetry, and the shout is his call for support of his new genre.

In "Ay Adamha" (Hey People) (1941), the narrator addresses a crowd enjoying the safety of a shore and exhorts them to go to the sea to save someone who is dying:

Ay adamha keh bar sahel neshasteh shad o khandanid!
Yek nafar dar ab darad miseparad jan.
Yek nafar darad keh dast o pay-e daʾem mizanad
ru-ye in darya-ye tond o tireh o sangin ke midanid. (301–302)

[Hey you, sitting on the shore, happy and laughing—
Someone is drowning in the water,
Someone is constantly struggling
In this heavy, dark, turbulent sea,
the one that is also known to you.]

Again, the reason that those on the shore should join the man in the water is that he is making sacrifices. The drowning person is Nima himself in one of his emotionally and even economically depressed moments. If his sacrifices were to go unrecognized, they would not result in any change.

Through a set of binary oppositions between the sea and the shore and between the night and the day, several other poems by Nima depict a contradiction between the old and new poetry and convey the poet's life story. This dichotomy very often transcends poetic form and includes the questions of lifestyle and social orientation that were associated with the traditionalists and the modernists. To be sure, Nima had begun to embark upon his lifelong attack against traditionalism even in his first old-style poem, "Qissih-i Rang-i Paridih" (The Story of the Paleface) (1921), in which he uses an autobiographical text in the traditional masnavi form to present a nonconventional self-image. And soon in "Afsaneh" (1922), his first work in New Poetry, this same dichotomy and life story repeat themselves, as the beloved becomes the poem. Like the mermaid, she instigates a change in the protagonist through words of hope. Throughout the story, which shows a similarity to the narrative of the mermaid in Manali, the title character, Afsaneh, has a function similar to that of the mermaid. She too symbolizes New Poetry. The piece then turns into a eulogy to New Poetry. Here, New Poetry acts both as the object and the tool, as well as a solution for a stagnant culture. The poet states that the Afsaneh of his poetry is the remedy for his heart, medicine for his pain.

Nima's theoretical writings about New Poetry further explain his notion of the dichotomy between the old and new poetry as he elaborates on the concept of form. His assertions about literary form and his ideas about aesthetics prove that his notions of form and suffering are connected—Nima promotes form as an ideological element that, on the one hand, reflects natural suffering and, on the other, causes him to suffer throughout his career.

Nima's Aesthetics

Nima's discussion of aesthetics is presented primarily in two works: *Arzish-i Ihsasat va Panj Maqalih-i Digar* ("The Value of Feelings" and Five Other Articles,) (1939) and *Harfha-yi Hamsayih* (The Neighbor's Word,) (1969).[51] Form in these theoretical writings is the central ideological element in the explanations of his aesthetics. It dominates the central stage of his quest to reshape literary discourse and to present Persianist ideology.

To Nima, ideology means more a system of emotions than a school of thought. It consists of "a collection of feelings, memories, and details that are stored in the brain."[52] Although he believes that time and place condition the ideas that artists share, he does not consider ideology a conscious process. This view differs from the Marxist definition of ideology as a set of ideas associated with certain social classes and a hierarchy of values used to justify human actions. Nima's notions of ideology are so different from Marxist ones that the idea of associating him with Marxist aesthetics should be dismissed, as well as the idea that suffering is inflicted upon Nima as a result of his observations of people's misery.

In these theoretical writings Nima explains the inevitable confrontation between avant-garde artists and reactionary conservatives.

He states that such confrontations represent a universal struggle between old and new.[53] Those who exceed the limits set by the old poets will improve poetry. Those who fail to do so are doomed to stagnate or "only move toward the grave."[54] Nima asserts that commonly shared feelings, the basis of creativity, and their distribution among artists bring these artists together and initiate new forms: "Time has created you and you have to know your time. The individuals who support you are similar to you."[55] Artists must acquire knowledge of their time, he believes, before any social change can occur. Moreover, Nima maintains that the advocates of new ideas, the artists, share a common attitude or, more precisely, a common "manner of social feeling."[56] He contends that the translation of foreign literary works affects and inspires us, thereby producing new feelings (a theoretical justification for his basing "Manali" on "Urashima").[57] He concludes that this social feeling is also conditioned by biological characteristics and personal joys.[58]

Nima was especially inspired by French symbolism, which holds that verse forms best evoke and suggest meaning if they are not too rigid. He believed in such ideas in both theory and practice. As expressed in his theoretical works, form mirrors the period, satisfying its needs and conveying its meanings. An inappropriate form disrupts all of these functions. Form is relevant to the general methods of perception that dominate an age. Nima demonstrates this point by drawing examples from Western, Japanese, and Persian literatures and concluding, "If there is no form, there is nothing else. . . . You can make the most trivial subject interesting through form."[59] However, it seems that by "form" he often refers to genre and by "new form" he means New Poetry specifically. This fascination with the concept of form led him to infuse even poems with his theories. In "Manali," Nima uses the metaphor of "clothes" in reference to form similarly to the way he uses it in "The Value of Feelings." The cover, then, comes to stand for the things it conveys in both the poetry and theory of Nima. For him, form is destiny: "It is created, it lives, and it dies."[60] This infusion of theory into poetry explains why Nima prefers narrative verse to other forms and why "Manali" resembles an epic. Like a storyteller, Nima retells his own life story through narrative verse.

It is not surprising that Nima's criticism of the old poetry revolves around the question of rhyme and rhythm and its relation to form. He believes that the old poetry lacks rhythm altogether. Each single line has a rhythm of its own, resulting in a piece without its necessary harmony. That is, the old poetry is disjointed; each line is disconnected from the others. Even the rhyme at the end of each verse, which supposedly helps the rhythm, often fails to do so.[61] He states:

> It is the traditional poem that is devoid of meter and rhyme, even though the opposite seems to be the case. But I believe that, metrically, a hemistich or a line cannot be a complete verse when it cannot reproduce the natural rhythms of speech. . . , rhyme acts as the organizer of the rhythm; it separates the melodious sentences; it is like the conductor of an orchestra.[62]

Nima also believes that the old poetry is so subjective that it does not allow the poet to depict the natural world in a natural way. It is, he says, "as subjective as our music."[63] Contrary to the old poetry, he continues, his own New Poetry must have a rhythm throughout the poem, enabling poets to better depict what they see. Therefore, he concludes, poets should change their poetry because their lives, the lives they "see," are changing. As life changes, the structures of the Persian language and literature that are to reflect this new reality must also change.[64]

Such was the way that Nima contributed to the Persianist movement theoretically as well as through self-portrayal in his poetry. As Manali, this is the mission he takes upon himself. He performs the role of the artist who eventually overcomes the "putrescence" of the old thoughts in favor of "future virtues." Not only his definition of ideology and form but also the kind of binary opposition that Nima creates in "Manali" differentiates him from advocates of Committed Literature. Writers of such literature represent social issues in terms of class, but Nima explains them in terms of new and old poetry. In an article about his book of poetry *Faryadha* (The Shouts), he refers to the poems in the book as suppressed shouts and to himself as the supporter of those who need to shout. And he declares that his book represents a battlefield not for the poor and the rich or the happy and the miserable, who may occasionally appear in a poem, but rather for the struggle between New Poetry and old rhetoric. The poems distinguish the "New Poetry's" "volunteers for the battlefield" (*davtalabha-ye maydan-e jang*) from those they must combat, the defenders of old poetry.[65] The enemies, he writes, consist of "the teachers of rhymes and the old devices who restrict people in their enunciation."[66]

Nima's Suffering

None of this was easy for Nima. Despite the encouragement that he received from some friends to promote his new forms, his aesthetics, and his ideology, Nima felt lonely and suffered from harsh opposition throughout his career. His poems abound with references to these experiences; such as the following passage from "Manali:

> Man beh rah-e khod bayad beravam,
> kas na timar-e mara khahad dasht.
> Dar por az keshm a kesh-e in zendegi-ye hadesehbar,
> gar cheh guyand nah har kas tanhast.
> An ke midarad timar-e mara, kar-e man ast.
> Man nemikhaham darmanam asir.
> Sobh vaqti keh hava roshan shod,
> har kasi khahad danest o beh ja khahad avard mara,
> ke dar in pahnehvar-e ab,
> beh cheh rah raftam o az bahr-e cheh am bud azab? (353)

> [I have to go my own way,
> no one cares for me.
> In struggling against the happenings of this life,
> everyone is alone, even if they deny it.
> What nurtures me is my work.
> I do not wish to remain captive.
> In the morning when it grows bright,
> everyone will know, and see me,
> on this vast sea,
> Which path I have taken and why I have suffered so.]

Nima also alludes to his struggle and suffering on behalf of New Poetry in his introduction to the poems he read at the First Iranian Writers' Congress in June 1946, about the same time he was writing "Manali." In it, Nima gives a brief account of his childhood, stating that it was relatively normal, with all the usual problems that children face during their school years. He then describes his successful career, asserting that his knowledge of the French language "opened new horizons before [his] eyes."[67] Responding to his opponents—the advocates of old poetry—he proclaims that, for the sake of his country and for the benefit of the younger generation, he has opened the path for New Poetry. He briefly explains his innovations in the rhythm and rhymes of his New Poetry, finally concluding: "I resemble a river from which one can silently get water at any spot" (64). Then he abruptly states, "The main source of my poetry is my suffering. In my belief the real poet must have that source. I write poetry for my and other people's suffering. My life, words, rhythm, and rhymes are only tools" (64).

The statement "the source *(mayih)* of my poetry is my suffering (or tribulation) *(rani)*" has become a part of Nima's literary patrimony and has appeared as an epigraph in several works and anthologies of modern Persian poetry.[68] Unfortunately, the inherent vagueness of this statement has encouraged misinterpretations of Nima's ideological orientation, aesthetic discourse, and his poetry.

The word "suffering," nonetheless, has been taken since the 1950s as the definitive declaration of Nima's commitment in literature.[69] Miskub, a literary critic, does not consider "Manali" a successful work because, he argues, although Nima is a great socialist and leftist humanist and suffered from the observation of poverty, starvation, ignorance, war, and oppression, "Manali" fails to be sufficiently expressive. According to Miskub, the work is too ambiguous in the representation of these socialist ideas. Dastghayb, who also believes that Nima in "Manali" and other works means to focus on social life and reveal the truth about social problems,[70] writes, "Nima describes the nature and the people who work and suffer with a new perspective."[71] Falaki too argues that Nima's poems are the articulation of the people's (the working class's) suffering, maintaining that Nima uses the epic form in "Manali" to demonstrate the relationship between a fisherman and the sea and thereby to express the need of the fisherman, who represents the working class, for a decent life. According to Falaki, "Manali" represents only Nima's own commitment to people.[72] Tahbaz ties Nima's work directly to political and social realities, declaring that "Nima in many of his poems reveals the frightening situation under the monarchy."[73] Kasrai, still going further, locates "Manali" specifically within Nima's struggle for a revolution similar to the 1917 October Revolution.[74]

The inaccuracy of such an interpretation becomes obvious when one considers the subjective mode of the statement created by the use of first person singular, which would not have appealed to writers of Committed Literature. It is also questionable because the concept of suffering presented in "Manali" and his other poems does not confirm it. Moreover, *The Neighbor's Word* demonstrates rather different expressions of this suffering: "My suffering and sorrow are profound. I wear myself out every day. I don't think I will have enough opportunity to express myself."[75] Nima, in fact, spent much time alone struggling, thinking, and working to develop the substance and style of his poetry. This new style "did not exist in my country and in my language. I spent a whole, laborious life under the burden of old forms, old words, and old methods, and under the pressure of the classical way."[76] These efforts culminated in what he believed was the preparation of an avenue for others to follow. "I, now, lay this road down in front of the new generation."[77] On this occasion it is possible that Nima remained intentionally ambiguous to satisfy certain political concerns of the members of the Congress. That is, because of the socialist ambience of the First Congress of Iranian Writers, which was dominated by the Soviet Union–Iran Cultural Association, Nima may have been incited to make the ambiguous suggestion that he, too, produced his literary work fully aware of the flaws of society and the suffering of poor people.

Nima's suffering, on the contrary, originated from the problems he faced during his own career in regard to the promotion of New Poetry rather than from his specific concern for people's poverty and other political problems. Such a clarification of the nature of suffering can alleviate the difficulty of understanding his ideology of representation and the style of his poetic self-portrayal. Inspired by a foreign text, Nima in "Manali" created a more complex and certainly a more allegorical text than his source. By means of allegory he asserted his ideological concerns about the situation of the New Persian poetry in opposition to the traditional practice and about the role he must play in the conflict. Through self-portrayal in "Manali" and in his theoretical assertions, Nima expressed his belief that one way to overcome the obstacles hindering modernity was to promote a new, simpler, and more direct Persian language and fresh aesthetic forms.

Above all, Nima emphasized literary form as an ideological element of modernist discourse. He perceived form to be a derivative of a dominant mode of sensibility, a specific condition unique to each period. An artist who does not adjust to each period's conditions will be unable to articulate the urgent questions of the time. But how should the future be? And what was the urgent question of the time for Nima? Why did he place so much emphasis on form? As a product of Persianism, Nima believed that the writer overcomes the old by exposing and subverting its forms. Like his contemporaries Sadiq Hidayat and M. A. Jamalzadih, Nima believed that cultural backwardness was the main barrier to literary evolution. All three writers saw language as the vehicle of culture and dedicated themselves to releasing it from outdated, formulaic styles and artificial rhetoric. They all favored simplifying language, disparaging religious superstitions, and promoting Western literary styles and new aesthetic forms.

Nima acknowledged that there were other writers who advocated change. In fact, many younger poets responded positively to his innovations. Partaw, for example, replied to an encouraging letter that he received from Nima, "As you have guessed, I also started years ago to create new works of Persian literature and have been trying to simplify and improve the Persian language."[78] Nima especially appreciated his friend Sadiq Hidayat's efforts as the editor of *Majalah-i Musiqi* (Journal of Music) to publish a number of his poems. He also congratulated Hidayat for writing *Afsanih-i Afarinish* (The Myth of Creation: A Puppet Show in Three Acts, a fictional work that ridicules the fundamental religious beliefs about Creation) and encouraged Jamalzadih to continue writing works like *Yiki Bud Yiki Nabud* (Once Upon a Time), a Persianist collection of short stories. Nima believed that these works provided a precise picture of the "general customs and code of conduct" of Iranian society particularly those aspects of the culture that Persianists believed needed to be modified.[79]

Muhammad Ali Jamalzadih: The Pioneer of Short Story Writing

M. A. Jamalzadih (1892–1997) was a satirist who often created humorous situations with characters by using all manner of diction and dialects that played off one another. By employing this technique, in the process of creating a large number of Persian colloquial idioms, he not only blazed a new trail in Persian short story writing but also expanded the vocabulary of the Persian language. Of even greater significance was Jamalzadih's pioneering role in combining Persian and Western literary aspects as he wrote about very indigenous issues in new forms.[80] Theory thus contributed to Persianism.

His collection of short stories *Yiki Bud Yiki Nabud* (Once Upon a Time), (1921), which in great part determined the early course of modern Persian fiction, provides an excellent example of how Jamalzadih contributed to Persianism. In it, he drew inspiration from foreign styles while also defending the Persian language against Arabic and Islamic influences. This work was offensive to traditionalist elites, religious and conservative people who all found his writing blasphemous in terms of both national pride and religion.[81] Jamalzadih nevertheless developed loyalty to what he called "sweet Persian," a passionate feeling that links his diverse and at times contradictory works together.

In "Farsi Shakkar Ast" (Persian Is Sugar)—the most famous short story of this collection and the first short story written in a simple, precise, and informal Persian language—Jamalzadih distinguishes three cultural tendencies: Islamic tradition, Western influence, and "genuine" Iranian culture. He represents these through four characters: a narrator; a Westernized Iranian man who speaks Persian with a French accent; an Iranian shaikh (a clergyman) who speaks a mixture of Persian and Arabic; and an ordinary Iranian man named Ramazan who speaks a simple, colloquial Persian. The narrator, a middle-class Iranian man who has come back from Europe, is taken to jail immediately after he disembarks at a northern port. His "crime" is that although he looks like a foreigner, he carries an Iranian passport. In prison, he encounters the shaikh, the Westernized man, and Ramazan.

Describing his encounter with the Westernized man, the narrator says, "First my eyes fell upon one of those Western-oriented fellows who will remain the symbol of coddling, idiocy, and illiteracy in Iran until the day of resurrection."[82] He then describes the shaikh: "A hissing sound was coming from a corner of the cell, and I turned my head in that direction. Something caught my attention in that corner, which I thought at first was a shiny white cat curled up on a black bag of charcoal. But it turned out to be a shaikh, who was sitting cross-legged with his arms hugging his legs and wrapped in his cloak as if he were in his mosque. The shiny white cat was his disordered, wrinkled turban and the hissing was the sound of his salutations for the holy family of the prophet (salavat)" (281–90). Finally the narrator introduces Ramazan: "suddenly, the door to the jail opened noisily and they threw a poor young man into the cell" (281–90).

Like the narrator, Ramazan does not know why the authorities have arrested him.

Trying to figure out what has happened, he, with the shaky voice of someone who has been oppressed and violated, turns to the shaikh for answers: "Shaikh, for Imam ʿAbbas's sake, tell me, what the hell have I done?" The shaikh, with "perfect declamation and composure," utters: "Believer! Deliver ye not the reins of thy rebellious and weak soul to anger and rage for those who control their wrath and are forgiving toward mankind."[83]

Ramazan is stunned by the shaikh's speech. He can follow the shaikh's voice but not the meaning of his words; he can relate neither to the mixed Arabic or Persian words nor to the religious terminology. The only word he recognizes is *Kazem* (a name meaning "one who controls in Arabic"). Thinking that the shaikh is calling him by that name, Ramazan says, "No, reverend, Kazem is not your servant's name. My name is Ramazan and I only want to know why I have been buried alive." The shaikh, "with the same consummate declamation and composure," replies:

> May God reward ye who believe. The point is well taken by your advocate's intellect. Patience is the key to release. *Spero* that the object of our imprisonment shall become manifest *ex tempore;* but whatever the case, whether sooner or later, it most assuredly will reach our ears. *Interea,* while we wait, the most profitable occupation is to recite the name of the creator, which in any event is the best of endeavors.[84]

Sure now that he will not receive any useful information from the shaikh, Ramazan turns to the Westernized man. However, here too he meets with confusion. He is not able to understand the man's Persian, which is spoken with a thick French accent. Ultimately, the narrator, despite his own Western appearance and exposure to European life and language, is able to speak the "true, sweet language" of Persian and thereby help Ramazan.

Through the interaction of these four characters, Jamalzadih presents one of the most central concerns of Persianism: the conflict between Persian, foreign, and Islamic cultures. The focus of the story, however, is Ramazan's struggle to understand the shaikh and his religious phraseology. The shaikh lacks a means of clear communication, even though he does not cease to produce words. His "hissing" suggests he is alienated from and oblivious to Persian culture and language. He only perplexes Ramazan, a "poor," "desperate," "browbeaten" fellow Iranian. Ramzan's own prayer and his recitation of holy names make him sound naïve, ignorant, and slavish. He begins to think the two other prisoners evil and mad. Only the secular protagonist/narrator, in all likelihood standing for Jamalzadih himself, can fully understand what is transpiring in this cell. He is a "true" Iranian who adopts the positive aspects of Western culture and yet remains Iranian. He provides Ramazan with insight into the situation in the prison: "Little brother, they're neither devils or madmen, only Iranians with the same country and faith as you and I." To which Ramzan responds, "If they are really Iranians why do they speak languages that have nothing to do with human speech?"

The characters, their modes of expression, and the satirical tone of the story demonstrate that simple, pure Persian language is superior to that "contaminated" by Arab-Islamic terminology. With these tools the author defends bewildered Iranianness against what he perceives as a cultural invasion. The contrast between the shaikh's language and that used by the narrator represents this Persianist ideological concern. Jamalzadih openly scorns Arabic influence in favor of a "pure" Persian in order to promote the idea of literary modernity.

To solve some of the difficulties facing Persian culture, Jamalzadih advocated using the people's language. In his preface to *Once Upon a Time*, he explains that Persian literature can change social conditions if it is made more accessible to the masses, if it uses colloquial language and dialects, and if it adopts new literary forms. These arguments seem revolutionary when compared to the then-prevailing disdain in Iranian literary circles for the use of colloquial language. His writing demonstrates his conviction that a new literary language is essential to convey emerging modern sensibilities on both linguistic and imaginative levels. This conviction surfaces not only in "Persian Is Sugar" but also in many of his other works, such as "Dard-i dil-i Mula Qurban Ali" (Mula Qurban Ali's Grievances) and "Rajul-i Siyasi" (Political Men). In short, the themes of his works, his incorporation of the colloquial language, his critical stance regarding religion, his experimentation with new forms, and his dedication to modernity all serve to categorize him as an advocate of Persianism. Regardless of all of the changes that he and his environment underwent, his attachment to the Persian language remained constant.

Sadiq Hidayat: The Legend of Modern Persian Literature

Sadiq Hidayat is Iran's most renowned short story writer. Born in Tehran in 1903, Hidayat spent several years studying in France before returning in 1930 to pursue his writing career. Best known as a short story writer, he is also known for his famous novella *Buf-i Kur (The Blind Owl)* (1936). Hidayat was a major figure in the revival of folklore studies, producing a number of works on this topic. Besides several collections of his works, Hidayat wrote two plays and translated Kafka *(The Metamorphosis)* and Jean-Paul Sartre *(The Wall)*. In addition he co-edited *Majallih-i Musiqi* (Journal of Music) and was a member of the executive committee of the First Iranian Writers' Congress of 1946. He later returned to Paris and, after a period of extreme depression, committed suicide in April 1951.

Hidayat's writings exemplify the Persianist ideology of representation in their bold confrontation of traditional culture and religion. He found folklore attractive because of its indigenous, pre-Islamic origins; the tales he collected contained a great number of antireligious terms and colloquial expressions, as his own writings did.

In the short story "Talab-i Amurzish" (Seeking Absolution) (1932)[85] Hidayat's imaginative satire ridicules what he believes to be the most unequivocal manifestation of backwardness. In this story Karbala serves as a symbol of the cultural tendencies Hidayat wants to eradicate. Karbala has been a meaningful symbol in Iran since 680 C.E., when Husayn, the third Shiite imam, and most of his small group of supporters and family were murdered by the Umayyad Yazid in the Battle of Karbala. Before that bloody day, Husayn's group of seventy-two had been attacked by the troops of Ubaydullah, led by ibn Sa⁽d. Shut off from water and food sources and thus weakened, Husayn was forced to negotiate a truce. His entreaties were rebuffed even though he came forward carrying his baby son and asking for water. The child was shot in the throat with an arrow while in his father's arms, and the battle ensued. Only one son of Husayn, who had been too sick to fight, his mother, and some other women and children survived. They were delivered—along with Husayn's head—to Ubaydullah, who eventually released them to Medina. Shiites continue to commemorate this day with mournful ceremonies, processions, self-flagellation, cursing of the earlier caliphs,[86] and performances and theatrical reenactments of the public slaughter of Husayn and his supporters *(Ta⁽ziyeh)*. The latter, the equivalent of the Passion Play in Christianity, is an event of great magnitude for Shiite Muslims in Iran, Iraq, Afghanistan, and elsewhere.[87] Because of its entrenched religious significance among Shiite Iranians, Karbala appears in many cultural texts and even in political speeches. It is a simple fact that the manner in which Karbala is portrayed can indicate the religiosity of a text, its author, and ultimately the community from which it arises. For Hidayat, in particular, the theme of Karbala serves as a means for promoting Persianism by disdaining the concepts and rituals surrounding the event.

In "Seeking Absolution" a number of pilgrims travel across the desert to visit the tomb of Imam Husayn in Karbala, Iraq. After a long, difficult trip with storms, dust, and the burning sun assailing them, the pilgrims arrive at Karbala, where they encounter a confusing "sea of people: filthy Arabs, people selling all kinds of goods, people with stupid faces, with turbans on their heads and with cloaks and slippers who are trying to speak Persian, grating Turkish, or speaking Arabic which rolled out into the air from deep in their throats or even from their intestines" (79). The pilgrims become only more confused and lost as they come across a "crowd of sellers attracting customers in several ways: one is singing *Nuhah* wailing, mournful songs, one is beating his breast, one is selling prayer beads and sacred shrouds, one is claiming he can catch genies, one is writing prayers, and another loudly soliciting patrons for his rental rooms. And one local Arab is just sitting in front of a coffee house, picking his nose with one hand and cleaning between his toes with other, his head covered with flies and lice" (80).

The narrative continues with each pilgrim relating a story in turn. Each has committed a crime for which he or she has come to Karbala seeking forgiveness. The first tale belongs to Aziz. Barren, she allows her husband to marry another woman but later kills their baby out of jealousy by inserting a needle into the baby's brain. Over the next few years, they have two other boys. Aziz kills the second child in the same way but eventually decides to kill the new wife instead of the third child. Upon relating her story, Aziz feels better and soon after even begins to laugh when she hears the pilgrims' stories and anecdotes, which are similar to hers. Mashhadi Ramazan, a carriage driver, confesses that once, when carrying two passengers, his carriage broke down, killing one of them, so he then killed the other one and stole his money. He came to Karbala to give some of the money to the Ulama so that they might make the rest *halal* (lawful) for him. Khanum Gulin, the third pilgrim, confesses that she has just killed her sister on the way to Karbala in order to be their father's sole inheritor. Aziz is surprised to hear these confessions, but Khanum Gulin states that she has heard "in a mosque, that as the pilgrims decide to depart for a holy place, all of their sins are forgiven even if they are as many as the leaves on a tree" (89).

These confessions reveal that none of the pilgrims is genuinely pious. Hidayat depicts them all as sinful hypocrites who only pretend to be righteous in their communities. The pilgrims, however, are not the only persons or things disparaged in the story. In fact, nothing in the story is depicted positively. The old, half-ruined city, the dusty roads, the crude scenes, the deceitful intentions of the pilgrims; and filthy local residents are all unappealing. Hidayat conveys the reader to Karbala by means of a long, tiring journey through the desert only to arrive at a ruined, backward, filthy town. Hidayat's imagery tries to create a sense of disgust; through such details as *makhlut-e khak va shen-e dagh* (a mixture of hot dust and sand), *ab-e gandideh* (stagnant water), *surat ha-ye ahmaq-e fineh beh sar* (stupid faces beneath fezzes), *magas* (flies), *shepesh* (lice), *cherk cheshm va la-ye angoshtha* (dirt around the eyes and between the toes). Both his recitation of religious verses related to the Passion Play and his metaphors describing the dreams of one of the characters has about a divine being who shows the way to Karbala serve to denounce the pilgrimage and its related rituals as superstitions. With this portrayal Hidayat demystifies Karbala. The pilgrims who arrive from elsewhere only heighten the sinister atmosphere because of their corrupted lives. This depiction of Karbala is in sharp contrast to the usual reverence for a site so exalted that it no longer seems to exist in actual time and space, yet so divine and so familiar that its foreign location becomes irrelevant. Hidayat's subversion of Karbala's image was in line with the government's policy that banned the performance of the *Ta'ziyeh* in 1931 but is even more obviously comprehensible in the context of Persianism. Such ideological affinity between the oppositional intellectuals and the state disappeared in the next episode of Persian literary history.

In "Hikayat-i Ba Natijih" (A Story with a Moral, 1931),[88] Hidayat again criticizes traditional and religious culture, focusing in this case on veiling and the pretense of chastity. In this story a mother complains to her son about his wife, accusing her of behaving promiscuously and not in accordance with religious law. Because of listening to his mother's advice, the son beats his wife. In bitter revenge the wife pushes the mother-in-law into a fire.

This one-page story also points to Hidayat's preoccupation with Persianism. The mother and the son represent religious culture, and

the wife and the fire represent opposite forces and change. Fire is especially significant because it was considered sacred in pre-Islamic Iran's
predominant religion, Zoroastrianism. The characters' names also suggest this dichotomy The man's name is Zolfaqar (after the sword of Ali,
a seventh-century Shiite Muslim imam), and the mother's name Guahr
Sultan or "Sultan's jewel," a common name in the Qajar period. With
their traditional and religious connotations, both of these names stand
in contrast to the secular name of the abused wife, Setareh, a Persian
word meaning "star." Finally, because of its satirical and sarcastic tone,
the story amounts to the ridicule of traditional culture. The mother's
comment that, in her time, young women placed stones under their
tongues to disguise their voices when a stranger came to the door (dis-
guising voice being analogous to the practice of veil) constitutes a
mockery of a once serious practice because of her flippant tone and its
lack of context in the story.

"Sag-i Vilgard" (Stray Dog) (1942) provides another example of
Hidayat's critical eye toward religion. Pat is a mixed-breed dog, well
groomed, raised in a safe environment, and close to his master's family. All this, however, comes to an end one day when his master takes
him on a trip to the town of Varamine near Tehran. There, in the heat
of the day, he smells the scent of a bitch and sets off into a garden to
search for her, deaf to his master's call. Inside the garden he confronts
the gardener, who beats him up and shoos him away. Forfeiting his
sexual quest, he begins to search for his master, but to no avail. He
leads the rest of his life in lonesome misery. He is constantly beaten by
the townspeople, feels alienated, and is unable to make sense of his
cruel surroundings. One day, the dog comes across a man who not only
does not beat him but even offers him food. Pat follows the man as he
drives away, only to end up in the middle of a desert, thirsty, tired, and
hungry. There he lies down and dies.

As simple as the story may sound, it contains sharp criticism of tradition. A dog is considered a particularly impure creature, which Muslims are encouraged not to touch. Hidayat, however, describes Pat
sympathetically.[89] "In the depth of his eyes a human spirit was dis-
cernible. In his benighted life something eternal undulated in his eyes
and had a message that could not be conveyed, for it had been trapped
just behind his pupils."[90] The townspeople, however, were not able to
see this: "In their eyes, the torture of an unclean dog, cursed by religion
and possessed of seven lives, was quite natural and worthy of eternal

reward. So to please Allah, they beat him."[91] Because the dog suffers a hideous pain, even the gardener and garden, positive images that were associated with cultivation and beauty in the classical period, are here negative. The scenes of people beating the dog are tediously repetitive and yet in their excess convey the author's sense of the grotesque in what he is attacking.

Displaying complicated formal and stylistic innovation, Hidayat's *Buf-i Kur* (Blind Owl) (1936) has become Iran's most controversial and celebrated work of fiction.[92] The novel, representing Persianism, involves an Iranian artist who dislikes traditional religion and the Arabic influence on Iranian culture. It is a two-part story about the life of an antireligious pen-and-ink artist who, as an outcast of society, struggles to come to terms with his own identity and a life of opium addiction and impotence.[93] The first part depicts his destitute situation as a man unfulfilled in life or love. After he catches a real or imagined look at a beautiful dark woman, the only image he is able to paint is of that woman handing a lotus flower over a stream to an old man beneath a cypress tree. Haunted by the memory of this woman and an intense love for her, he runs madly around town trying to find her. Unsuccessful, he returns home to find her waiting on his doorstep. Although she allows herself to be ushered inside, he is not enticed by her body on the bed. Instead, he pours a glass of wine into her mouth, and she dies. Not wanting any other living soul to look upon her beauty, he chops her up and transports her to a graveyard in a suitcase with the help of an old hunchback. Once this act is completed, he feels somewhat relieved, though the guilt over the dead woman weighs on him. Upon their parting, the old hunchback gives him a jug. After he goes back to his room, the man realizes that adorning the jug is the picture of the same woman and old man beside the stream that he himself has drawn. This strange coincidence makes the man imagine he might have existed centuries before as an artist who drew the same scene. Feeling alone in his agony and realizing that nothing has changed, the man slides into an opium-induced unconsciousness.

The second part of the novel begins at that point. After falling down a well and going far, far back in time, the man wakes to find that he is an Indian dancer who is the impotent husband of a prostitute wife. She is willing to sleep with the worst individuals society can produce but refuses him. He detests her but desires nonetheless to sleep with her. In an attempt to gain favor with her, he even acts as her pimp and brings her "human scum from the streets." He hopes that by learning what allure they have for her he can eventually endear himself to her. But she does not lift her personal ban on him. In desperation, he thinks of killing her while dressed as one of her suitors but decides instead to try to make love to her in the guise of her frequent visitor, the seller of odds and ends. He has forgotten to put away the knife hidden in his wraps, and while embracing her, he accidentally stabs and kills her with it. Horrified by what has happened, he is brought out of his shocked state only when he looks in the mirror and discovers that he has actually become the seller of odds and ends. He immediately begins to search for the ancient jug but just misses the old hunchback running off with it. He returns home once again with the weight of another dead person on his heart.

This novel has been the subject of many different and contradictory interpretations. No matter how the story is read, however, it is clear that Hidayat portrays a man and a society that have both lost their identities. Rahimieh aptly states that "The lack of an effective transition between the old and the new is that which gives rise to the narrator's increasing sense of isolation and eventual madness. He continues to feel alienated from his own art and fails to realize any other possibilities."[94] The man seems to be living a nightmare, and society seems to be torn apart. The owl in the title of the work foretells an even worse condition for him and for society. In Persian folklore the owl is an omen of bad luck that lives in ruined and desolate places.[95] Moreover, by applying the adjective "blind" to the owl, Hidayat distorts, undercuts, and completely overturns other conventional folkloric connotations of owl imagery. The title suggests the impotence of absurdity of the main character: the owl is an effective nocturnal predator because of its keen sense of sight, but a blind owl would be completely ineffectual.

The language of the text speaks against Arabic language and portrays the protagonist as an antireligious intellectual who is made to suffer by traditional and Islamic culture. When the protagonist's nanny talks to him about the miracles of the prophet, his only thought is: "I was merely envious of her inferior level of thinking and of her foolishness." When she brings him a dusty prayer book, he states: "Neither the rabbles' prayers nor any of their writings or thoughts was useful for me." He then asks himself, "What use did I have for their nonsense and their lies? Wasn't I myself the outcome of many successive generations, and didn't I inherit their suffering? Wasn't the past in

myself? Never have any of the mosques, the calls to prayer, the ablu-
tions, the noisy spitting, the bowings and prostration in front of the
Almighty, or Absolute creator, with whom one could speak only in
Arabic, ever had any effect upon me."[96] Moreover, once when he
attended a mosque, he was not able to harmonize his thoughts and
feelings with those of other participants: "I realized that my eyes were
scanning the glazed tiles and the intricate designs on the walls, designs
that relieved me from the duties of the mosque and transported me
into a realm of delightful dreams. . . . In this imagined night I said my
prayers as if they were some vacillating words uttered in a dream"
(88–89).

Hidayat scrutinizes the superstitious aspects of the traditional and
religious beliefs that the protagonist encounters everywhere he turns.
This line of thought underpins characterization in the novel:

> They were carrying a coffin in front of my window. The coffin was
> covered with black cloth and on top of it two candles were burning.
> The sound of *la ilaha illa Allah*, there is no god but God, drew my
> attention to the procession. The merchants and the passersby halted
> their activities and walked seven steps behind the coffin . . . even the
> butcher, for the sake of having performed a ritual good deed, fol-
> lowed the coffin for seven steps. (97)

In contempt, he turns away from the window only to encounter the
nanny who is bringing herbal extracts to him. "She was sliding the
large beads of a rosary through her fingers and praying first silently
and then aloud in a contemptible way, reciting, *allahmma, asllah illa*. (97)

Many people who cite these religious phrases seem to have no
knowledge of what the words mean. They recite them solely because
they think they will receive a spiritual reward. Thus the narrator makes
explicit and derogatory references to the Qur'an and its Arabic language: "It was yesterday or the day before when I yelled and my wife
appeared in the half-open door of my room, and I saw with my own
eyes the marks of the old man's filthy, yellow and decayed teeth, teeth
from between which Arabic verses of the Qur'an flow, on my wife's
cheek" (197). The old seller of odds and ends epitomizes the cultural
backwardness that, in the author's eyes, plagues society.

By slandering the religious beliefs, rituals, and leaders that are often
referred to in Arabic, Hidayat reinforces a Persianist dichotomy
between pious culture and Persian culture: "My pronunciation of the

terms of the prayer was devoid of inner meaning because I preferred to speak to a friend, or an acquaintance rather than to God or to an all-powerful One—God was too much for me!" (197) The author uses terminology such as *kitab-i du^ca* (prayer book), *du^ca* (prayers), *arabi* (Arabic), *masjid* (mosque), *qadir-i muti^cal* (Almighty), to describe what he sees as a rotten culture and a corrupt religion. The classical images of the garden, the old man by the brook, and the young woman with a wine glass appear in this book, but with meanings quite different from those of the classical period. Weary of them as clichés Hidayat employs them in a novel, if gloomy, fashion. The atmosphere is very sad and none of the usual love scenes of the classical period appear. These essential elements of classical aesthetics seem to bring nothing but melancholy to Hidayat.

Hidayat's other stories also divulge his attitude toward Islam and the Arabic language. Sometimes he creates antireligious characters who are often very explicit in expressing their (and his) nontraditionalist beliefs. Faridun and Farangis, the two major figures in "Shabha-yi Varamin" (The Nights of Varamin), Hasani, in "Ab-i Zindigi" (The Water of Life), and Dash Akul, the protagonist of "Dash Akul" (Dah Akol) all dispute the value of religious culture. Other times, he creates religious characters of Haji Aqa and Alviyeh Khanum and subjects them to his ridicule.

Hidayat's dislike of religious tradition reaches a climax in his long stories *al-Bi^csah al-Islamiah ila al-Bilad al-Franjiah* (The Islamic Mission to the Western World) (1933), *Zamharir va Duzakh* (Intense Cold and Hell) (1934), *Tup Murvarid* (Pearl Cannon) (1947), and *Afsanih-yi Afarin-ish: Khaymih Shab Bazi dar Sih Pardih* (The Myth of Creation: A Puppet Show in Three Acts) (1933). In these works Hidayat mercilessly ridicules religious principles and superstitious beliefs. He often utilizes an elaborate mixture of Arabic and Persian to accentuate the beauty of pure Persian over Arabic, much as Jamalzadih does in "Persian Is Sugar." For example, Hidayat uses *al-Faranjiah*, an Arabized form of the word *Farang* when referring to Europe (*g* has become *j*, and the Arabic ending *-iah* has been added). This has, rather, a sense of convolution and a comical sound to a Persian ear. None of the satire is directed at Europe, Europeans, and their affections for Persians. In *The Myth of Creation*, Hidayat most directly insults the religious beliefs regarding the Creation story and other rituals, practices, and principles as mere superstitious.[97] The phenomenon of Persiansism explains how Hidayat could have written both a serious, melancholic, esoteric novel such as *The Blind Owl* and a satiric, sarcastic, uncomplicated story such as *The Myth of Creation*.

He offers passionate glorification of Iran's pre-Islamic history in works such as *Parvin Dukhtar-i Sasan* (Parvin, the Daughter of Sasan) (1930), *Sayih-i Mughul* (The Shadow of the Mughuls) (1931), and *Maziyar* (1933). He delves into history to give his own fictional account of the Arab and Mughul invasions of Iran. He searches the Sasanid period for a Persian identity and when he does not find it, he attacks the invaders. In *Parvin*, for example, Hidayat writes on the Iranian's tragic tale of resistance against Arabs and portrays it as the last true cultural movement. He focuses on the fate of Parvin, the heroine of the book, as a means of grieving over the termination of that empire. The story reiterates the nostalgic memory of the pre-Islamic era in a way that makes it seem as if the invasion had occurred only days ago.

Even though Hidayat did not find a Persian identity or an ancient Persian "Superman," his profuse, innovative, and provocative fictional works showed him to be an iconoclastic advocate of Persianism. His contribution to the rise of Persianism and to the emergence of the modern Persian language is immense. He deeply influenced a large number of subsequent authors, especially in their ideology of representation, though none ever approached the issue as boldly as he.

Persianism in Other Writers' Works

Persianism surfaced in the works of later writers in this episode of Persian literary history. For example, Jalal Al-i Ahmad in his early works *Sih Tar* (Seh Tar) and *Khasi Dar Miqat* (Lost in the Crowd) and Khusraw Shahani in "Murdih Kishi" (Pallbearing) wrote critically about religious aspects of the culture. These works in particular imitated Hidayat's satirical style in mocking religious characters and his satirical style.

An erstwhile journalist, Al-i Ahmad was the youngest writer to establish himself as a fiction writer and essayist between 1941 and 1953 before joining the Committed Literature movement and adopting a new leftist, revolutionary mode of expression. He began by advocating Persianism and criticizing traditional culture and backwardness.[98] He admired Hidayat and wrote a few critical pieces about him and his works.

Al-i Ahmad's early book *Sih Tar* (1948) includes thirteen short stories in which he deprecates Islam and the Arabic language. In the title story he depicts a musician who, after working very hard and earning enough money, finally purchases his own instrument. But soon afterward the instrument is broken into pieces by a fanatic Muslim trying to prevent the musician from going into a mosque. In another story the narrator becomes fed up with Arabs and their behavior toward him while he is on a trip to Baghdad: "Oh, how much I hated those Arabic words, those Arabic names with their difficult pronunciation; so many glottal ʿayns and qafs and so many palatal tayns and zayns!"[99] Like Hidayat, he uses an Arabicized title, "al-gumarak va al-mukus," merely to ridicule the situation and provide a bit of "humor". Several other characters deride the Arabic language, especially as the language of prayer, in some other stories in this collection.

Khusraw Shahani was a lifelong journalist and one of the founding members of the Iranian Press Association. His works of fiction, written in the 1960s and 1970s, include nine collections of short stories and two novels. His writings appeared in the many new literary journals that arose during the prerevolutionary period. He was a master of using familiar Persian folk characters for satirical purposes in the short story form. In "Murdah Kishi" (Pallbearing), a man walking to work encounters a funeral procession. Step by step, he becomes more involved in the procession. Probably because of his more urban appearance, other participants eventually ask him to fill out an application for a burial certificate, a document necessary for the burial. To do this, he is requested to attest that he is a relative of the deceased. Although hesitant, he complies because he feels it is his duty as a good Muslim. This involvement leads to a new set of problems when the actual relatives who have come to the city from their village in the hope of gaining a hefty inheritance invade his home, seeking the dead man's estate. The protagonist must prove to the family that he had not only not received anything from the deceased but that he had never even met him.[100]

Through this story, Shahani portrays the entire ceremony as a nonsensical process and the Arabic terms associated with the Islamic funeral as decadent. He manipulates language to ridicule the Islamic tradition of public pallbearing by assigning a negative, destructive meaning to religious terms such as *mordeh keshi* (pallbearing), *qari* (Qurʾan reciter), *mayyet* (the deceased), *shahadat* (to say the Muslim creed), *shariat* (religious law), *fataha* (first Surah of the Qurʾan), *sawab* (divine reward), *rawzah* (mourning ceremony), and *majles-e khatm* (final mourning ceremony). He depicts participation in religious activities as not only superstitious but also harmful, associating them with backwardness, hypocrisy, and injustice. The protagonist wastes his time and his money, and is forced to lie, only to be accused of stealing money from the deceased.

In sum, Nima Yushij, Muhammad Ali Jamalzadih, Sadiq Hidayat, Jalal Al-i Ahmad, and Khusraw Shahani represent the Persianist literary movement.[101] This movement was a struggle against the Qajar Islamic tradition and the influence of Arabic language as manifested in poetry and fiction. Literature, especially poetry, had regressed during the Qajar dynasty, consisting almost exclusively of treatises on the lives of the prophet Muhammad and Imam Ali in repetitive, traditional prosody. There were two other issues that, although not the major concerns of the authors in this episode, were significant in terms of the way they helped to distinguish this episode from the ones that follow it. First is the portrayal of the West, especially America, toward which there was no opposition or hard feelings expressed in the literary works during this period. On the contrary, the tacit understanding among the authors was that Iranians should follow Western models in their effort to modernize. The second regards women. Postconstitutional literary products demonstrate a strong sympathy toward the liberation of women. Sadiq Hidayat, M. Jamalzadih, and before them, P. Itisami, A. Lahuti, F. Yazdi, and Iraj Mirza in their own way show support for the liberation of women. In a poem, Mirza says, "Tamam-e in mafased az hejab ast / hejab ast ancheh iran zan kharab ast"[102] (all this rottenness is from veiling / veiling is what has destroyed Iran), a comment that exemplifies such enunciations in fiction and poetry. In a sense, it could be argued that some early novelists, such as Mushfiq Kazimi in *Tehran-i Makhuf* (The Dreadful Tehran) (1925), Yahya Dawlatabadi in *Shahrnaz* (1925), Abass Khalili in *Ruzgar-i Siyah* (Dark Days) (1924) and in *Intiqam* (1925), have tried to portray women's condition as part of their overall criticism of the traditional or corrupt modern culture.[103] Journals such as *Danish* (Knowledge), *Zaban-i Zanan* (Women's Tongue), *Alam-i Nisvan* (Women's World), which were all published for some time during the first three decades of the twentieth century, devoted themselves to the women's cause. Women, in fact, participated in the publication of many of these journals.

This episode began to wane when the First Iranian Writers' Congress convened and shifted its attention to Marxism's call for socialist realism among literary communities. The demise of Persianism was all but assured after the reestablishment of Muhammad Reza Shah's rule in 1953, when censorship pushed all the major writers inexorably toward the Marxist left.

3

Revolutionary Literature: The Committed Literary Movement Before the 1979 Revolution

THE ALLIES' OCCUPATION OF IRAN during World War II ended the regime of Reza Shah in 1941, and his abdication allowed his son, Mohammad Reza Pahlavi, to continue the Pahlavi dynasty. However, the political situation became chaotic. The monarch became nothing but a figurehead. Mohammad Mossadeq (d. 1967), who became prime minister in 1951, began a series of fundamental reforms and a push to nationalize the economy.[1] From 1941 until the shah's coup d'état that overthrew the government of Prime Minister Mossadeq in 1953, political activists experienced freedom of expression and free elections, both of which had previously been absent. The nationalists, led by Mossadeq's National Front, and the Marxists, led by the pro-Soviet Tudeh Party, competed for power. Although the nationalists—with their promise to nationalize the Anglo-Iranian Oil Company—were successful in gaining the political power and forming a government, the Marxists were active in all areas of culture endeavors; their literary activities included the publishing of numerous journals and periodicals. There were also some religious activists, led by Ayatollah Kashani, but their political and cultural influences were minimal.

This situation gave rise to the second episode of modern Persian literature, which was to last until the 1979 Revolution. In this episode, literary activists believed that there were two kinds of literature: one that defended the people and was committed to their cause, and another that disregarded serious social and political issues and remained "pure" literature. They supported the former and engaged in Committed Literature *(Adabiyat-e Moteahed)* that derived its principles from Marxism or, more precisely, from what they perceived was Marxism.

The themes of this literature revolved around equality, justice, and freedom. The figurative expression of these issues and the glorification of heroism and martyrdom were the constitutive elements of the language system in most fiction and poetry. The strident antagonism to religion that had characterized the writings of Persianism disappeared. Writers of Committed Literature, in fact, became somewhat supportive of Islam. Influenced by leftist organizations such as Organization of Iranian People's Fada'i Guerrillas (OIPFG) (Sazman-e Fadaiyan-e Cherikha-ye Fedai-e Khalq-i Iran), which sought an ally in revolutionary Islamic forces in its struggle against the regime, literary authors considered Islamic forces to be potentially revolutionary and therefore portrayed Muslims as oppressed people. The leftist authors indeed witnessed the emergence of such revolutionary Islamic groups. For example, the Organization of People's Mojahedin of Iran (OPMI) (Sazman-e Mojahedin-e Khalq-e Iran) began its struggle against the Pahlavis' rule in the late 1960s and joined the OIPFG in the armed struggle. The emergence of OPMI, highly influenced by Marxism, marked a shift in the way Islamic forces were involved in politics. Previously, Muslim activists had not developed any long-range revolutionary strategies, but the OPMI became fully engaged in radical oppositional activities.[2] The OPMI was also relevant to the rise of Islamic radical activities in the Middle East.[3] By this time, a divide in the Islamic camp (excluding the Mojahedin) could be discerned. Secular writers supported this shift and discontinued their defamation of Islam. Following this, literature in this episode became the medium most appropriate in the eyes of all groups for communicating the revolutionary messages about sociopolitical change,[4] which they envisioned would improve the condition of the Iranian people.

Directly sponsored by the political parties, new journals such as *Ruzgar-i Naw* (New Era), *Payam-i Naw* (New Message), *Jahan-i Naw* (New World), and *Mardum* (People) politicized poetry, prose, and literary criticism to an even greater degree. They introduced Soviet authors and other international Committed writers to provide examples to follow and to convey a message about the urgent need for a new society and a new political system. Most translation activities in this period were for the purpose of addressing this need.

The literary activism in this period culminated in the organization of the First Iranian Writers' Congress, which took place in the Iran–Soviet Union Cultural House in Tehran in 1946.[5] This event helped the dissemination of Marxist literary theory and the upsurge of Committed Literature. During the conference more than seventy authors presented their works. Even though traditionalists had a strong presence, the leftist discourse succesfully advanced its political messages. Most of the poems read by leftist authors treated themes related to the proletariat, socialism, or social criticism. Even those poems related to morality and education had a critical tone toward the current social and political system.[6] One of the delegates, Faridun Tavaluli, read a poem entitled "Farda-ye Enqilab" (The Revolutionary Morrow), which typifies the dominant voice in the conference:

Fardy-ye Enqelab
Por jush o por khorush
az noqteh ha ye dur
miayadam beh gush
migiradam qarar
mibakhshadam omid
miaradm beh hush
Farman jonbeh ast.
hengameh-ye nabard.[7]

[The morrow of the revolution
enthusiastically and with glamour
from a point in distance
reaches my ears.
It calms me,
gives me hope,
revives me.
It is the summons to move.
It is the time to fight.]

No revolution, however, would occur in the near future. The royal court continued to pressure Mossadeq, and finally, with some outside help, Mohammad Reza Shah overthrew Mossadeq's popular government through a coup d'état in 1953.[8] Immediately, the government of Mohammad Reza Shah began a policy of repression against Iranian liberals, the Tudeh Party, and eventually every oppositional member. This policy succeeded in dismantling all organized opposition. For a long time Mossadeq and other national leaders were imprisoned and democratic activities came to an end. In this coup d'état, the United States supported the shah, creating an unpopular image of the West for the first time among the opposition forces.

In the late 1950s, Iran began to experience rapid economic growth, industrial development, and the widespread Westernization of its society. The shah's so-called White Revolution brought changes—beyond his father's reforms—in land ownership, industry, education, and the treatment of women. Later, skyrocketing oil revenues enabled his government to engage actively in reform and modernization. However, none of these reforms helped to create a positive image for the shah.[9] The government's policies, which focused on the interests of the wealthy upper class, created dissatisfaction among the other sectors, such as the workers, urban dwellers, migrant workers, and the bazaar. The opposition considered policies of economic development a service to foreigners. The clergy and the merchants united and immediately began to use the leftist's revolutionary rhetoric. The shah, on the other hand, used propaganda, censorship, and his secret police, Sazman-i Ittila'at va Amniyat-i Kishvar (National Security and Information Organization), known by its Persian acronym as SAVAK, to control the opposition.

As a result, new revolutionary radical-Marxist organizations that admired the Cuban and Chinese revolutionary styles emerged in the late 1960s. They soon wielded influence over intellectuals, students, and authors. This new radical opposition sought earnestly to undermine the ruling power of the shah, whom they saw as a puppet of the West. In addition, several smaller groups such as Shoaiyan's Group, Golshorki's group, Setareh-e Sorkh (The Red Star), and Arman-i Khalq (The People's Ideal) embarked upon a new wave of physical and ideological attacks on the state, believing that their revolutionary actions would not only weaken the ruling class but would also result in a mass uprising. In contrast to the earlier opposition, the new radical groups believed armed struggle would play a major part in the political campaign to overthrow the shah.

In this milieu revolution and political change became the goals of literary activity, giving rise to the second episode of the history of modern Persian literature. Writers overthrew the regime many times allegorically and symbolically, in order to encourage people to rise against their situation. Allegory, symbol, and most importantly, metaphor became useful tools for veiling meanings meant to be conveyed to readers despite censorship efforts. Many remained anonymous for years, and some (such as A. Sayeh, A. Bamdad, and Omid) were known only by pseudonyms. When exposed, many of these writers were persecuted. In this episode, a myriad of fiction writers, such as Hushang Gulshiri, Samad Bihrangi, Ghulam Husayn Sai'di, J. Mir Sadiqi, Sadiq Chubak, M. Dawlatabadi; poets, such as Ahmad Shamlu, M. Akhvan Salis, Faridun Mushiri, and Hamid Musadiq; and other writers, such as Ahmad Riza Ahmadi, Muhammad Huquqi, Ismail Khui, Nasim Khaksar, Hamid Riza Rahimi, Said Sultanpur, and Siyavush Kasrai, described and criticized the Iranian society under the monarchist state. At times they were directly involved in revolutionary activities organized by underground organizations. Literary journals such as *Faslha-yi Sabz* (Green Seasons), *Arash* (Arash), *Kitab-i Jum'ih* (Friday's Book), *Kitabi Zaman* (Book of the Time), *Daftarha-yi Zamanih* (Books of the Era), *Andishih va Hunar* (Arts and Ideas), *Alifba* (Alphabet), *Sadaf* (Shell), *Sukhan* (Speech), *Nashriyih-i Kanun-i Nivisandigan-i Iran* (Journal of the Writers Association of Iran), and *Vizhih-i Hunar va Adabiyat* (For Art and Literature) published and promoted Committed literary works and criticism. These journals were especially successful in keeping constant contact with their audiences through an informal network. Indeed, that is how these journals were able to support themselves financially, because they refused financial assistance from the government.

As a result of these authors' tendencies toward Marxism, a socialist realism became a distinctive feature of literature in this episode, and Committed writers deemphasized form, as opposed to content, arguing that the latter has a larger capacity to serve the people. Their fascination with substance was derived from Marxist literary criticism, which, as Eagleton explains, opposes literary formalism and attacks the technical aspects of literature that allegedly reduce literary creativity to a game of aesthetics.[10] Those who later constituted the network of Iranian Committed writers learned about Marxist literary discourse through the translations of the literary works of Brecht, Gorky, and Sartre and through partial translations of classic Marxist texts. Sartre's *What Is Literature?* they found interesting for its conception of the role of literature as *litterature engagée* (Committed Literature) and the role of the writer as social critic. The works of Brecht and Gorky provided them with actual examples of commitment. And in the translation of the works of Mao Tse-tung and Lenin, Iranian literary activists were fascinated by the these communist leaders' decisive tenet that art and literature should "serve . . . the millions and tens of millions of working people."[11] From these ideas, Iranians developed a guideline for the literary activities, believing that they should write for only "the workers, peasants, soldiers and urban petty bourgeoisie."[12] From the popular translated works of Herbert Marcuse, they learned that there was "a definite connection between art and the material base, between art and the totality of the relation of production between art and social class," and that "the only authentic, true, progressive art is the art of an ascending class" and that "realism (in its various senses) is the art form which corresponds most adequately to the social relationships, and thus is the 'correct' art form."[13] From Ernest Fischer's book *The Necessity of Art: A Marxist Approach*, translated into Persian as *Zarurat-i Hunar dar Ravand-i Takamul-i Ijtimai* (The Necessity of Art in the Process of Social Evolution), they learned a concise version of Marxist literary theory, even though it was translated into a vague language to escape censorship.[14] After this discovery, the Iranian writers through their fiction and poetry began to teach the growing readership the responsive and "responsible" social roles that they should play in the struggle against the "cruel political system" of the shah.

The Iranian critic, poet, and writer Muhammad Ali Sipanlu, like other prominent critics of his time, believed in socialist realism, and he published an anthology of Committed literary works with commentaries to support his choices for reading. According to Sipanlu, one criterion for selecting these pieces for inclusion in his anthology, was that they "contain the essential elements of our time and general aspects of the peoples' lives." In his introduction to *Baz Afarini-i Vaqiyat: bist u haft qisih az bist u haft nivisandah-i muasir-i Iran* (The Interpretation of the Reality: Twenty-Seven Short Stories by Twenty-Seven Contemporary Iranian Writers) (1988), Sipanlu categorizes contemporary literature according to nine themes and subjects. The first represents life in Iran's countryside before the land reform in the stories of Buzurg Alavi and Mahmud Dawlatabadi and the influence of the landlords after land reform in a story by Amin Faqiri. The second is city life in the stories of Gh. Davud, Mahshid Amirshahi, Esmail Fassih, and Jamal Mir Sadiqi. The third contains the oil industry and its employees in the stories of Ebrahim Gulistan, Naser Taqvai, and Ahmad Mahmud. The fourth includes the petty functionaries' lives and the inside and outside views of their class in the stories of Bihazin and Taqi Mudarrisi. The fifth encompasses the urban squatters and the poor in the stories of Gholam Husayn Saiʿdi and Abdu Rahim Ahmadi. The sixth includes Iranian youth, some of whom are hopeless and nihilistic in the stories of Bahram Sadiqi, Reza Danishvar, and Ahmad Massudi; others are active in student movements in the works of Nadir Ebrahimi, and still others appear in clashes with the police state in the stories of Hushang Gulshiri. The seventh category examines the plight of the traditional Oriental woman in the stories of Sadiq Hidayat and Simin Danishvar. The eighth category examines the religious problem in a story by Jalal Al-i Ahmad. The ninth category, tending to be purely literary works, includes only stories by Javad Mujabi and Amir Husayn Ruhi.[15] Sipanlu concludes, "In these works the reader can detect the fictional version of most of the problems of our society which led to historical changes, e.g., the recent revolution of Iran."[16] Sipanlu's priorities and his understanding of contemporary literature exemplify the dominant ideas of his time.

Revolution and Fiction

Well versed in the Committed literary theory, Hushang Gulshiri (1937–) published his early works, including *Shazdih Ehtijab* (Prince Ehtejab) in the literary journal *Jung-i Isfahan* (Literary Miscellania of Isfahan). He wrote a total of three short story collections and four novels and; like many other writers in the 1970s, he was imprisoned. The reason for his imprisonment was that in his works he rather openly portrayed issues related to the revolutionary struggle against the shah's regime.

In Gulshiri's short story "My China Doll,"[17] a five year old girl, Maryam, narrates a fragmented tale of the incidents that have recently shaken her family. As she plays with her dolls, she dramatizes some of these sad events and describes the characters, places, and scenes that she has encountered. It becomes apparent that her father is confined in a building to which it is difficult for Maryam or (anyone else) to gain access. The one time she visits her father, she is not able to make physical contact with him because they are separated by physical barriers. Maryam's mother, uncle, and grandmother strive to convince Maryam's father to agree to certain conditions in order to get him out of the building. Maryam does not realize exactly what is happening, but she does sense that she is losing the father she loves dearly. In her rehearsal,

Maryam intends to give the role of her father to her favorite doll, a china doll, but she can't do that because the doll is broken. Her father had promised her to buy her a new china doll, but Maryam realizes that he will not get a chance to fulfill his promise. Now Maryam has lost both the father and the doll.

This short story displays an engaging ambiguity about the physical site where Maryam's father is confined. Ambiguity is a distinctive feature of modern Persian literature of this period, not only because of the restrictive rules of censorship but also because of the kind of metaphors the writers used—the china doll may have something to do with the revolution in the socialist republic China. Gulshiri certainly used such metaphors to convey a sign system that promoted a specific ideology. The metaphor's appeal, universal and particular, derives from its ambiguity.

Maryam's lack of access to her father may speak to a more universal father-daughter problem found in all cultures. One might conclude that the father was terminally ill and hospitalized. (This interpretation is not only possible but also allowed the text to pass censorship.) However, an interpretation of the text in the light of textual and historical particulars shows that Maryam's father is nowhere else but in a prison. His family tries to convince him to appear on television and express his regret for opposing the regime. After the coup d'état, the regime forced the members of Tudeh Party to capitulate. Later, during the 1970s, this practice continued by forcing the political prisoners to appear on television and to speak in support of the regime. Here in the fictional version, Maryam's intellectual father would not concede to such a humiliation: a lesson for all radical political activists. The story carries another effective political message: the state's power to incarcerate a political dissident also deprives an innocent child of a loving father.

Living under a totalitarian regime, the community of readers who now appreciated Committed Literature read "China Doll" as a protest against the shah's rule. For them, there was enough evidence. Maryam says to her doll, "If I put my hand under your skirt, do you like it? The lady did it with Mama and grandmother too. Grandmother said, '"God forbid."'"[18] The Committed reader's interpretation would immediately allude to her family being searched before entering prison to visit her father. With uncompromising resistance, the china doll would sacrifice its life for the sake of his goals and would not recant. The text was supposed to provoke the readers to act upon their feelings and rise up against the oppression of an innocent family. This was one of the basic premises of leftist ideological activity that was used in Committed Literature to depict the regime's oppressive policies.

Like other Committed works, this short story presents a different approach to religion from the one presented by Persianist works. For example, although the political father is a secular leftist, his mother is portrayed as a devout Muslim who even prays to God for her child's release—and she is not mocked for doing so.

Another piece of literature that deals directly with the strategies of revolution is the story "The Little Black Fish" (*Mahi Siyah-i Kuchulu*) by Samad Bihrangi (1939–1968), a Marxist writer and activist.[19] He published not only several collections of children's short stories but also numerous essays and some collections of Azari folklore. Later he became very active in the Committed literary circles in Tehran and Azarbayjan until he drowned in the Aras River in 1968. Some Committed literary activists, including Al-i Ahmad, portrayed Bihrangi's death as a political assassination by the SAVAK, and the OIPFG included Bihrangi on its list of martyrs.[20] These two factors contributed to the continuing popularity of Bihrangi, not only as a writer but also as a leftist, a Marxist, and a national hero. Bihrangi wrote *The Little Black Fish* as children's literature, no doubt hoping the authorities would permit its publication.

The Little Black Fish begins with a grandmother fish telling a bedtime story to her 12,000 children and grandchildren. In her story a young, intelligent fish, after living with his mother in a small stream, decides one day to embark on a journey to explore what lies beyond his small world. His mother and the other neighboring fish ridicule him for his unrealistic decision, but he is not intimidated and stands firm. He embarks upon his journey and faces many obstacles before he reaches the sea at the end of the stream. He meets a number of creatures, some of whom are extremely hostile. One lizard, however, gives him a dagger to defend himself should he confront a bigger enemy. Eventually a heron catches and swallows him. The heron's stomach contains another fish. The little black fish bravely saves the other little fish by killing the heron with the lizard's dagger, but he dies in the struggle. The grandmother's story ends at this point, and the children say good night. All but one of the 12,000 small fish fall asleep. The last one, a little red fish, cannot sleep because he is thinking about the sea all night long and with this Bihrangi's story ends.

Bihrangi's allegory of a little black fish that rebels and decides to search for a new way of life clearly speaks to rebellion against social status quo. He tries to convince his mother that he has to find the end of the stream because his life is meaningless in that pond. The cries of his mother do not stop him. The little black fish asks for her forgiveness and tells her to cry not for him but for the old fish who stay behind. Then through his journey he matures to such a degree that he can sacrifice himself for the sake of others.

The production and success of this story were not accidental. The fictional story of the little fish paralleled the arguments of those intellectuals of the time who advocated radical action against the shah's regime. They too felt that maintaining the organization and trying only to survive until the right moment for a revolution was not enough to create any change. As Marxists, they not only desired to analyze the sociopolitical condition but also wanted to take action to change these conditions. During his struggle the little black fish uses revolutionary slogans and gives philosophical advice.[21] By example, he teaches the younger red fish how to sacrifice his life for the cause. The little black fish's dagger suggests this period's tendencies toward armed struggle, which was soon considered the most effective way of opposing the regime and widely endorsed by major political groups. The story exemplifies the belief that in order to change society, one must take radical action. In the course of action, one will face the reactionary and tyrannical powers that will hinder progress and the truth. However, once action is begun, it will be continued by others (the red fish) who follow the same path even after the pioneers have passed on.

More precisely, this story can be seen as a fictional prelude to a political book about the revolution entitled *Mubarizih-i Musalahanih, Ham Stratigi Ham Taktik* (Armed Struggle; Both Strategy and Tactic) by Masud Ahmadzadih, the leader and one of the founders of OIPFG. According to Ahmadzadih, under a totalitarian regime avant-garde intellectuals must engage in the armed struggle in order to mobilize the people for the final confrontation with the oppressor's army. The intellectual guerrillas' task is to form small cells and mount an attack on the army of the regime in order to destroy the regime's repressive atmosphere and thereby to encourage people to support the armed struggle as the only path to freedom. In other words, a small engine begins to run so that the larger engine—the masses—can start moving.[22] The little black fish represents that small engine and the rest of the fish, especially the little red one who could not fall asleep, represent the large engine.

Bihrangi, in contrast to the writers of Persianism, did not ridicule or reject Islamic culture categorically because the paradigm of armed struggle outside "The Little Black Fish" encompassed myriad revolutionary activists with diverse ideological tendencies. For example, as long as they believed in the necessity of overthrowing the regime through armed struggle, Islamic activists were considered to be among the forces of revolution. Wealthy Muslims were exceptions, as they presumably supported the regime and opposed revolutionary activities. The Haji character, which in the previous period represented Islam and was treated as a symbol of backwardness, represents the affluent class in Bihrangi's work and is criticized for this, not his religious ideology. The Haji in "Pisarak-i Labu Furush" (The Little Sugar Beet Vendor) represents a bourgeois business man whose class identity overshadows his religious traits. His actions are the result of his social status, not his religious beliefs.

During this period the dominant Marxist ideology extends to novels. Literary activists cherished the idea of writing a novel dealing with the theory of dialectical materialism, a work requiring a combination of realism and revolutionary romanticism, if an ideal guideline for actual life is to be created. In socialist realism, the hero strives to change society into an ideal form. He is aware that the creation of a new order usually requires the destruction of the old one. In socialist novels the protagonist takes all necessary steps to help the revolutionary group he or she supports. Personal interests, religion, love, family, and life are all secondary to political and social responsibilities. Writers creating this type of novel depict personal life as being insignificant in comparison to the party's political goals. One's personal life and the party are linked only through sacrifice. Although the government in Stalin's Soviet Union supported this theory of the novel, during the shah's regime it was the intellectual opposition who espoused that approach. This concept of giving up one's life for an eternal utopia already existed in classical Persian philosophical and Sufi texts. Modern literature, however, required people to assume greater social and revolutionary responsibilities, and to sacrifice a great deal more. After all, the ultimate message of the literature of this period was that it was easier to accept death than to live under the humiliating oppression of a dictatorial regime.

Death became a theme that modern Committed writers praised. Death for one's principles was accepted without hesitation. Even children's literature, which was often designed to speak to adults, valued death. A portion of Bihrangi's "The Little Black Fish" reads: "Death can come upon me very easily now. But as long as I'm able to live, I shouldn't go out to meet death. Of course, if someday I should be forced to face death—and I shall—it doesn't matter. What does matter is the influence that my life or death will have on the lives of others."[23] This sentence became the axiom of a whole generation that went out to meet death—first in small groups and later in masses during the course of the 1979 Revolution. This also corresponds to the Shiite concept of *Shahadat*, of dying for a religious cause. Accordingly, it is difficult to distinguish secular martyrdom from that of the Shiites among the young revolutionary generation during the course of the 1979 Revolution, because both secular leftists and religious activists died in their fights with what was a common enemy.

Another example of militant literature is the novel *Tangsir* by Sadiq Chubak (1916–), with its central character Zar Mohammad.[24] A simple southerner, Mohammad has already fought against British occupation in his area. Now he has lost all his savings to members of the ruling elites in his village, but his peaceful attempts to get his money back go unnoticed. He decides to kill the four or five people who have deceived him. From then on, his struggle is no longer merely personal because his enemies are part of the oppressive ruling class. His rebellion against the establishment makes him the leader of the oppressed people of his community. As he fights for justice and equality, he benefits from the support of the villagers, who likewise can no longer tolerate the injustice. He kills all of his enemies and escapes with his wife and child. The novel was successful and was soon turned into a successful movie that signaled the beginning of the production of a series of similar movies, such as *Safar-i Sang* (The Stone's Travel) and *Khak* (The Soil) by other secular film makers.[25] The regime tolerated these productions, believing that they were solely against the landlords, with whom the shah also had grievances, especially regarding his ideas for land reforms. People, however, welcomed these productions as expressions of the activist and revolutionary spirits.

The fiction of Mahmud Dawlatabadi (1940–), one of the most prolific as well as one of the most acclaimed writers of modern Persian literature, exemplifies the tendency of Committed Literature to close the gap between diverse understandings of revolution. His short stories and novels portray the situations of oppressed classes, especially peasants and rural workers; regardless of their religious beliefs, his characters are the victims of their social conditions. The class traits of all his characters comply with Marxist models of class society and historical materialism. He represents the elite and the bourgeoisie, peasants, proletariats, and intellectuals according to the classical definition of these classes but realistically enough to present individual characters as religious, if necessary. In *Klidar*, Dawlatabadi's ten-volume novel, depicting life and class struggle in northeast Iran, the peasants, urban petite bourgeoisie, and intellectuals—Muslim or not—unite in the fight against landlords and capitalists and the oppressive forces who support them.[26] Dawlatabadi portrays all these characters according to their social class and their position regarding sociopolitical issues.

The story occurs in the years between 1946 and 1948 in and around Klidar, a village in the province of Khorasan in northeastern Iran. Golmohamad is the oldest son of a large peasant family. His life changes dramatically after he and several men in his family attack a rival family in a nearby village for the purpose of retrieving a woman named Soqi with whom one of the men, Madyar, was in love. Soqi's fiancé and his father resist, and in the ensuing fight one man from each family is killed. This incident drives Golmohamad to kill two gendarmes who visit his tent for some trivial investigation. Golmohamad is imprisoned but manages to escape with the help of a Marxist activist, Satar, who is indirectly associated with the Tudeh party. Golmohamad becomes rebellious, leading an armed struggle against the government forces with some of his family members and Satar beside him.

All of the residents of Klidar are affected by this rebellion, which grows bigger rapidly. Some become active in the movement and prepare to sacrifice their lives; others oppose the movement and support the landlords, the bourgeoisie, and the government. Some classless characters, such as Qadir and Abbas Jan, change sides in different situations. They have been exposed to revolutionary speeches and the writing of the supporters of the peasant movement and therefore occasionally relate to them. However, because of their economic needs, they finally side with the landlords and the government.

The government eventually takes the movement more seriously and calls out more troops. Ultimately, Golmohamad's guerrilla army slowly loses the ground they had gained earlier and disintegrates. The government troops utterly defeat them in a final dramatic encounter. They massacre Golmohamad, members of his family, and his friends after tormenting them under a long siege with no food and water. They decapitate Golmohamad and send his head along with the women of his family to a city near Klidar.

The novel sets out to portray tribal and rural communities during a period of rapid social change. In this period, in a class-based society as complex as Klidar's, armed struggle may not be the best form of resistance. Perhaps the time for a peasant struggle has passed and the rapid social change in urban areas is affecting the village. Perhaps the result of Golmohamad's movement would have been different if Satar's political party had played a more active role in organizing and educating people and not leaving everything to Golmohamad.

This story has even more political significance because it was written in the mid to late 1970s. Dawlatabadi, along with other intellectuals, sought change in the political system through action. Even if because of severe dictatorial conditions, they could not openly discuss the nature of the necessary action for such change, they could still talk about it in fiction. The author has in mind the armed struggle when he portrays Golmohamad as an armed guerrilla. Through courageous battles, a group of thirty fighters exhausts the enemy for a period of time and recruits a great number of peasants and workers. They gain the support of an urban revolutionary group consisting of workers and students led by Akbar the ironsmith: what the leftist revolutionary in the late sixties and seventies wished to achieve.

Islam as a political paradigm or as an ideological force does not play a negative or determinative role. Although Dawlatabadi's political mapping complies with Marx's classical writing that holds the economy as the force behind social behavior, he has no quarrel with Islam. His underlying belief complies with the left's class analysis at that time, which insisted that Islamic forces could potentially become revolutionary and join the people's movement in overthrowing the ruling elite. Thus Dawlatabadi as a Committed literary writer refrained from directly opposing Islam or even discussing it. In his writing, people are religious, but their religiosity is expressed only in their casual references to God and holy leaders.

A good example of this change of modern authors' attitude toward Islam can be found in the definitions related to the events of Karbala.

As members of the larger society who opposed the shah's rule, literary activists assumed responsibility for promoting the cause of the oppressed Muslims. They found relevance in the Islamic notion of martyrdom and its archetype, Karbala. After all, according to socialist novels, heroes are so dedicated to their cause that they do not hesitate to embrace martyrdom. The historic events of Karbala have nourished the concept of martyrdom *(Shahadat)* in Shiite political discourse, providing it with holiness and divine countenance. Husayn's martyrdom has given Shiism "a whole ethos of sanctification through martyrdom."[27] Najjar, a scholar of Arabic literature, writes: "Acts of martyrdom undermine superordinate power by demonstrating that defiance is thinkable and do-able and set an example of sacrifice that can be imitated by an oppressed group inclined to rebel in the name of a principle."[28] Both secular oppositional activists and modern Persian authors in this period used this notion and even alluded to Husayn's death to arouse a sense of guilt and rebelliousness.

In the final scene of *Klidar,* the government forces massacre the protagonist and most of the central characters, just as Imam Husayn and most of his family were martyred in Karbala. Dawlatabadi makes this connection to provoke a stronger antagonistic feeling toward the government. As in Passion Plays or the religious ceremonies in which the devastation and martyrdom of Husayn and his troop mark the climax, *Klidar* too culminates in the moment of bloodshed. Moreover, the novel makes two indirect assertions. First, even though Golmohamad's armed struggle was defeated, his ideals, his spirit, and his cause for the spread of justice remain, just as those of Husayn endured. Second, the novel insinuates itself as a substitute for the Karbala tale. The author very indirectly, and in a nonconfrontational manner, tries to reduce the significance of Karbala by creating Klidar. Yet Karbala and Klidar reinforce each other even as they compete for an eternal space in the contemporary readers' memories.

The novels of Ahmad Mahmud, also devoted to socialist realism, are even more compatible with Marxist theories of literature than Dawlatabadi's works. Mahmud was affiliated with a socialist party and wrote only to present his party's policy in the form of literature. As an omniscient narrator, he leads his characters toward the party's ideological goals. Sadiq Chuback's short stories and novels (such as *Tangsir* mentioned earlier) also show the ugliness of society under the Pahlavis, while mostly describing petite bourgeois life and its particular social problems. Chuback's works, which ratify the characters in their individual or group rebellions, are noteworthy for their portray of women's and children's problems. Likewise, some of the short stories of Hamid Rahnuma (1920–), such as "The Rain," compare the living conditions of the rich and the poor to expose the inequality and injustice that dominate society in the most obvious way. Ghanoonparvar describes the role of these writers as becoming "that of a prophet, a prophet whose mission concerns not the next but the present world."[29]

Gulam Husayn Saiᶜdi (1935–1985), a psychiatrist by training, began writing in the 1950s and gained prominence by the mid-1970s. As a founder of the Association of Iranian Writers and the author of at least nineteen plays, one novel, and eight short story collections, he was one of the more significant and influential writers of this episode. He wrote much of his work under a pen name, Gowhar-e Morad. In addition to his fiction, Saiᶜdi edited a journal whose political outspokenness led to his eighteen arrests in the 1970s.[30] A successful playwright with a leftist viewpoint and public appeal, he was equal within his genre to those writing poetry and fiction. Like other Committed writers, he owed some of his popularity to his opposition to the government of Mohammad Reza Shah and its Westernization policies. He symbolized the anti-Western tendency and overall revolutionary convictions of the episode. He was devoted to representing the repressive strategies of rulers, the lives of villagers, and the urban poor as accurately as possible.

Like other Committed authors, Saiᶜdi gained more popularity after imprisonment. And, like the others, he supported the armed struggle by writing fiction that promoted the use of violence. In *Azadaran-i Bayal* (The Bayal's Mourners) (1978), the poor residents of a village are tormented and have no choice but to use violence against their oppressors.[31] Writing so clearly in support of the use of violence to establish democracy, he was forced to deny on television that he was affiliated with armed political groups. The secret police understood the relationship between Committed Literature and the growing opposition. This explains why the secret police arrested Dawlatabadi even though his writings had permission to be printed and had passed censorship before he published them.[32] These and other writers were arrested on the assumption that their works were connected to the growth of oppositional movement, and some were forced to express their support for the system.

Jalal Al-i Ahmad (1923–1969), in his later works, is an extreme example of a secular author who advocated Islam. When Persianism lost its prominence in the 1950s because of the new sociopolitical conditions in which intellectuals developed a strong anti-Western sentiment, Jalal Al-i Ahmad changed from being a Persianist to becoming an advocate of Committed Literature. His loyalties were first to the Tudeh Party and then shifted to the Third Force (a small political group that separated from Tudeh Party and supported Mossadeq's national government) before he devoted himself exclusively to writing in 1953. He aligned his desires with those of the anti-establishment intelligentsia at all times, and in a sense he acted as a spokesman for his contemporaries in the 1950s and 1960s. In his ideological commitment during this period, however, Islam played an important role. He was one of the few prominent authors who openly supported Islam as a potential force for fortifying the movement against foreign domination and as a means of defining Iranian cultural identity.[33] Because of his boldness, his fame as an intellectual activist increased rapidly in the late 1960s.

Al-i Ahmad's novel *Nun va Alqalam* (The Letter "N" and the Pen) (1960) signaled his shift away from Persianism. At this time, authors found it difficult to be directly involved in political activities, but their influence as social critics could be strongly felt. Al-i Ahmad successfully used fables, allegory, and folklore to pass along political messages in his works that both influenced and engaged his readers. His personal style was marked by an agitated and aggravated mood. This tone was present in both his most important nonfiction work, *Gharbzadigi* (Westoxication) (1962), and his best-known piece of fiction, *Mudir-i Madrisih* (The School Principal) (1958). In the former, he claimed that consumerism and women's emancipation were the result of the subversive Western influence on pure, indigenous Iranian-Islamic culture. In the latter, Al-i Ahmad sets the school up as a representation of society with all its problems. He takes an anti-American sentiment in defense of Islamic society. The narrator tells a teacher who has been run over by an American's car, "Don't you know you shouldn't be on the streets? Don't you know that the streets, the traffic lights, the civilization, the asphalt all belong to those who, driving in their cars, have spread all over the world?"[34]

With such writing, Al-i Ahmad helped the dissemination of an even more favorable attitude toward Islam. He spread the idea that intellectuals should recognize Islam as a major identifying element in their culture, differentiating them from the West. However, it should be remembered that he was not himself a devoted Muslim. He remained critical of aspects of the religious culture that he found regressive. His short story "Ziyarat" (The Pilgrimage) and his diary of his pilgrimage to Mecca in 1964, *Khasi dar Miqat* (Lost in the Crowd), demonstrate his ambivalence. The former offers a critique of these repressive aspects, and the latter describes an inner spiritual journey instead of offering the conventional definition of Hajj (pilgrimage). No historical material suggests that Al-i Ahmad observed any tenet of the religion. He nevertheless ended up helping Islamic forces in their attempts to gain a place among oppositional voices because he no longer believed that Persianism or socialism would solve the problems of Iranian society. As a Committed writer, and in terms of his beliefs about the role of literature, Al-i Ahmad claimed that "if you want to have fun with poems, if you want to waste your time, if you see poems as a means of becoming famous you are mistaken in this country. Art is a holy war."[35] Like other authors he perceived "literature as an antenna so tall that it could help to predict future events."[36]

As the way the meaning of the metaphors should be perceived changed, the social and discursive factors that played an essential role in the rise of this episode of literary history also created a new figurative mode of reading, resulting in a sort of mutual consent among the writers and readers. By the mid-seventies, it was clear that authors and readers were working together toward a revolution.

The leftist organizations (especially those engaged in the armed struggle) emphasized the relationships between their underground members and the literary communities. They encouraged these literary communities to write only revolutionary poetry, militant fiction, and eulogies for their martyrs, and they urged their followers to use revolutionary literature as a guideline for their social activity in the absence of open party platforms. Such use of the literary arena and the emergence of socialist literary didacticism during the decades before the 1979 Revolution successfully established the predominance of leftist revolutionary discourse. Literary activists cooperated with the leftist oppositional groups to mobilize people against the shah and his authoritarian rule but they did not present any clear ideas about democracy or an explanation of how society should look after their imagined revolution. Rather, they advocated a new social agenda in which they had no real experience. Committed Literature simply maintained that freedom did not exist in society and that there was an urgent need for revolution. Everyone agreed that the fighting must continue until the shah was overthrown and that everything else could be deferred until his deposition.

Revolution and Poetry

Poetry in this episode convoyed even more provocative revolutionary messages than the prose. In this episode, as Reza Barahani (1970–) another Committed literary figure of this time, writes, "Ideas about society were so promoted in some poems that they became a social and natural philosophy. Most poets after Nima showed the necessity for social change even better than he did. . . . Contemporary poetry represented the contemporary history for this century."[37] Barahani concludes that the poet must know what period of literary history he is living in and must also know that his mission is to produce a perfect literature.

Committed literary critics prepared numerous anthologies of modern Persian poetry that included a number of poems from earlier periods to support the new leftist ideology of representation. Nima's poem "Ay Adamha" (Hey People), which reappeared in a number of anthologies and in many journals, became a favorite. The critics intended its character's call "Hey you, sitting on the shore, happy and laughing— / Someone is drowning in the water" to be read as a call for a social revolution.[38] On the literal level, the narrator is asking those who are enjoying the safety of the shore, acting happy and laughing, to go to the sea to save someone who is struggling alone and drowning in the water. This someone is like all of us: "Someone is constantly struggling. In this heavy, dark, turbulent sea, / The one that is also known to you."[39] According to the new reading, the safety of the shore, referred to the comfortable conditions of the people who stayed out of the conflict with the regime and enjoyed its financial generosity.[40] These "people" were from potentially revolutionary classes, and they needed to be encouraged to get involved. The turbulent sea referred to nothing but the society. The heavy dark sea stood for the despotic political regime, and the drowning person was the person who wanted to inform the people that the dark, turbulent condition of society could change through their concerted effort.

This Committed literary movement also reinterpreted Nima's theory of form. Writers were now collectively convinced that because

Nima refuted classical poetic form in favor of free verse, form no longer held a position of significance. Nima, now older, remained silent on this interpretation of his theory of form. Even if he had wanted to challenge it, he would not have been able to do so because of an obvious contradiction: if form is important, why did he ignore the fact that form plays a central role in the classical poetry; and if form is not significant, why did he invest so much energy in the promotion of form as an ideological issue central to Persianism?[41] Now he had to either revise his emphasis on the importance of form or dismiss his previous argument against classical poetry. He once quietly insinuated that thoughts and ideas were what the form had to reinforce.[42] This was sufficient conceptual means for the Committed literary community to use Nima as a legitimate source of reference. For example, Dastghayb concluded that because Nima did not stress form over content, his work expresses people's misery, and Barahani's opinion was that Nima's works were all about "the history of this century."[43]

The debate over the new poetic style, with its growing emphasis on content, continued into the 1960s and early 1970s. At this time the members of the Committed literary community went beyond presenting social criticism and providing the appropriate interpretations—they directly participated in revolutionary practices. Khusru Gulsurkhi, a revolutionary Marxist poet and writer, first contributed to these debates by arguing: "poetic style and form are not important. The effect of poems on the senses and conduct is, on the other hand, important. We need to provoke through poetry."[44] Marxist criticism in general, especially before Lukacs and the Frankfurt School, opposed using literary formalism to approach literature outside an historical context,[45] and in Iran, Gulsurkhi reinforced these ideas through his poetry and literary criticism, often to the point of instigating government reprisal.[46] He believed in a "Soviet Union kind of modernism that complied with the deprived classes."[47] In the early 1970s he formed a revolutionary group and attempted to kidnap the crown prince. He was tried and then executed. During his trial he announced that he believed in Marxism and that Ali, the first Shiite imam, was the first Marxist—a statement that was intended to unite secular and Muslim opposition groups. Because of this statement and his death, he quickly became a national hero.

Saᶜid Sultanpur (d. 1981), another Committed poet and critic, began his literary career with the belief that as "the bourgeois class uses literature to ensure the survival of the class dependent on imperialism, we have to use literature to regain the stolen rights of the proletariat."[48] He also wrote, "If we all somehow manage to write and publish, the walls of censorship will break down. If we don't, it means we censor our own thoughts about our love and faith. And that means taking our children's eyes out at birth."[49] He was imprisoned for his beliefs and his sympathy with the OIPFG, and after he was released he officially joined that organization. He was executed after the Revolution.

This combination of pen and action progressed to the point where all poets' lives were potentially in danger because their poetry aimed directly at the Shah's regime. Ahmad Shamlu (1925–) knew the risks of writing such incisive poetry, yet he did not fear death or imprisonment. He wrote in *Bagh-i Ainih* (The Garden of Mirrors):

Cheraghi be dastam, cheraghi dar barabaram,
man be jang-e siyahi miravam.
Gahvarehha-ye khastegi
az keshakesh-e raft o amadha
baz istadehand,
Khurshidi az amaq
kakeshanha-ye khakestar shodeh ra
rushan mikonad.[50]

[A light in my hands, a light before me,
I go to fight the darkness.
The cradle, tired,
has stopped,
from the struggle of rocking back and forth.
A sun will arise from the depth,
will light up the gray galaxies.]

The light in the hand of intellectuals represents poetry itself, a weapon with which the protagonist sets out to fight the darkness of oppressive rule. The sun serves as a metaphor for the Iranian revolution and indicates that this revolution will transcend even Iran's borders. In fact, the political organizations widely believed that, because of Iran's strategic importance, a revolution would affect the "dark galaxies," or the whole region, eventually changing the international balance of power.

Shamlu politicized the question of poetic form even further in a leftist sense. In "Shi'ri Kih Zindigist" (Poetry That Is Life), demonized the

advocates of old poetry, such as Hamidi Shirazi, as if they belonged
to the antirevolutionary camp—for the sheer reason that they did not
address critical sociopolitical issues.

Muzu^c-e she^cr-e shae^cran-e pishin
az zendegi nabud. . . .
. . . .
hal ankeh man be shakhseh, zamani
hamrah-e she^cr-e khish
hamdush-e Chin Chow koreh-ʾi jang kardeham
yekbar ham hamidi-e she^cr ra
dar chand sal-e pish
bar dar-e she^cr khishtan avang kardeham
Muzu-e she^cr
emruz
muzu-e digarist
imruz, she^cr harbeh-ʾe khalq ast
zira keh sha^ceran
khod shakheh-ʾe ze jangal-e khalqand. . . .[51]

[The subject of the earlier poetry
was not life.
. . . .
whereas I myself had once
fought beside the Korean Chin Chow
with my poem
And once
a few years ago
I hung Hamidi the poet
from the gallows of my poems.
The subject of today's poems is different.
Today, poetry is the people's weapon
because poets
are themselves a branch of the people's forest. . . .
Today
a poet must.
. . . .
find the subject, rhythm and rhymes of his poems
carefully, one by one,
from among the pedestrians of the streets.)

Hamidi Shirazi, a traditionalist literary activist, is treated as an enemy here because he opposed Nima and New Poetry.[52] Shamlu uses the gallows metaphor to send a clear message: if the traditionalists maintain their safety by not engaging in political activities, they could be written off.

These metaphors were mostly related to the criticism of social problems, injustice, and lack of freedom. *Sokut* (silence), *khab* (sleep), *faramushi* (forgetfulness), and *dard* (pain) stood for the social circumstances and issues that the political opposition criticized. In other Committed works these metaphors also appeared in various elaborated forms to describe circumstances of life. For example, night *(shab)*, which referred to dictatorial conditions, spawned many related metaphors, such as *zharfa-ye shab* (the depth of the night), *shab-e harzeh darayan* (the night of idle talkers), *shab-e lashkhoran* (vultures' night), *shab-e dard alud* (the painful night), *shab-e khunin* (the bloody night), *shab-e ashkalud* (the tearful night*)*, *shab-e sangi* (the stony night), *shab-e asman-e sard* (the night of cold sky), *shab-e barani* (the rainy night)*, and* *shab-e por az setareh-ha ye zendani* (a night full of imprisoned stars). It seems as though these Committed activists saw no stars in the sky in the time of the shah. Their metaphors were optimistic only when they talked about the future or about their heros*: bidari-e shab* (the awakening of night), *payan-e shab* (the end of the night), *shab-e por setareh* (the night full of stars), *sepidehdam* (the dawn) *khorshid* (sun), *khorshidha-ye shabaneh* (nightly suns), *rastakhiz* (resurrection), *shekufeh* (blossom), *moj* (wave), and *ofoq* (horizon). With these opposing metaphors, the poets created a striking dichotomy between the shah and his critics, between what was the shah's regime and what was not, between what the shah advocated as a Western model and what the opposition advocated as a non-Western model. Two camps could hardly have been more distant from each other in their views than the shah's regime and his opponents in both literature and in actuality during this period.

In the winter of 1971, the OIPFG's guerrillas attacked a gendarmerie post in the small town of Siyahkal in the forests of the Caspian Sea area, confiscated the post's arms, and ran into the forest. This action signaled the beginning of armed struggle by the left. Soon other Marxist and Islamic groups joined the armed struggle, which lasted until the shah's government was toppled. Following the Siyahkal incident and after the beginning of armed struggle, a new set of metaphors emerged. Literature now took its own autonomous course, in the sense that it continued independently to promote the cause of Siyahkal, with poets using metaphors for rage, violence, and combat in their poems. As Ismail Ko'i put it in "North Too," a poem written in 1969: "At this time now, I am expressive and explosive." All major poets talked about the forest, trees, rivers, and high mountains. Their writings became filled with metaphors such as *jangal-e yaghi* (the rebellious jungle), *ghobar-e dud-e mosalsal* (smoke of the machine gun), *khun* (blood), *vazheh-e khunin* (the bleeding words), *vazheh-e sorkh* (the red word), *vazheh-e golgun* (the rose-colored word), *safir-e goluleh* (whistle of a bullet): an arsenal of words with which they could subvert the shah's portrayal of the country as a stable society. Anything associated with the Caspian Sea or forested area near it alluded to Siyahkal: Roaring sea, roaring Caspian, the cry of Caspian sea, the sea movement, the laughter of the Caspian, high waves, red forest, the mourning forest, epics of the jungle, standing trees, standing cypress, and the like.[53] Historical and mythical heroes such as Kavih, Arash, Hallaj, and Siyavush came to personify the new heroes, and the arsenal of words expanded even more. A dozen of the poets, including Shamlu, Kadkani, and Khui, wrote poetry on its anniversaries every winter to commemorate Siyahkal and the glory it left in the minds of the intellectuals and workers.[54] In his poem "Zarurat" (The Necessity), Kadkani (also a prominent scholar and not even known primarily as a leftist) wrote,

Miayad, miayad:
Mesl-i bahar as hameh su miayad.
Divar,
ya sim-e khardar
namidanad.
. . . .
Ah,
beguzar man cho qatreh-e barani basham,
dar in kavir,
ke khak ra be maqdam-e u mozhdeh midahad,
ya hanjareh-e chekavok-e khordi keh
mah-e day
az puneh-e bahar sukhan miguyad
vaqti kazan goluleh-e sorbi
ba qatreh
qatreh
qatreh-e khunash

musiqi-e mokarar va yekriz-e barf ra
tarji^{c}i arghavani mibakhshad.[55]

[He comes, he comes:
Like Spring, he comes from all directions.
Walls,
Or barbed wire,
He does not know.
. . . .
Oh,
Let me be a drop of rain
in this desert,
who shall give glad tidings of his arrival
Or let me be the throat of a small lark
who in winter
speaks of the spring pennyroyal
when from that lead bullet
with drops of his blood
winter adds a purple strophe-poem
to the snow's repetitive and monotonous music.]

The guerrilla is compared to a spring whose coming cannot be prevented. He does not fear the "barbed wire" of prison and will not be hindered by any other threat. The poet is, on the other hand, a sacrificing messenger. He takes it upon himself to inform the people about the arrival of the guerrillas, represented by spring. They will bring change to the barren desert and the cold snowy days of this time.

After the armed struggle began, more and more prominent poets of this Committed literary movement came to hold identical sentiments and address the various revolutionary issues that came to the foreground. The ideology propelling this literary movement implied that the revolution would not succeed without the full participation of everyone. Hamid Musadiq (d. 1999) addressed all Iranians:

Man agar bar khizam,
to agar bar khizi
hameh bar mikhizand.
Man agar benshinam
to agar benshini
cheh kasi bar khizad?

cheh kasi ba doshman besetizad
panjeh dar panjeh har doshman
dar avizad.[56]

[If I rise,
if you rise,
all will rise.
If I sit down,
if you sit down,
who will rise?
who will fight the enemy,
who will
grapple with the enemy?]

The message could not be clearer: this is an open invitation to revolt. The unwritten agreement among poets—to lead the masses toward social change—surfaces most blatantly in Musadiq's poetry. He too had to pay for his assertiveness with imprisonment, which in turn only added to the popularity of his works.

The popular poet Faridun Mushiri (1925–), was also influenced by the Committed literary movement. In his poem "Yaghi" (The Rebel) the protagonist rebels against everything. He vows, "I am not afraid of death since life / has poured nothing but the poison of sorrow into my glass / If I have rested a moment of this long, boring life / Let it be taken from me."[57] Similarly, Faridun Tavaluli (1918–), who participated in the First Iranian Writers Congress in June 1946, wrote: "The sound of revolution, loud and clamorous / From far away / Comes to my ear / It soothes me / Gives me hope / And makes me conscious."[58]

The revolutionary activities of these poets culminated in the Ten Poetry Evenings of October 1977 in Tehran, organized by the Kanun-i Navisandigan-i Iran (The Association of Iranian Writers) at the Iran-Germany Cultural Center. About seventy poets and writers recited poetry and gave lectures, drawing thousands of intellectuals who were mostly students. The content of the meetings, whether expressed through poetry or speech, revolved around freedom of expression, support of the Iranian people, praise of revolutionaries, and discontent with social conditions. The writers also discussed some of the ramifications of Committed Literature. For example, more openly than ever before, Simin Danishvar said, "The philosophical perspective of an artist is derived from socialism, Marxism, and Existentialism."[59] Hushang Gulshiri said in a closing remark, "We promise you and we swear to the pen, swear to the rain, swear to this night, and to the coming morning that we will be a worthy guardian of freedom of the pen and ideas. We promise to be with you everywhere. You promise us that you will take our word to every town and village."[60] The statements that outlined the relationship between the author and his reader echoed, very publicly, the principles of Russian Marxist literary theory and socialist realism.

These ten meetings grew increasingly radical and finally turned into riots. Thousands of intellectuals, students, and technocrats—clearly leftist secular in their appearance—participated each night and commended the ideological messages that were carried in the literary works. The resulting revolutionary ambience went beyond the nights, however. During the day, others also gathered around the institute and discussed the issues surrounding the events. After the ten nights, the discussion of current events continued in the *News Bulletin* of the Association of Iranian Writers and in other journals, such as *Friday's Book*.

The protests and debates were perfectly timed, as they followed an earlier uprising regarding housing issues. In the summer of 1977, the Tehran mayor's office had ordered the destruction of houses that were built illegally outside the official city limits. The destruction caused a massive rebellion, during which the people not only violently attacked the government offices but also reconstructed their houses during the night.[61] The leaders of the poetry nights' movement were encouraged and provoked by the housing movement. Together, the events of the "ten nights" and the "housing" decisively fueled the popular uprising that marked the last two years of the shah's rule.[62]

Once Muslim activists noticed the growing secular opposition to the shah, they became more active as well and eventually overwhelmed the secular revolutionary movement. Even though their literary activism was minimal, they began to mobilize their supporters, using religious institutes such as mosques, and during the last eighteen months of the shah's rule, Islamic forces gained hegemony over the movement. They gained it almost too easily, because the secular literary activists and culture producers and their readers were not averse to Islam. Muslims were also attracted to the revolutionary movement because it promised change. As was discussed earlier, the Marxists had chosen a sympathetic approach to Muslim activists. In addition, the shah's systematic attack on Marxist organizations and leftist activists resulted in the elimination of many of the top opposition leaders, creating a vacuum in the leadership of the movement. Islamic activists and the clergy stepped in to fill this void and gained complete political hegemony nearly a year after the Revolution. Now Marxist, leftist, and other secular groups came under attack from Islamic forces and many were imprisoned and/or murdered. Many of the Marxist and leftist authors who did not lose their lives were forced to live in exile. At this point, the episode of Committed Literature declined rapidly toward a tragic end.

It is thus certain that the works of Committed writers informed a generation of intellectuals who created the revolutionary events of the 1970s. Literary communities, in cooperation with leftist and other secular revolutionary activists, mobilized a revolutionary movement just as they had prophesied it in literature. They taught the generation to question sociopolitical problems in a metaphorical yet bold language. They also taught the generation how to counter the regime and to doubt the reforms that it had accomplished. In the end they were defeated and physically eradicated by the postrevolutionary religious ruling elites. However, the change they effected in the political and literary cultures of their society was too strong to be dismissed even by the physical eradication of the authors. The culture they created remained alive in many individual writers for several years after the Revolution. That culture even reproduced itself in the culture of the ruling elite, this time wearing the shroud of Islam. In short, this prerevolutionary left has still remained, for many, a point of departure, a context for comparison, and for this reason, the discussion of Committed Literature will continue later in this book.

Social Issues and Revolutionary Themes in Prerevolutionary Women's Literature

Under the sway of the dominant literary movement, prerevolutionary women's literature emphasized sociopolitical issues more than specific gender issues. To be sure, authors chose themes related to women but in the context of male-dominated social concerns. Women's literary works before the Revolution did not have a distinct identity but were subsumed within the dominant paradigm of Committed Literature and leftist ideology. The Iranian Revolution of 1979 ended this trend and, as chapter 5 will discuss, gave rise to a feminist literary episode in women's literature.[63] The literary production by Iranian women thus demonstrates a discontinuous process that has proceeded in two episodes. The literary meanings produced by women in these two episodes reflect periodically changing sociohistorical conditions and discursive context. I here analyze the works of three prominent female literary figures who represent the prerevolutionary literary episode—Simin Danishvar, Furugh Farrukhzad, and Simin Bihbahani—to illustrate the affinity of their writings with the dominant literary movement. Such an analysis, I must make clear, does not intend to slight women writers whose works did not as overtly advocate women's causes. On the contrary, it will attest to their heterogeneity and complexities in their roles on whatever convictions they advocated. A close reading of their texts uncovers what they wanted to reveal about their time. It shows both how they helped to shape the literary movement of which they were a part and how they were influenced by that movement. I must also more clearly spell out the sociopolitical issues versus those of gender. In a strict sense, gender is socially constituted and gender issues are in fact a type of social issue. In this book, the distinction between *social* and *gender* is an empirical one: the problems defined in terms of class and politics, and those that belong to the realm of men-women relationships and the institution of male domination. I must further mention that the distinction between gender issues and social issues is not my invention. Others have also drawn upon such analytical distinctions in discussing women's fiction. For example, Tierney-Tello explains how women's writings in several South American countries question sociopolitical, generic, and textual forms of authority.[64]

The secular trend unleashed by the Constitutional Revolution (1906–1911) continued under the Pahlavis (1924–1979). Along with this trend came the construction of the bureaucratic and administrative structure of the state, the emergence of modern social institutions, and the decline of certain traditional social organizations. The state played a central role in implementing social reform, including a change in women's social conditions. The Pahlavis were committed to improving the status of women by improving social mobility, education, and employment in the modern (state) sectors of the economy and by removing obstacles that had traditionally hindered women's participation in public life. Reza Shah's new policy of mandatory unveiling in 1936 was a bold attempt not only to eliminate what he considered a custom impeding women but also to promote a Western lifestyle among women. Although this policy was abandoned under Mohammad Reza Shah, the encouragement of women to be active in the public sphere continued. Through the reforms of the early sixties, women were also "enfranchised."[65] One outcome of these policies in the 1960s and 1970s was an increase in the number of women with advanced degrees and greater participation in the labor force.[66] Some women even came to occupy the highest echelons of the state bureaucracy at the cabinet, parliament, and ambassadorial levels.[67]

The state's reforms with regard to women were viewed differently by diverse groups within the opposition. They were opposed by the religious conservatives for their Westernized nature and for the way that they undermined clerics' traditional authority. To the left the reforms appeared superficial and limited to small groups of urban women who in fact symbolized the shah's White Revolution and Westernization.[68] These reforms, in the view of the left, prevented the growth of a grassroots movement of working women.[69] Liberals also had their own misgivings about these reforms. They considered a monarch talking about the liberation of women to be totally anachronistic, if not ludicrous.[70] For women activists, these reforms were at best a simple Westernized substitute for traditional feminine roles.

In this oppositional context, women and men alike committed themselves to Committed Literature in their literary activities. The professed ideology of the loosely connected circles of authors who followed this trend was their commitment to action. Literature was to address the problems of social inequality and political oppression. In these circles, writers took it upon themselves to observe and record the problems of society and to encourage their readers to engage in activities for future change.[71] Women's literature was an integral component of Committed Literature; and women writers, skillfully engaging the canons of the literary establishment, wrote social realist, romantic, and didactic novels as well as political poetry.[72] In their writings, as in those of men, the figurative language, style, and literary stance of Committed Literature remained dominant until the 1979 Revolution.

Simin Danishvar: Emblem of Commitment

Simin Danishvar (1921–) established her reputation as one of the best-known female fiction writers of modern Persian literature with the publication of the best-selling novel *Savushun* (1969) and two collections of short stories, *Bih Ki Salam Kunam* (To Whom Can I Say Hello?) (1974) and *Surat Khanih* (The Playhouse) (1961).[73]

Set in the province of Fars after World War II, *Savushun* depicts the life of a woman named Zari who is married to Yusof, a political activist involved in a resistance movement against the Allied forces.[74] Zari has had a happy childhood and experienced personal freedom while growing up and during her school years at a British missionary school. She is somewhat religious, loves her husband, wants a comfortable life, and is willing to work hard for it. Yet in her married life Zari experiences a nagging internal conflict. On the one hand, she is a loving wife, cherishes her children, and enjoys her beautiful house. On the other hand, she yearns for her past freedom and independence. These conflicting feelings, however, are reconciled through her husband's revolutionary heroism and eventual martyrdom. After his death she even emulates him by taking up his cause, adopting his philosophy, and following his path. She turns her husband's funeral ceremony into a public demonstration.

At the end of the novel, one of Yusof's friends reassures Zari of the righteousness of her new path: "Do not cry, sister. A tree will grow in your house and others in your city and even more in your land. And the wind will convey the message from tree to tree, 'Did you see the dawn on your way?'"[75] With this inclination toward courageous political activism, her personal conflicts come to an end, and her long search for a purpose beyond her home comes to fruition.[76]

The explanatory logic that permeates the novel seeks to reason out the problems of social oppression, foreign domination, and the men's need to defend their homeland. Women's specific problems appear here and there only to be subordinated to the more serious and lofty issue of national emancipation. Even before she joins the movement, Zari herself values the men's struggle above her own as she performs her wifely and motherly duties. Yusof's ideas reflect the national aspirations of that time, and his death is a metaphor for the defeat of nationalism. Zari, who sympathizes with and later joins the resistance movement, represents the hope that the struggle will continue. The novel forces a patriarchal notion of the Revolution upon the story, a notion that associates the Revolution with the territory of the father. Even when Zari is ready to engage fully in the movement, her role does not transcend that of the traditional sister or wife who publicly mourns the loss of her man.[77] She constantly regrets that she lacks a high level of awareness and commitment and that she has not been capable of giving a gun to her beloved son. Here, it is the dominant language system of Committed Literature that permeates and shapes the relationship between Danishvar and her themes and characters.

As in socialist novels, the heroes of *Savushun* take all the steps necessary to accomplish their most honorable goal of helping the movement. Religion, love, family, and the personal interests of life are secondary to one's social and political responsibilities. Life and the movement are linked only through death, and death itself becomes another subject of praise. The figurative expression of this devotion to the social movement and the glorification of heroism and martyrdom are the constitutive elements of the language system in Danishvar's *Savushun*.

As Dawlatabadi was doing, Danishvar strove to update not only the form, meanings, and metaphors of Committed Literature but also the religious concepts related to Karbala. In the final scene of *Savushun*, Zari speaks out after the martyrdom of her husband and vows to continue in his path of political struggle. In these final scenes, Zari resembles Zaynab, Imam Husayn's sister.[78]

In the short story "Bih Ki Salam Kunam" (To Whom Can I Say Hello?) Kawkab, a lonely elderly woman, recalls her memories in a stream of consciousness style. She has lost her husband, her job, and even her pet spider, and has been forced, in complete despair, to marry her daughter off to a disreputable and abusive man who forbids her to see her mother. This situation further isolates Kawkab from the world and causes her to become very cynical. Then, on one snowy day, while returning from the market, she slips and falls and is unable to get up. A young couple helps her, and for a moment she again feels closer to people and greets everyone around her. The story suggests that Kawkab's loneliness and pessimism are consequences of the social system and individual misfortune. Clearly, the author presents men as the source of the old woman's misery. However she insinuates that women are responsible for the men's faults by "turning them into *na-mard*," one who lacks manliness and masculine superiority. That is to say, true men do not beat their wives, and it is because of women's mistakes that Kawkab's son-in-law is atypical. Although Danishvar creatively uses the concept of *mardanigi* to criticize the son-in-law, it is portrayed as a normal and positive characteristic. Later, during the postrevolutionary period when feminist discourse gained predominance in women's literature, the author revised this short story in order to change this conciliatory approach toward abusive men.[79]

Danishvar's male characters sometimes occupy the center of her stories. The short story "Tasaduf" (The Accident) (1961), about the consumerism that Western culture promotes, is told from the male protagonist's point of view.[80] Nadereh (or as she prefers to be called, Nadia) likes to imitate the radio reporters and actresses in dubbed movies. She presses her husband, Akbar, to buy a car. Akbar, the protagonist, is a modest office worker who cannot afford or understand his wife's passion for cars and luxury. He realizes that Nadia is under the influence of Sedigheh, a woman in their neighborhood who, wearing white gloves and dark glasses, drives a car.[81] He nevertheless accepts an extra assignment out of town to get an advance to pay the expenses for Nadia's driver's license. Then he obtains a mortgage on his inherited house to purchase the car. Nadia, however, creates a problem every day thereafter. She gives him headaches and stomachaches as she drives him to work. She gets involved in accidents on a frequent basis. She constantly quarrels with police officers. Eventually Akbar is forced to apply for another out-of-town assignment to pay for some of the damage she has caused. While out of town, Akbar continues to hear about her adventures with the car through extensive letters she writes to him. But at one point the letters stop, and when Akbar returns, he finds out that her car has been totaled in an accident with an army colonel's car. The wreckage is put up on public display by the police as an example of the consequences of bad driving, and the colonel is hospitalized. Nadia, however, becomes involved with the colonel and asks Akbar for a divorce. Akbar remains alone, strapped with installment payments to the loan institutions.

The author maintains a critical view toward materialism and consumerism. The female represents Western culture and the invasion of technology. She is portrayed as assertive but destructive, outspoken but abusive, and modern but disrespectful of tradition. She "wipes on purple lipstick, and put on a white scarf with purple spots, dark glasses and white gloves," an outfit ridiculed by the author for being out of place. To convince her husband to buy her the car, she mocks and teases the bus and taxi drivers and the pedestrians, especially the veiled women on the sidewalks. When she can, she tries to park her car by an embassy, suggesting that she prefers the foreigners or foreign domination. The man, on the contrary, represents both the nation and the victimized. He is just being abused. In the context of this East-West antagonism, he even seems justified in beating the woman.

Not exclusive to "The Accident" or *Savushun*, the West and metaphors that refer to it are ideological representations that constitute the theme of stories such as "'Id-i Iraniyan" (The Iranians' New Year) (1961) as well.[82] Thematically, these representations are consistent with Al-i Ahmad's anti-Western exposé *Westoxication*.

Another example of the centrality of male characters is the "The Playhouse" (1961), which is about a man who plays the role of a Siyah and is referred to in the story as Siyah. Literally, "Siyah" means "black" but the word also refers to a popular, clever theatrical character in traditional Iranian folk shows who has the same function as the Shakespearean fool, in the sense that he is allowed to say things that ordinary characters may not express openly.[83] While working as a playwright, director, and general troubleshooter at a theater, Siyah falls in love with an actress and tries to solve the many problems she faces. Pregnant by one of her admirers, the actress is not able to continue performing unless she undergoes an abortion she cannot afford. Siyah manages to help her keep her job and tries to find money for her abortion. He becomes a symbol of humanism and, by taking care of the woman, appropriates feminine archetypal qualities of the helper. The woman is so helplessly dependent upon others and so incapable of speaking on her own behalf that he must even mediate between her and the reader by expressing her problems.

Some of Danishvar's prerevolutionary writings, like this story, portray the plight of women in society. In depicting these women, however, she places a greater emphasis upon the effects of class and foreign oppression than upon male domination. All of her works manifest her commitment to explain the root causes of these social problems.[84] They publicize revolutionary political activism and criticize Western cultural infiltration but overlook the role of patriarchy. She casts her characters as advocates of humanism and assures the advocates of Committed Literature that, although gender issues are important, they will not hinder the greater collective quest for political change. The author herself achieved a more prominent position in the community of writers when she was elected the first president of the organization of Committed writers, the Association of Iranian Writers.[85]

Furugh Farrukhzad: Concerns for Human Beings

Furugh Farrukhzad (1935–1967) was one of Iran's most acclaimed and iconoclastic poets of the prerevolutionary period. Her writing can be categorized into two general groups. Her early collections, *Asir* (Captive) (1955), *Divar* (The Wall) (1956), and *Isiyan* (Rebellion) (1957), contain images and sensual depictions of love, passion, and suffering. Her two collections, *Tavaludi-i Digar* (Another Birth) (1964) and *Iman Biyavarim Bih Aghaz-i Fasl-i Sard* (Let Us Believe in the Beginning of a Cold Season) (1969), address human suffering and inequality and are primarily concerned with the social conditions of the time.[86] These last two works clearly reflect the social themes of the dominant Committed Literature.

In her early poems Farrukhzad reveals her feelings about men. In "Revolt," she exhibits her dislike for the man she does not love: "You man, selfish creature, / don't say my poetry is shameful."[87] In another poem, however, she writes confidently in a confession to her lover, "You made me a poet, O man," appreciating the relationship.[88] The first man resembles her husband whom she disliked and later divorced, the second man a loving friend who supported her. Farrukhzad's poetic representation of these two relationships underpins many of her poems. Through this dichotomy, she splits her aesthetic efforts between describing what is imposed upon her in an unhappy marriage and depicting her wish to participate in an active social life, to associate freely with the man she does love, and to join the community of Committed artists.

The elegy "Leaving: The Poem," which displays Farrukhzad's personal approach toward gender relations and her quarrels with men, is perhaps a reflection of her own romantic experience with the second man after her first marriage failed. The protagonist of the poem spends a night with her lover. Even though she deeply wants him to stay with her the next day, she lets him go.

> Hameh shab ba delam kasi migoft
> "sakht ashofteh-ʾi ze didarash
> sobhdam ba setaregan-e sepid

miravad, miravad, negahdarash"
Man beh bu-ye to rafteh az donya
bi khabar az farib-e farda-ha.
Ru-ye mozhgan-e nazokam mirikht
chashmha-ye to chun ghobar tala
tanam az hes-e dastha-ye to dagh
gisuyam dar tanafos-e to raha
mishekoftam ze ʿeshq o megoftam
har keh del dadeh shod beh deldarash
naneshinad beh qasd-e azarash
beravad, chashm-e man beh donbalash,
beravad, eshq-e man negahdarash
Ah, aknun to rafteh-ʾi o ghorub
sayeh migostarad beh sineh-e rah
Narm narmak khoday-e tireh-e gham
minahad pa beh maʿbad-e negaham.[89]

[All night something was telling my heart
"How excited you are to see him.
When the stars whiten at dawn,
he will leave, he will leave—hold him tight."
Lost to the world I was with the scent of you
heedless of morning's betrayal
Like golden dust,
your eyes were pouring on my eyelashes.
My body burning beneath your touch
My hair abandoned to your breath
I blossomed in love and I said
She who gives her heart to her love
never thinks of ways to hurt him.
Let him go, my eyes will follow him
Let him go, my love will protect him.'

Now you're gone and, ah, the twilight
sheds shadows across the crest of the road
Ever so slowly the gloomy god of sorrow
enters my eyes' shrine of worship
and writes on each wall
black words (verses) all in black.][90]

In the initial stanzas of the poem, the protagonist relates her internal conflict over whether she should let her lover leave. She then ponders the joy she has had while being with him. The man is apparently compelled to leave in the morning, and staying would inconvenience him. She advises herself to let him go. She makes every sacrifice because "She who gives her heart to her love never thinks of ways to hurt him." In the end, she nonetheless laments over his departure.

In these poems Farrukhzad wrote revealingly about love and the nature of her relationship. Her boldness was something quite new in Iranian women's literature. It was unfamiliar, if not outrageous: public expression of this sort was confined to male writers. Yet Farrukhzad's poetic expression could go only so far. In the final analysis she adheres to the traditional notion that a woman should sacrifice herself for her love—that is, a man. The notions underlying her poetic expression often display a close affinity with the cultural context of male domination that promoted sacrifice for another person or for the Revolution.

This adherence to the existing framework of literary discourse becomes paramount in Farrukhzad's later works. "One Like No Other" from *Let Us Believe in the Beginning of a Cold Season* demonstrates her commitment to the social movement. In the following extract, she envisions the arrival of a savior.

Man khab dideham keh kasi miayad
man khab-e yek setareh-ye qermez dideh-am
va pelk-e cheshmanam hey miparad
va kafshhayam hey joft mishavand
va kur shavam
agar dorugh beguyam.
Man khab-e an setareh-ye qermez ra
vaqti ke khab nabudam dideh-am
Kasi miayad . . .
kasi ke namishavad girft
va dastband zad ve be zendan andakht
Kasi az asman-e tupkhaneh dar shab-e atashbazi miayad
va sofreh ra miandazad
va nan ra qesmat mikonad.[91]

[Someone's coming, I dreamed dreaming of a red star.
And now there's a flutter in my eyelids

and my feet are out the door.
And if I'm lying
may I be struck blind.
I dreamed of the red star wide awake.
Someone's coming . . .
Someone who can't be arrested
and handcuffed and thrown in jail . . .
Someone's coming out of the sky over Artillery
Square, on the night of the fireworks
And he'll spread the tablecloth and divide the bread.][92]

She shows excitement about a dream in which a savior arrives. The savior is a man who will bring justice and divide the food equally among the people. The dismembered community will be reconstructed by this savior, who is none other than the leader of the future revolution. In her portrayal of this leader, the poet employs the rhetoric of Committed Literature. The jail and the handcuffs refer to the state; the lack of equal distribution of food refers to society's injustice; and the red star and the fireworks foretell future change. This rhetoric is not exclusive to this poem. Throughout *Another Birth* Farrukhzad employs, on the one hand, metaphors such as coldness, silence, death, and, above all, those of the night and darkness, to describe the social condition. On the other hand, she uses metaphors such as warmth, lightness, day, tomorrow, water, rain, and flight to refer to the movement, to imply hope, and to hint at a better future.[93] Her choice for the place where "Someone" will land is the Artillery Square, a famous downtown square in Tehran frequented by ordinary people. The words "artillery" and "fireworks" are sensitive metaphors in support of the armed struggle.

Farrukhzad's presentation of this "Someone" in "One Like No Other" reflects the dominant discourse because it follows the pattern of a male figure of authority and a dependent female figure. It reflects the stereotypical view of male and female roles: one gives, one takes. He is "someone" who is "better," "taller," "braver," and able to bring light and justice. She, on the other hand, has to wait to receive her share. This hierarchy was also present in "Leaving: The Poem," in which the woman must accept the man's decision to leave, while she remains at home behind a window from which she looks and mourns her loss. Like the works of other Committed authors, Farrukhzad's "One Like No Other" shows sympathy for Islam as here she talks about a "neon Allah sign" and "Qazi Al-Quzat" (The Judge of the Judges), using an Arabic phrase with an Islamic connotation.

In "Delam Baray-e Baghcheh Misuzad" (I Pity the Garden), Farrukhzad speaks the language of the supporters of armed struggle more directly:

> ....
> Hayat-e khaneh-e ma tanhast
> tamam-e ruz
> az posht-e dar seda-ye tekeh tekeh shodan miayad
> va monfajer shodan.
> Hamsa-ye ha-ye ma hameh dar khak-e baghche ha-yeshan be ja-ye gol
> khompareh va mosalsal mikarand[94]
> ....

> ....
> [Our backyard is empty
> all day.
> From behind the door, I hear the sound of shattering
> and explosions.
> Instead of flowers in their little gardens, our neighbors now plant
> mortar shells and machine guns.]
> ....

As she leaves behind the uncomplicated rhetoric of her early poems, changes her marital status, and constructs a political consciousness, the individual in her poem is also replaced by members of her family and members of society.

In accordance with the tenets of Committed Literature, she even begins to deemphasize form. She explicitly states, "Form and style are not important; the content is."[95] This deemphasis of form in favor of content (the discursive context) reflects her shift from individualism to commitment. The individual loses her status to the power of the collective, a result of the suppression of subjectivity on behalf of the socialist collectivity.[96]

Even if Farrukhzad's notion of literary criteria were in fact indicative of her feminist leanings, they were interpreted by the prerevolutionary readers to mean that men and women must unite and put their differences aside for the sake of victory in their common endeavor. Huquqi, a literary critic, writes, "Furugh Farrukhzad in her *Another*

Birth is a different human being and a different poet than in her other works,"[97] summarizing the general attitude of the critics who then welcomed her to join the community of Committed Literature.[98]

In an important sense Farrukhzad's work may be construed as a feminist assertion, if one assesses her poetic activities and life within the context of the male-dominated culture of her period.[99] Farrukhzad's poems about women's emotions and feelings are straightforward. She brings love to relationships between man and woman. In her poems and her deeds she destroys the walls of her confined life. Yet her overall literary discourse does not revolve around the problematic of gender hierarchy. Her most important works speak to social rather than gender issues. In an interview Farrukhzad stated: "if my poetry has a degree of femininity, it is quite naturally due to the fact that I am a woman. I am fortunate to be a woman. However, if my poetry is judged in terms of artistic criteria, then I do not think gender can be a determining factor. . . . The essential issue is the human being. To be a man or woman is not the issue." She believes that "discussing this matter is not right in the first place," and thereby complies with the Committed literary notion that honored sexually objective criteria in literary criticism.[100]

Simin Bihbahani: The Expression of Social Problems

In terms of innovative style and mastery of the poetic expression, Simin Bihbahani (1927–) ranks with Farrukhzad.[101] She is a prolific poet, whose prerevolutionary works alone include five volumes.[102] In their themes, these works have much in common with those of the prerevolutionary movement and participate in the same struggle to promote the leftist cause as, the prerevolutionary literary movement. "The important and interesting part of my work," says Bihbahani, "has been to explain people's pain and dissatisfaction. I must say that since I have presented my poems for public judgment, I have been encouraged by critics and have been welcomed by the people, especially those from deprived and oppressed classes."[103]

Ja-yi Pa (The Footprint) (1956) portrays the lives of prostitutes, dancers, washers of the dead, sick children, and poor students. The poems in this book occasionally feature female characters, but the author's main concerns remain those of social injustice, which affects men and women alike. Bihbahani is an individual touched by tragic aspects of social life, whose voice speaks passionately in support of oppressed people. Of an imprisoned pickpocket in "Jibbur" (Pick-pocket), she writes,

Man nadanam keh pedar kist mara
ya koja dideh goshudam be jahan,
keh mara zad o keh parvard chonin
sar-e pestan-e keh bordam be dahan.

. . . .
Khofteham ba hasrat-e nan,
gusheh-e masjed o bar kohneh hasir.[104]

[I don't know who my father is
or where I opened my eyes to the world,
who bore and fostered me,
nor at whose breast I suckled. . . .
I have slept hungry, begrudged a piece of bread,
in the corner of the mosques, on torn mats.]

Bihbahani portrays this man's crime as the result of poverty and the lack of family support and social welfare. This point of view informs the entire collection. She dedicates another poem, about prostitution, to "the ill-fated men who in escaping from their own suffering seek shelter in the embrace of women who are more ill-fated."[105] In yet another poem, "Raqasih" (Dancer), a female entertainer awaits a man to rescue her and improve her life.[106] Bihbahani never holds patriarchy responsible for any of the related problems she describes but, rather, portrays men as victims among whom a savior may one day be found.[107]

Bihbahani's protagonists do not speak of themselves. They are too worried about the poor and downtrodden—workers, peasants, pris-oners—to worry about themselves, and they subordinate their per-sonal interests and desires to their concern with social issues. Her characters are prepared to sacrifice on behalf of those who suffer. The gender identity of the narrator, protagonist, or other character loses its importance because it is not essential to their struggle for freedom, pro-gressive change, and the future. Their resolution resonates with the prevailing thought that unity must supersede division to make the Revolution successful.

Raising her voice in rebellion against injustice, Bihbahani predicts, in symbolic language, a revolution in the political system. In the introduction to one of her collections, she writes, "I have seen the rainbow laughing in the minute particles of the rain. I have read the hidden secret in the green book of the spring, the change of the fruitless season to flowering and the bearing of fruit."[108] Like other writers of the prerevolutionary period, she employs coded signs of Committed Literature, using metaphors such as fruitless, cold, and silence to refer to the dictatorship; spring and rainbow to refer to the revolution; and sunshine and laughter to refer to freedom.

Like other prerevolutionary women writers, Bihbahani approaches gender issues in her works in the context of the socially Committed literary movement. She employs Committed Literature's realistic outlook, figurative language, and metaphors to address concerns about social problems, class, and political freedom. Her individual advocacy of oppressed men and women did not result in a feminist literary enunciation any more than on a broader social level women activists' efforts gave rise to a grassroots women's movement.[109] The dominant discourse she supported, in fact, encouraged women to join men in the Islamic movement of 1978–79. Consequently, women massively participated in this movement not as women particularly but as members of the force opposing the Pahlavis.

Prerevolutionary women's literature, as exemplified by the works of Danishvar, Farrukhzad, and Bihbahani, displays a remarkable sensitivity toward social issues, though issues related specifically to women were treated as secondary. The explanatory logic underpinning their works was that of Committed Literature, in which the narrative was to provide explanations of the existing social problems—and, of course, the way out—in figurative and symbolic language. Whether these authors were themselves feminists is not the issue. In all likelihood, each author experienced gender prejudice and discrimination in her social environment. Yet they were still confined within the literary framework set by male-dominated, socially conscious Committed Literature. Their discourse was derivative and necessarily implied a male solution. When this discursive context changed in the postrevolutionary period, women writers began to formulate increasingly independent literary expressions.

4

Revolution and Literature: The Rise of the Islamic Literary Movement after the 1979 Revolution

In 1979 the shah's secular authoritarian state was replaced with a religious regime whose central objective was a total reorganization of society according to the normative and regulative rules of Shiite Islam. The new theocratic multifaction regime soon transformed Iran into an Islamic state in which Shiite clerics, often opposing one another, held the key governmental positions. The fundamentalists, with their spiritual leader Ayatollah Ruhollah Khomeini, gradually pushed liberals out of the government and forced the first modernist Muslim prime minister, Mehdi Bazargan, to resign. In 1981 they ousted the first elected president, Abolhassan Banisadr, who did not fully comply with their Islamization policies, and pushed other liberal Muslims out of power. In a marked contrast with the liberal interpretation of Islam, the fundamentalists categorically rejected Western models. They insisted on unconditional devotion to Islam and its cosmological doctrine. They implemented Ayatollah Khomeini's theory of the Islamic State, which is based on the governance by jurisprudence, a theory that was in sharp contrast with Islamic modernism's attempt to rationalize religious dogma in its attempt to show the compatiblity of Islam with modernity.[1] Because of the ruling clerics' zeal for the Islamization of the society, there were significant shifts in all aspects of social life in a country which had only recently experienced several decades of secularization. They denounced Western culture, established systems of Islamic law and jurisprudence, imposed severe censorship, banned alcohol and music, and made the veil mandatory.

The new ruling elite claimed all the credit for making the Revolution in order to facilitate the elimination of leftist and secular opposition, which wanted their share of power and recognition for their roles in advancing the revolutionary movement against the shah. In the first few months after the Revolution, oppositional groups, including the Organization of Iranian People's Fada'i Guerrillas, the Organization of People's Mojahedin of Iran, the Paykar Organization, the Union of Communists, the Union of Socialist Workers, the Democratic Party, and the Komeleh Organization of Kurdistan, were recruiting new members and holding street demonstrations. The regime used all its newly formed police forces to repress them. They suppressed any ethnic movement for autonomy. They violently closed down the universities for several years to deprive intellectuals of their most important base of activities. Later they attacked Marxist and other leftist activists, including the secular writers, physically and ideologically. Respect for diversity, human rights, freedom, individuality, modernity, and cultural diversity became rare. Many leftist and Marxist literary activists died, were imprisoned, exiled, or became inactive.

Those writers who survived the attacks realized that the Revolution had not helped them achieve any of their goals. Instead, they began to question the revolution that had given rise to such an upsurge of cultural backwardness. This remnant of Committed writers wondered what happened to the revolution they had dreamed about so many times for so many years. Yet they had no desire for another revolution nor could they see the possibility of overthrowing the new regime. They began to focus on cultural issues. The literary community found itself widely dispersed and falling into individual units, each of which faced different problems. However, they found their previous style of representation inadequate for rendering these new issues. Once again, the old metaphors no longer suited the new conditions. Persian literature—most notably, poetry—faced a crisis.[2]

For a decade after the Revolution, some secular writers wrote about the effect of the Revolution and its repercussions in their individual lives. Fiction writers like Asghar Abdulahi wrote on previously uncommon themes, such as the life of ethnic and religious minority groups.[3] Ali Khudai, Abass Marufi, Riza Jula'i, and Riza Farkhal wrote introspectively to address the psychological and emotional aspects of life under the new conditions.[4] Farkhal, for example, captured the melan-

choly of literary activities in the 1980s in the short story "Ah Istanbul."
In it, the editor of a publishing company cannot decide whether to
accept or reject the translation of a novel for publication. He even struggles with the idea of talking about the manuscript with his close friend,
a bookseller downstairs: "Behind the lighted window of the bookstore,
the shadows of passersby's bodies were walking fast with their heads
fallen. I attempted to talk to Fazli about that woman and her translation. Fazli knew all of these literary and artistic figures well. He even
knew the forgotten literary corps."[5] At the end, only the fact that the
story of the novel occurs in Istanbul, somewhere outside Iran, prompts
the editor to accept it for publication. In reality, writing about other
places became a way of escaping some of the burdens of home.

Similar moral themes and frequent references to the precarious situation of intellectual communities appeared in the collection of poems
Shi'r bih Daqiqih-i Aknun (Poetry in This Minute) (1988) and in the
poetry of authors such as Shams Langrudi.[6] Langrudi wrote:

Bar mikhizim va mineshinim.
Bar mikhizim va mineshinim.
Va in bazi-e bi rahm,
ta hafr-e marg zir-e qadamhaman
hamchenan jaryan miyabad. . . .
. . . .
Ah,
In zoraq-e bi bud o bi setareh koja miravd?
In tekeh ha-ye qalb-e zaman koja mirizad?
Dar in siyahkhaneh-e na iman,
na seda'i miayad,
na moj-e khun-e tabah shodeh-i darha ra baz mikonad,
na parandeh'i mikhanad,
na bad-e khazani,
par-e simorghi ra
hamrah-e setarehha be hava mirizad.
Inja
Faqat seda-ye shekastan-e ostekhan ast o
omid o arezu-ye hadar shode'i ke be ham mikhorand.[7]

[We rise and we fall.
We rise and we fall.

And this cruel game,
continues
until death digs under our steps. . . .
Ah,
Where does this shapeless, starless boat go?
Where do these pieces of the heart of time fall?
In this unsafe black house
no sound can be heard
nor does a wasted wave of blood open the doors.
No birds sing.
No autumn breeze takes a feather of a phoenix into the air.
Here
the sounds belong to the breaking bones
and to the wasted wishes and hopes.]

In Committed Literature the "rise and fall" was part of the revolutionary process was viewed optimistically, with the belief that the sequence will end with the masses rising. And the phoenix symbolized that process. Now, in Langrudi's postrevolutionary movement, the rise led only to a fall, to death, and the phoenix was of no help.

These postrevolutionary authors also faced a crisis in the press and publication industry, which struggled not only with suppression but also with the lack of paper, ink, and other materials and equipment. These authors often needed to mute their attitude toward Islamic leaders in order to avoid prosecution and to assure their publishers that the book would not be banned. In Karimi-Hakkak's words, "In the 1980s the state's policy toward the press and publishing industry has reflected both fundamental fear of secular ideologies and a deep desire to push the intellectual community into greater conformity."[8] This censorship and the intellectual writers' interest in the reinterpretation of Persian literature and Iranian culture resulted in the invention of new metaphors, allegories, and other tropes in the language of modern Persian literature causing further variance in literary production.

While ambivalence marked the work of the remnant of Committed authors, the work of Islamic authors who in one way or another and to various degrees, supported the state ideology gave rise to new literary activities in 1980s. Some of these Islamic authors had been writing before the Revolution but became more active in the 1980s. Although some were more fundamentalist than others, they were all inspired by the dominant Islamic discourse in their fiction and poetry. They provided the ruling elite with ideological support of Islam or with outright political support of the government. The state in turn found these Muslim authors a valuable political resource and consequently acknowledged the importance of literary and artistic expression in advancing its religious ideology. The state thus provided a social space and a readership in schools, religious schools, Islamic associations, and mosques for Muslim writers as long as they worked within the state-supported Islamic discourse. The Ministry of Islamic Culture and Guidance frequently sponsored the publication of what it considered to be " Islamic literary work," whether by experienced or inexperienced authors. Islamic writers enjoyed relative freedom; because they had easier access to facilities and supplies and were unencumbered by censorship, they were able to assert their ideas about social events. The state supported these writers, and their literature supported the state, both opposing the secular sector of society. They published an enormous amount of poetry and fiction.

As a result, for the first time an episode that may be called modern Islamic Persian Literature or the Literature of the Islamic Revolution (*Adabiyat-i Inqilab-i-i Islami*) appeared.[9] In this episode, authors depicted the events of the 1979 Revolution and its aftermath, the events of the Iran-Iraq war (1980–88), and many new religious themes, all in accordance with the state's conception of Iranian history. These authors not only acknowledged God as the creator of the world, commonplace for a religious text, but also portrayed God or his representative clergy as the ultimate rulers of people's daily life. It was God and his representatives who guided people, cured their sicknesses, helped the poor, rewarded those who did good, and, if need be, put people to the test by having them face difficult problems, such as the war with Iraq. This situation led to a literary movement characterized by a strong commitment to Islamic ideological premises.

The works of fiction writers such as Muhammad Nurizad, Nusrat Allah Mahmudzadih, Mihdi Shujai, Muhsin Makhmalbaf, Valid Amiri and poets such as Taymur Gurgin, Musavi Garmarudi, Tahirih Saffarzadih typify this episode.[10]

This Islamic literary episode was highly influenced and informed by prerevolutionary Committed Literature in terms of its expression of commitment (although different in its goals) as well as in its use of similar metaphors (although with different meanings) and many of the same themes. That is, the authors of the Islamic episode, deliberately or not, imitated prerevolutionary Committed Literature in terms of content, form, and even some aspects of its figurative language. These imitations, however, served the state's overall effort to subvert the ideological and historical significance of Committed Literature.

Just as Marxist literary theory and an oppositional movement had determined the dynamics of prerevolutionary Committed Literature, the Council for Cultural Revolution of the Islamic Republic and other newly created cultural institutions regulated artistic and literary activities among Islamic writers after the Revolution.[11] The Council's bylaws provided the guideline for rewarding cultural and artistic activities. Section 6 of item 8 enumerates the criteria for award-winning works:

> Producing or compiling an outstanding work on Islamic culture and art. Translating an outstanding work on Islamic culture or art. Establishing an institution for promoting Islamic culture and art. Cooperating effectively with art and cultural institutions for the realization of the government's cultural policy. Introducing Iranian Islamic art and culture on an international level.[12]

Each year the representatives of the Ministry of Islamic Culture and Guidance present these awards on the anniversary of the Islamic revolution. The similarity of these policies to the concept of "party literature" is not accidental. The government of the Islamic Republic was born of a revolutionary movement as well.

Mirmudarris, an Islamic journalist and writer, expressed the Islamic notion of art, especially that which determined the level of commitment, in a journal published in Qum by the Islamic clergy. In his article Mirmudarris argues that the most important quality of "Islamic art" is its mission, which should always be divine in nature. The history of art, according to Mirmudarris, demonstrates that religiosity has shaped the concept of commitment in artistic works. Contrary to the claim that commitment forces art to stray from its pure aesthetic goals and even signs its death warrant, one cannot, Mirmudarris claims, avoid seeing that art has always communicated specific ideals. When that message is a divine one, art becomes eternal. Conversely, when the message belongs to the material world, it assumes an inferior quality. A religious work of art is therefore one that contains a religious message, whether it is direct, as in painting about Ashura (The martyrdom of Imam Husayn) or indirect, such as a movie loosely tied to a theme about the holy war against Iraq. He advises artists to be aware of the Islamic requirements regarding art, such as the need for women in movies to be properly veiled. To doubt the necessity of such requirements is an indication of one's ignorance about religious teachings and the divine creeds.[13]

Thus "Islamic literary theory," like that of Marxism, adheres to the notion of commitment; however, the difference lies in the kind of ideology that the authors in each episode promote—the kind of ideology that inspires them. Other differences lie in their concept of history. Marxist writers apply historical materialism, whereas the Islamic authors motivate their audience to reread history through their Islamic fiction, to believe more wholeheartedly in their faith, and to advance the immediate political agenda of the state.

The theme of Karbala, which had been both ridiculed for its religious importance and praised for its revolutionary quality in previous episodes, gained an entirely new significance in the Islamic literary episode. In Islamic writings Karbala not only reclaims its historical legacy as the place of the massacre of the third imam and the location of his tomb but also redeems its holiness by becoming a place capable of miracles. Some believed that the souls of imams were capable of performing miracles. The secular prerevolutionary literature did not represent such beliefs; but in postrevolutionary Islamic literature, miracles performed in the name of Karbala, even in very distant places, became repeated literary themes.

Moreover, the historical events of Karbala have nourished the concept of martyrdom (Shahadat) in Shiite political discourse and have provided it with a particularly potent holiness and divine countenance.[14] Najjar, a scholar of Arabic culture and literature, writes: "Acts of martyrdom undermine superordinate power by demonstrating that defiance is thinkable and doable and set an example of sacrifice that can be imitated by an oppressed group inclined to rebel in the name of a principle."[15] Secular oppositional activists used such rhetoric to arouse a sense of guilt and rebelliousness in apolitical people and to convince them to make sacrifices for an ideal society. Islamic activists used it to win loyalty to the Islamic state, to curtail Western influence, and to provide support for war against Iraq. During the war, martydom was referred to as "the key to Paradise."

In addition to themes related to Karbala and religious faith, Islamic writers presented themes related to the events of the 1979 Revolution, the battles of the Iran-Iraq war, and the government's campaigns against ethnic uprisings. War became an especially popular theme in the final years of the Iran-Iraq war, when many of those Muslims who fought on the front or lost someone to the war began to write about their experiences.[16] Perhaps because of the propagandist nature of their work or the oversimplicity of their memoir writing, Islamic authors' renditions of these themes, however, did not lead to any works of great literary value.

Muhammad Nurizad's "Mard va Karbala" (The Man and Karbala), a short story about poverty and faith, brings some of the themes together. It features a rural, seasonal construction worker who seeks a better life for his wife and son in a city foreign to him but fails to find work.[17] He had abandoned his land in the village because he could no longer tend the farm alone, and it would embarrass him to return to the village. He thinks he will be humiliated by his relatives and neighbors for his failure to succeed in the city. The winter is severe, he is out of work, and his son, Asghar, is very ill. "The child's constant coughs turn him blue and his chest rattles from the ravages of whooping cough. The reproachful look in his eyes makes the man even more desperate. It pained him to watch the boy's twisting, skinny body and his black lifeless eyes, full of blame and complaint"(9). The worker's wife, desperate, sits at the boy's bedside, crying in silence and speaking to the child in short sentences. The man decides to continue his search for a job in the city. He walks around looking for work for a long time to no avail. He then prays: "Oh, God, for the sake of all that is holy, don't take this child from me. He is all I have. I have spent all my savings on his medicine without any effect. For the sake of the torn throat of Ali Asghar [a child martyred with Imam Husayn in Karbala], keep this child for me. . . . Oh, Imam Husayn, for the sake of your Ali Asghar, cure my Asghar" (12–13). He remembers, while walking, that during his first years in the city he used to go back to the village to visit his family. Everything was better then.

While thinking, praying, and walking, he happens upon a house where the owner is hosting a preacher, who is in the process of delivering a sermon. It is the first time that he has come upon this kind of meeting in the city. The preacher, coincidentally, is one from his home village. The man recognizes the old preacher and thinks that since this pious man has left his village all of God's blessings have departed the place with him. In his sermon the preacher recites the events of Kar-bala and the martyrdom of Imam Husayn, narrating some of the dia-logues in Arabic. He also recites from the Qur'an and urges the audience to put their faith in God. As usual, the sermon centers around the suffering of Imam Husayn and quickly induces the men and women in the audience to weep uncontrollably. "Today in this meet-ing, I want to take you to Karbala," the preacher continues. "Let me show you the heart-breaking scenes of Husayn's farewell. He is left alone and all his friends and young men are martyred. He sees in front of his eyes the bodies of Habib ibn Mazhir, Muslim ibn Awsjih, Ali Akbar, Qasim, Abu al-Fazal al-Abbas . . . , martyr after martyr lying in a designated tent. Ali Asghar and Abu al-Fazal had already been buried beside the tent. Imam Husayn had chosen that spot to keep the fragile body of Ali Asghar from lying where it was certain to come under the beating of horses' hooves" (23).

The man, affected by the recitation of Karbala's events, begins to sob. In no time, he realizes that his difficulties are trivial compared to those of the imam's family. When he compares his Asghar's coughing to Ali Asghar's cut throat, he began to cry so hard that the rest of the audience, moved by his grief, all start to cry in sympathy—even the women in another room downstairs. After the preacher finishes his ser-mon, he comes to the man to calm him down reminding him that he must have trust in God but commending him for expressing his emo-tions so fervently. The man walks home with a heart so full of hope that he no longer feels the cold winter weather, and so confident that he believes that he can single-handedly take care of his land back in the village. Upon arriving at home, he finds his child sitting up and eating food, feeling well enough to greet him: "You're home, dear daddy!" (27). He notices a picture of himself, his wife Asghar, and his grand-parents on the wall, and is even more resolute to return to the village. He utters to himself, "With trust in God . . ." (27).

Traditionally, people attend religious services to gain blessings. They are more likely to relate closely to sermons when they are facing a problem. Although the protagonist of this story arrives at the house quite accidentally, the story suggests that fate has drawn him there because of his good heart and righteousness. And because he has the opportunity to cry for the events of Karbala—an act that the pious strongly believe will help in a time of desperation—a miracle occurs: his child recovers from his sickness.

The significance of Karbala in this story thus differs from the way that it appeared previously in the works of Persianist or Committed writers. Hidayat created grotesque images of the city and other concepts related to it. Dawlatabadi parodied the scenes of Karbala in order to offer a potent writing to the readers in the context of the oppositional struggle. Conversely, Nurizad appeals directly to the sacredness of the city of Karbala that enables miraculous changes in the lives of devout believers. The notion that the city itself can perform miracles is novel in modern Persian literature. Moreover, the text itself, in its use of Arabic words and Islamic phrases is in sharp contrast with the Persianist writing. Arabic is no longer avoided or mocked.

This story, like many other Islamic literary works, displays a nagging similarity to prerevolutionary Committed Literature. The structure of "The Man and Karbala," for example, is similar to prerevolutionary Committed socialist realism, in which authors portrayed rural peasants and seasonal workers as they dealt with socioeconomic problems. This short story suggests that the shah's land reform is responsible for the worker's situation and for his inability to produce in the village. He has no choice but to leave his piece of land behind. In the city he cannot find a job because there are too many workers for the few jobs available. However, the solution to the problem is somewhat different from the one offered by Committed writers. Committed authors would imply that sociopolitical change was necessary in order to improve the condition of peasants and seasonal workers; "The Man and Karbala," however, does not seek the solution in social change but in an adherence to fervent religion and a deeper personal association with the tragedy of Karbala. The author's subversion of prerevolutionary realism begins by adding a high degree of religiosity to the story and ends by seeking the solution in returning to the village and his roots. This story is a good example of the way the fundamentalist movement appropriated the leftist agenda for its own ends.

Nusrat Allah Mahmudzadih, another Muslim writer, published a somewhat fictional memoir, *Marsiah Halabja* (The Elegy of Halabja) (1989), in cooperation with a governmental publishing organization for what at that time was an unusually large printing of 20,000 copies.[18] The book depicts the author as an Iranian soldier arriving in Halabja, a city located in the Kurdish region of Iraq, soon after it was bombed with chemicals by the Iraqis during the war with Iran. The Iran-Iraq War began in September 22, 1980, when Iraq's army invaded the southwestern province of Khuzestan and ended in August 1988 when Iran accepted a cease-fire mediated by the United Nations. During this period, the two sides gained and lost control over several towns. Iranian troops claimed to have captured Halabja after the attack and saved it from further destruction. The book opens with a message from the Ayatollah Khomieni about the just causes of that ongoing war. Different chapters of the book allude to major events in Islamic history. For example, the first chapter, "Tragedy of Ramazan," refers to the assassination of Imam Ali in the early Islamic period. The author then presents an account of the city's rebellion against Iraqi rule, which had resulted in its bombardment. As the story unfolds, he searches the city and finds a child who has turned red from the poisonous gas and is unable to breathe normally. The fighter begins to talk to the child. The story consists of the soldier's monologue to the child, who eventually dies in his arms. One of the last passages reads:

> Look how your small face has become red. Your soft skin made the effects of the chemical bomb work faster. Don't breathe for a minute. Everywhere we go, the air is poisoned. I wish my mask could fit you. Embarrassment is choking me. How can you endure such a slow death from a chemical bomb? But you won't truly die. You will be a martyr and go to heaven.(50)

The author's vivid description of the horrific scene of the child's death is derived from actual incidents. However, he holds to the belief that the Iraqi regime attacked the city because its population showed interest in Islam. By depicting the child as a martyr in that land, the author links Ramazan with Karbala, and this war becomes a continuation of Imam Husayn's rebellion—symbolism reinforced in this case by the shocking photographs accompanying the text. The book concludes with the description of a man who can no longer resist the chemicals that have poisoned him but who dies happy at seeing the Iranian Muslim troops arrive: "The man, as he spoke his last words, was looking at a small picture of Ayatollah Khomeini, and I noticed the admiration in his eyes as he gazed at the picture" (136).

The notion of commitment the book conveys through its depictions of death and martyrdom resembles that of the prerevolutionary episode of Committed Literature as well. Terminology such as *razmandeh* (fighters), *imperialism* (imperialism), *enqelab* (revolution), *shahadat* (martyrdom), *abar qudrat-ha* (superpowers), and *maydan-e nabard* (battlefield) hearken back to the metaphors of leftist writing. The author directly borrows passages from prerevolutionary rhetoric. While talking to the dying boy, the soldier says: "You will face death one way or another. It is better that you welcome it" (50). This resonates with the famous passage by Samad Bihrangi: "Of course, if someday I should be forced to face death—and I shall—it doesn't matter. What does matter is the influence that my life or death will have on the lives of others."[19] This resemblance, again, echoes the way the Islamic fundamentalist movement concerned itself with modern issues.

Another new writer, Mihdi Shujai, connects Karbala and the Iran-Iraq war in a short story entitled "Zarih-i Chishmha-yi Tu" (The Shrine of Your Eyes) (1985).[20] An old man and his son, Qasim, are fighting at the front when he hears that a missile has hit his home and has killed all of his family. Soon after that, Qasim (also the name of one of Imam Husayn's sons) dies far within the enemy's stronghold. The old man decides to bring the body of his son back and crawls to the spot where Qasim is lying in a pool of blood. But when he discovers other dead bodies as well, he decides it is wrong to retrieve his own Qasim while leaving so many other Qasims without anyone to bring them back. Thus he returns alone.

The name Qasim ties the event of Karbala to the present situation because it was the name of an actual victim of the Karbala massacre. The Iran-Iraq war is perhaps nothing but the continuation of Imam Husayn's rebellion against the unjust ruler. Like the writings of many other young Muslim authors, "The Shrine of Your Eyes" is based on their experience of war, often including wars against other enemies, such as unruly minorities. Miyanduabi, for example, in his short story "Maqtal" (Place of Slaughter), expresses scorn for the Kurdistan Democratic Party, claiming that party members participated in criminal acts against their own people and against Iranian national interests.[21] All Muslim writers supported the armed forces; in their stories the Iranian soldiers were combating either the Iraqis, the antirevolutionaries, or an imaginary American invasion in the Persian Gulf area.

Muhsin Makhmalbaf, a prolific Islamic novelist and film maker, has written about prison and SAVAK (the shah's secret police). The short story "Mara Bibus" (Kiss Me), portrays the interrogation of a male revolutionary, Mostafa, by SAVAK agents.[22] The investigator questions Mostafa about his identity, activities, and his relationship with a woman named Marziyeh. Mostafa does not answer, however; the story unfolds through the information available in seven of Mostafa's letters confiscated by SAVAK and through the comments of Mostafa's comrade and best friend, Hasan, who recalls what he witnessed in prison. As members of a revolutionary organization, Mostafa and Hasan had often disguised themselves, stood on a street corner in the neighborhood, and passed out revolutionary pamphlets to girls returning home from school. One day, one of the girls, Marziyeh, approaches them and starts arguing with Mostafa. But after a few such encounters, Mostafa and Marziyeh fall in love.

Mostafa has joined the anti-shah movement to protest poverty and the lack of freedom, but he is also so religious that he considers even looking at a girl to be improper. His friend tells him that for the sake of their movement he has to look into Marziyeh's eyes. He responds, "I am religious. And I know there will not be any marriage. I will therefore look into her eyes but only with reluctance" (20). With this looking, which results in love, his life changes. Now his duties and his love conflict with each other: according to the prerevolutionary leftist discourse, personal love could interfere with carrying out organizational duties. As a solution, he tries to perceive his love as a heavenly one. He writes to Marziyeh: "You are the fire that has been burning me for several months; it is increasingly burning my soul. A forgotten feeling for humanity has returned to me since I met you; love, not the kind that subsides with sex, but a divine feeling that makes my soul eager to remain pure forever" (21).

He recruits Marziyeh for his organization and continues to contact her until they are both arrested. In prison Mostafa and Marziyeh resist bravely. Marziyeh convinces one of the guards to bring Mostafa to her cell so that they can have a short meeting. She tells him, "I just remembered the time when I took away my scarf and you could have seen my hair and my neck in a glance and you wouldn't. I wanted you to see my face and I wanted to look into your eyes. But you closed yours" (21). Even in that short encounter, Mostafa's beliefs prevailed. The love relationship is the ascension of Mostafa's love from a simple feeling for the movement to a divine love. He talks to God:

> Oh God, a tiny piece of your creation is so beautiful that it has made me so loving, and transported; what will I do if I confront your whole beauty? Marziyeh is a manifestation of your beauty to the extent that I can understand it. My praise of the beauty of my beloved is praising you. Her innocent eyes are your holiness, chastity, and purity. Marziyeh is you, my God. (30)

Like revolutionaries in Committed novels, Mostafa suppresses his sexual drives in order to dedicate himself to a superior goal: to the movement. God has become the protagonist's beloved. In Committed Literature, the people would have taken the place of the beloved God.

Mostafa and Hasan are very similar. They are both young, devoted Muslims, committed to the struggle, loyal to their organization; they are in prison at the same time and both resist interrogation. Their only difference is in the degree of their dedication to the cause, and that is perhaps what qualifies Mostafa to be Marziyeh's beloved. Nonetheless, Marziyeh's character remains perplexing. In the beginning she seems to be crazy, especially when she verbally attacks Mostafa on the street. Later on she appears to be madly in love with him, and that is the only reason given for her decision to join the organization. In prison, she is a nonessential. Hasan says, "She fails to understand that there are dozens of important guerrillas in prison" (30). That is, in the presence of important guerrillas, one should keep quiet. The authorities finally execute her for making noise and singing songs. In portraying Marziyeh, the author goes beyond the leftist notion that women must comply totally with their organization rather than express their individual concerns. However, this portrayal implies that women's concerns with the revolutionary movement did not take women's involvement with it as seriously, and such a notion misrepresents the importance of women's role in the leftist movement.

Furthermore, the story, by appropriating some of the features of the Marxist movement, presents a distorted history of the armed struggle before the Revolution. Many of the traits of the religious protagonist in this story also belonged to the nonreligious revolutionaries of the Pahlavi period. For example, Mostafa introduces himself as a *Cherik* (guerrilla), a term that Marxist fighters applied to themselves; Muslim fighters were known as the *Mujahidin* (holy war soldiers). Moreover, the way the protagonist introduces himself—as an "unemployed guerrilla"—indicates that the author is not able to present a realistic view of the organizations involved in the armed struggle.[23] In the culture of these organizations, being a guerrilla was a full-time occupation. In addition, the author does not present a consistent portrayal of the central character when he has the ultrareligious Mostafa writing letters that abound with references to secular literature. At one point he writes, "You have planted your hands in the garden of my heart," echoing Furugh Farrukhzad's famous line " I will plant my hands in the garden."[24] One of Marziyeh's letters includes the romantic secular poem "Kuchih" (The Alley) by Faridun Mushiri. The title of the short song comes from the song "Kiss Me," which she sings in prison, with all the other Muslim prisoners joining in. This song was a favorite of secular prisoners and is not considered Islamic by the present ruling elite government, which, in fact, has banned broadcasting it.[25]

Two central characters of the story are, to some degree, modeled on historical figures. Marziyeh, the name given to the female character, is a reminder of Marziyeh Ahmadi Osku'i, one of the female guerrillas of the OIPFG, who was killed in 1974. However, this characteristic stands in sharp contrast with Osku'i's legacy as presented by the OIPFG. Mostafa was also the name of the Marxist guerrilla: the Marxist Mostafa Shoaiyan. Although Shoaiyan was not a member of the OIPFG, he was engaged in the armed struggle. Shoaian, whose legacy was related to his strong devotion to Marxist ideas, ideologically stands in sharp contrast to Makhmalbaf's Mostafa, even though they both share the advocacy of armed struggle as well as an uncompromising stand against the regime. It seems that Makhmalbaf's story has in fact appropriated the actual brief love affair between Osku'i and Shoaiyan (which went unnoticed among the revolutionary circles at the time), though, with huge modification of historical fact. Makhmalbaf's story, which represents Shoaiyan as a devoted Muslim and Osku'i as an incoherent and incompetent woman, subverts the history of the guerrilla movement in Iran.[26]

Like many Muslim writers belonging to this episode of literary history, Makhmalbaf imitates the prerevolutionary authors in their denunciation of the shah's authoritarian regime and its secret police. According to Islamic state discourse, the prerevolutionary period was marked by a conflict between the state and Islam. After the Revolution, every time other forces tried to declare their share in the making of the Revolution, the ruling elites claimed that the Revolution occurred only because of the struggle and sacrifice of Muslims. They urged the people to erase from their minds the memory of the leftist, liberal, and Marxist activities against the old regime. Besides the mass media, which constantly represented a reconstructed version of every incident, the state-affiliated organizations published numerous books on the Revolution presenting the official views.[27] This notion of the history of the Revolution has been promoted by some academic works both inside and outside Iran. However, Makhmalbaf's misrepresentation of the historical facts related to the armed struggle served to promote effectively the new state's understanding of the historical process of the 1979 Revolution. In his work he supports the Islamic order while subtly using leftist figures and themes.

Makhmalbaf has also written on the consequences of the war and martyrdom. His novel *Bagh-i Bulur* (The Crystal Garden) (1986) centers around the lives of those who were awarded housing by the government because they were related to a war martyr. Its events take place in Tehran. The war is not over yet, and every character has already lost someone to the war. In their various residences life goes on somewhat differently. In one of these houses, three families live together: Alieh, the widow of a martyr, who has two children and is pregnant with a third; Suri, the widow of another martyr, with her two children and her husband's family; and Hamid, a disabled war veteran with his wife. Alieh gives birth to a girl and marries a dishonest man and soon endures a bitter divorce. Suri marries Ahmad, her brother in-law, only to lose him to the war a while later. Hamid goes through a period of emotional upheaval and even insanity, but seeing the body of a martyr cures him. The war or its consequences has affected everyone's life. Some of the characters face psychological problems as well. The story ends with a miracle: Ahmad's old mother, who was forced to take in the children of both her sons, begins to have milk and is able to nurse the children.

Even though the story slightly criticizes the government's handling of housing for the families of the martyrs, it promotes the ideology of the state, according to which all those who died in the fighting with the shah's regime were considered martyrs (*shahid*) but only if they were Muslims. This ideology once and for all—as far as the literature is concerned, and at the hands of authoritative Muslim fiction writers—clarifies the confusion over those prerevolutionary revolutionaries who were killed in clashes with security agents or in prison. If they were not Muslim, they were not martyrs. Makhmalbaf's story portrays martyrs in their Islamic sense, defined in terms of their relation to God. The dialogues in the book abound with religious terms and connotations that reflect the dominant rhetoric about the "true path": martyrdom is the key to paradise. Even the children's dialogue reflects the state's cultural and ideological axioms. In one scene three children, two girls and a boy, are playing house.

Sareh said: Well, what is your job Mr. Salman?

Samireh said: I am a martyr.

Sareh said: Hey, martyrdom is not a job. I don't want to play anymore.

Samireh said: Then what is martyrdom? Is it unemployment?

Sareh said: Martyrdom is . . . is . . . Martyr is the one who has gone to God.

Maysam said: What is God's job?

Sareh said: God has made us. Has made these flowers. He has made everything. He is very big.[28]

Such passages are blatantly religious; however, as Makhmalbaf uses and misuses history in his ideological representation, he does not hesitate to use the rhetoric and scenes of the prerevolutionary literary movement in this story. He frequently appropriates passages from Farrukhzad's works. His *Crystal Garden,* also shows the influence of Dawlatabadi. He also uses images similar to those in Bihrangi's "The Little Black Fish." In form, however, his stories are not similar to those of Dawlatabadi and Bihrangi but rather marked with diversity.

Islamic poetry also treated issues central to state ideology and issues related to the Iran-Iraq war. The war poetry, old or new style, either expressed the experiences of Islamic fighters in battle or praises the fighters and martyrs. These foci gave rise to threnody as an important genre, not because it had roots in the Islamic tradition but simply because there were so many occasions for it during the war. Besides those who died during the war, many important individuals died at the hands of oppositional groups. Such events inspired Islamic poets. Two Islamic literary critics, Mahmud Shahrukhi and Mushfiq Kashani, point out the significance of the genre and try to promote it.

Threnody is the most original and natural speech which comes from the spring of a poet's feeling. Threnody is the language of the heart, a poem which comes from the depth of the souls of those overtaken by a calamity. Threnody is the sad groaning of the melancholic hearts who cry out at the departure of a dear one. Threnody is the natural utterance of a human's pain and suffering.[29]

Their collection of this type of poem, *Majmuʿah-i Shiʿr-i Jang* (An Anthology of Poems on War) (1987) includes poetry by numerous newcomers that varies from scenes of battles to expressions of tender feelings and survivors' states of mind. In the introduction Shahrukhi writes: "This collection is a handful from a ton of material, a drop from the sea, a small sample of the talents of the poets of this region. It is a humble gift to Islamic fighters of the army of monotheism and to the witnessing martyrs who have eternalized the name of Islam and Iran in world history.[30]

As is common in such collections, some of the poems attack those on the left who did not support the war. Valid Amiri's short poem, "Su'al" (Question), written in the new style of Persian poetry reads:

An ruzha ke nur
dar jireh bandi bud
aya kasi tashar zad
bar shaeran-e farbeh-e an ruzgar:
az shab sorudan
az marg goftan
digar bas ast!
Inak chera
arvah-e shab parast
paiz-ha-ye munjamed-e matruk
hushdar midahand
mazmun-e aftab
mazmun-e yek bahar, shaqayeq-e mazlum
mazmun-e shadmani va labkhand
tekrari ast?
yaran gonah-e man chist
vaqti keh qatreh qatreh-e khunam
ba nur khordeh payvand?[31]

[Those days when the light
was rationed
did anyone shout at
the fat poet:
that is enough
writing about the night,
talking about death.
Why now are
these night-loving ghosts
these abundant, frozen autumns
signaling that

the meaning of sunshine,
the meaning of one spring, a sinless anemone,
the meaning of happiness and a smile
are repetitive?
Friends, what is my sin
that all the drops of my blood
are bound with light?]

Here Amiri is arguing with secular or leftist authors, such as the authors who contributed to *Shi'r Bih Daqiqih-i Aknun* (Poetry in This Minute) (1988) (A. Shamlu, M. Mukhtarzadih, Y. Ruya'i, and S. Langrudi), over the metaphors of night *(shab)*, light *(nur)*, and spring *(bahar)*. These leftist authors used the metaphor of night to describe the shah's regime. With the shah now deposed, they should describe the new situation with the metaphors of light and spring to express happiness and joy. Instead, they claim that these metaphors are repetitive. Today secular poets avoid using the metaphors and figures of prerevolutionary Committed Literature. Many try to disassociate themselves from that episode even in their style of writing. To them, continuing the trend of commitment means to accept responsibility for the defeat of leftist projects.

Amiri, on the contrary, freely uses the metaphor of spring because according to state ideology, spring has arrived. Just as politics was a battleground for the confrontation of conflicting ideologies, poetry seems to have become a battleground for conflicting metaphors. Just as the Committed writer Shamlu metaphorically hung the traditionalist Hamidi Shirazi in his poems, so Amiri threatens the remnants of the leftist literary discourse with drops of his blood.

Najafzadih Barfurush is a literary activist who has contributed greatly to the formation of the Literature of the Islamic Revolution through the publication of several anthologies of short stories and poetry about the war. His four-volume work on the war, *Farhang-i Shairan-i Jang va Muqavimat* (The Poets of War and Resistance) (1993) is an encyclopedic collection of poems by dozens of authors. Various contributors of different ages and backgrounds write in various styles and forms, using the Iran-Iraq war as their unifying theme.

Taymur Gurgin's "Ru-yi Telex" (On the Telex) (1993), in Barfursh's collection, presents a picture of the alleged atrocities committed during the war. He claims that the leftist opposition, as Iraq's fifth column, stands responsible for the devastation.

Khabarha-ʾi ast. . . .
Khabarha-ʾi ast bar ru-ye "telex"-e jang.
Khabar az har koja ayad,
kafan pichideh, khunin ast.
Khabar in ast:
shomar kushtegan az har do su, sangin-i sangin ast
vali az pusht-e jebheh
yek khabar ru-ye navar-e kaghazin tekrar migardad,
pay a pay midahad hoshdar:
"sotun . . . panjom . . . doshman"
sotun . . . panjom . . . doshman.[32]

[There is news,
News on the telex of war.
The paper ribbon is receiving news;
The news is coming from all over.
Wrapped in shrouds and they are bloody,
The news says.
There is a battle raging on every front.
The number of the dead is high on both sides.
But from behind the front
One piece of news comes repeatedly,
A message, a warning:
The enemy's fifth column...
The enemy's fifth column.]

The author tries to recapture the notion promoted by the state that the imperialists supported Iraq from the outside and the leftists, Marxists, and liberals helped Iraq from the inside. In the poetic version, however, the fifth column seems to be the fiercer enemy.

Ali Musavi Garmarudi, in "Man Shiʿr-i Shiʿiam" (I Am Shiite Poetry), published in the collection *Inqilab-i Islami dar Shiʿr-i Shaʿiran* (Poetry of the Islamic Revolution) (1986), praises the Islamic Revolution as a divine political manifestation:

Man pasdar-e marz-e sharaf,
khun o hemmatam
shiʿr-e moqavamat,
shiʿr-e qiyamatam.
Man jam-e khunfeshan-e sharaf ra

chun kaseh-ye shafaq,
hamvareh por ze khun
bar astan-e shamgahan
bar dast
amadeh dashtam
shemshir-e shi'r-e khod
dar khak-e razmgah
ba khun-e sorkh,
ba ayeh,
kashtam.
Man shi'r-e shiiyam
dar dast-e man cheragh
fara ru-ye mardoman
ta marz-e shab be parto-e khod bar deram ze ham
tarikh pa beh pa-ye man az kuch-e ha gozasht
az dashtha-ye khun o jonun.
hamrah-e man sepideh-ye sadeq
hamrazm-e man shikasteh-ye asheq
hamsuhbatam kalam-e khoda bud.
Taghut ra hamareh rah az rah-e man,
hameh sakhti
bira-he bud o joda bud.[33]

[I guard the bounds of dignity, blood, and aspiration;
I am the poetry of resistance and of resurrection.
The cup of dignity filled with blood,
Like the bowl of twilight,
I ever raise readily
At the threshold of night.
The earth of the battlefield I sow
With the swords of my verses,
Watering them with my pure blood.
I am Shiite poetry;
With a lantern in one hand,
I march in front of the people,
So my light may pierce the heart of night.
History, keeping pace with me,
Crosses the streets
Amid the plains of blood and fury.

My company is the truthful daybreak.
My fellows, the combatant, the wounded lover.
With the word of God alone I communicate.
Never do I accompany idols
Whose crooked ways deviate from my straight path of suffering.][34]

Garmarudi states that he, exemplifying Muslim revolutionaries, has been able to guard the bounds of dignity, blood, and aspiration. He has kept the resistance and the faith alive in poetry. Holding the lantern of the words of Shiite poetry in one hand and a sword in the other, ready to be martyred, he has provided light for the people's path. In response to this religious and courageous act, hundreds of thousands of voices have risen. On his way, fellow combatants and lovers in the safety of God's words never cease to join the poet. Together they fight the idol Taghut, embodied in the Pahlavi regime. All those who made the Revolution belonged to one united Shiite front. In its sentiments, Garmarudi's poem mirrors Makhmalbaf's version of the history of the Revolution.

Metaphors and terminology such as watering a field with blood, the red garden of martyrdom, fellow combatants in love, and triumphal songs were all carried over from prerevolutionary literary discourse but were assigned new meanings determined by the dominant ideology of the time. That is, the new meanings attest to the discontinuity in the way literature is "produced" and "consumed." The repetition of "I am Shiite poetry" conveys the bold emergence of this political Shiite theme in modern Persian poetry. The repetition of the "sh" sound produces a harmony between the word *Shiite* and other elements of the poem, such as *Shihadat*. However, the poet makes it clear that this united front has nothing to do with the "crooked," "idolatrous," non-Muslim writers.

The prerevolutionary pioneers of the guerrilla movement believed that they, as the avant-garde intellectuals *(roshanfekran-e pishtaz)*, had to rise first so that the masses could respond to their political action.[35] In Garmarudi's poem the people also respond to the avant-garde Shiite fighter, however, a shout is sufficient to raise up the masses in Shiism. The prerevolutionary avant-garde promised change, freedom, and justice to provoke people to action. Garmarudi's avant-garde fighter has only to reiterate his faith to get the masses to follow.

Tahirih Saffarzadih (b. 1936) introduced a similar theme, pleading people to follow the Islamic avant-garde. Relatively unknown during the prerevolutionary period, she became one of the most famous Muslim poets in the postrevolutionary period. In one of her poems, "Chaharrah-i Shahadat" (The Roads of Martyrdom) (1986), she writes:

Ragha-y-man keshideh mishavad az dard
ragha-y-man keshideh mishavad az risheh
dar bikaraneh tarin hejran
to asmanguneh shekafti
va ma zamin guneh
gustardeh shodim
va negah afkandim
har cheh keh dar ma bud
az sabr az sepas
az boghz
az niyaz. . . .
. . . .
Hameh yeki shodehim
ba ham
ba rah
ba Allah
ba sarzamin-e khasteh o khunin
ba khalq-e qahraman-e flestin
dar bikaraneh tarin hejran
az chahar rah-e shahadat bar mikhizim
bar mikhizim
va az nahad-e sangar-e iman
beh su-ye dushman dirineh
do bareh hamleh miaghazim[36]

[Our veins twitch with pain,
Our veins are torn from the root,
When in a vast separation,
You split heaven-like,
And we, like the earth,
Expanded
And poured forth at once
Whatsoe'er was within us
Of long-suffering,
Of gratitude,

Of inarticulate rage,
Of supplication.
. . . .
All have become one
With one another,
With the road,
With Allah,
With the heartsick and bloodstained Land,
With the brave people of Palestine,
When in a boundless massacre
From the roads of martyrdom we rise,
And from within the faith's trench
To the ancient foe
Again make an assault.][37]

This poem alludes to feelings that may arise as one enters upon the "roads of martyrdom." Upon entering this path, one realizes that the new generation seeks nothing but martyrdom. This being so, one may become a leader who can help the generation earn a victory for Islam. The death of a fighter encourages others to rise against the enemy. On the road of martyrdom there is no defeat. The poem promotes the Islamic Republic's notion about the universality of its ideology. The mention of Palestinians in the poem, for instance, attests to the attempt to give the poem such universality as well. In her poem "Fath Kamil Nist" (Victory Is Not Complete), Saffazadih demonstrates the quality that according to Kamybee and Mirkiani made her work an "established example of poetry of resistance with Islamic inclinations and a manifestation of commitment in art in its real sense."[38] In "Victory Is Not Complete" she writes:

Sedaye nabe azan miayad.
Sedaye nabe azan
Safire dast-ha-ye mo'men mardist
Keh hese dur shodan gom shodan jazireh shodan ra
Ze risheha-ye salem-e man bar michinad.
Va man beh su-ye namazi azim miayam.
Vozuyam az hava-ye khiyabanstava rahhaye tireh-e dud.
Va qeblehha-ye havades dar emtedade zaman
Beh estejabate man hastand.
Va lake nakhone man baraye goftane takbir

Qeshre faseleh nist.
Va doa-ye mojezeh midanam
Doa-ye taghir.
. . . .
Va ust keh midanad
keh poshte khasteh-ye abr
beh lahzeha-ye tord shekastan niyaz darad
va dafᶜe totaʾe takhdir
beh lahzeh ha-ye vahshi-e rud.
Va man keh az qesavate nan midanam
midanam keh fath kamel nist.[39]

[There comes the pure voice of Azan.
The pure voice of Azan
Is the cry of the believing hands of a man
Which pluck from my healthy roots
The feeling of getting away, getting lost, becoming an island.
I am heading towards a great prayer.
My ablution is from the street air,
And the dark paths of smoke.
And the Kiblahs of events over time,
Grant my prayers.
My nail polish
Does not keep me
From uttering "Allah-o-Akbar."
And I know a prayer of miracle
A prayer of conversion.
. . . .
And He is the one who knows
That the weary back of the cloud
Awaits fragile moments of breaking down.
To counter the conspiracy of stupefaction
Needs the immediate moments of rain
And the wild moments of the river.
And I, who know about the ruthlessness of bread,
Know that victory is not complete.
And no calculating brain has yet been able
To count the syllables of the distance of the leaf

From the hidden spite of the wind.
And the greed for finding the pearl
Will allow the whole surface of the shell
To reject the affection of the sand.][40]

It should be mentioned that even through Saffarzadih's poem promotes the ideology of the state through its use of Islamic concepts and
themetization of political issues, it also emphasizes women's role in the
polity. The poem reflects the time when feminist discourse was becoming a popular mode in literary activities and had begun to influence
Muslim women authors as well. These women's works are far from
outright feminist assertions of women's concerns in Iran, however;
they occasionally contributed to the popularization of women's discourse through innovative means and by the virture of their reinterpretation of Islamic norms.

These analyses show that Islamic writers use literature as an informative medium to promote their religion as well as the state's political
agenda. In their works, they treat the questions related to the Iranian
Revolution, war, and history of prerevolutionary movements as divine
issues. Through the exploration of these themes, the authors promote
religiosity, and they also believe that they themselves get closer to God
by means of what they write. They thereby see themselves as taking
over the role of the avant-garde in promoting the state ideology.

Although this religious literature came into existence during the
postrevolutionary period, some of its constituent features were derived
from previous secular literary trends. The literary language of Islamic
writers abounds with the terminology of Marxists. Ayatollah Khomeini issued a decree to "break" the Marxist writers' pens, but Muslim
writers appropriated their rhetoric—"revolution," "spring of freedom," "imperialism" (cultural and all other sorts of imperialism),
"antagonistic," "conflict," "fight until victory," "rights of deprived
nations," "international revolution," and "exportation of revolution"—
to convey new meanings in favor of the new state ideology. Islamic
authors derived their notions of commitment, populism, anti-imperi-
alistic sentiments, and justice from prerevolutionary Committed Literature. The Islamic ideology of representation called for a
commitment to the community. Islamic writers, too, called for the commitment of the population (if only the religious ones) in supporting
their Islamic nation against enemies such as Iraq, the West, and the left.

This literature never gained the respect of any major literary critics, but it became a strong political tool in the 1980s for taking the place of leftist literature, which was weakened by the left's failure to gain power in the Revolution.

In the late 1980s and early 1990s, when the government relaxed its censorship and allowed some cultural diversity, the Islamic authors lost their privileged status, and this episode began to decline. Other changes in this literary episode came about because of the growth of women's writings and the profusion of a feminist literary movement. Even female Islamic authors such as Tahirah Aybud and writers for journals like *Zanan* (Women) and *Zan-i Ruz* (Today's Woman), who began with a devotion to the state ideology, have now taken up some women's causes.

5

Feminist Discourse
in Postrevolutionary
Women's Literature

IN 1979, WHEN A RELIGIOUS REGIME replaced the secular authoritarian state of the shah, many of the social reforms undertaken by the Pahlavis for several decades were undone by the new ruling clerics.[1] The new religious regime not only obliterated the old regime's family law but also imposed gender segregation and mandatory veiling.[2] Soon after the Revolution, women lost the right to divorce, the right to keep their children in the event of divorce, the right to freely travel, and the right to equality in the workplace. The state's Islamization of society and transformation of gender relations redefined women's position in society, in family, at work, and in public life. The state actively promoted gender segregation, and gender consequently became a social determinant. According to new laws, women can be stoned if they commit adultery. For merely appearing in public without the veil, a woman may be imprisoned for at least forty-five days, given seventy-six lashes, or fined. A woman charged with improper dress can also lose her job if she is working in the civil service. Strictly speaking, the law forbids social contact between the sexes and regulates sexual conduct.[3] The ideal roles for a woman are those of chaste wife and good mother, even if out of necessity she has to participate in economic and extrafamilial activities. Generally, according to the new leaders, veiled women symbolize Muslim virtue and the rejection of the West.[4]

The state argues that the freedoms that the Pahlavis granted women, including the right to unveil, were colonial in nature. Veiling therefore liberates Iranians from this imperialist control and rejects Western notions of women's freedom. As a result, the veil—or, more precisely, the woman's body—has become a locus of contention and a battle-ground between Western modernity and Islam. The veil, as Milani explains, "not only polarizes but delineates boundaries. It consigns 'power,' 'control,' 'visibility,' and 'mobility' to one social category at the expense of the other. It not only separates the world of men and women not related to one another by marriage or blood but also cre-ates hierarchies across this divide."[5] The Islamic state reestablished stronger "boundaries" between men and women by actively enforcing official edicts about the veil in order to separate women physically and socially.

Immediately after gaining power, the Islamic leaders initiated a campaign to enforce a public dress code for women.[6] It began with Ayatollah Khomeini's speech in Qum on March 6, 1979—two days before the International Women's Day—in which he called for the mandatory public veiling of all women. While the media hailed this speech during the days that followed, it produced a strong reaction among intellectual and educated women. Women who were already leery of the implementation of Islamic law assumed a more aggressive stance. Their opposition of the compulsory dress code culminated in a series of demonstrations in Tehran and other cities that were the beginning of the first independent women's movement in Iran.[7]

Activities in preparation for International Women's Day escalated. On March 7, 1979, a students' lecture series became unruly.[8] Students from Marjan Girls' High School marched toward the palace of the prime minister. A photography exhibition was organized at the Faculty of Fine Arts. Other students staged a play that depicted the situation. Lectures and gatherings took place at San'ati University.[9] On March 8, high school girls reacted to the Ayatollah's decree: in order to discuss the issue, students did not attend classes, and then they marched in the streets to protest the dress code. Female Iran Air workers protested the decree as well. Eventually, thousands of women marched toward Tehran University.[10] In a separate rally at the Faculty of Engineering of Tehran University, another group of women, including university stu-dents, listened to speeches by women activists condemning the codes and then marched into the streets, chanting slogans.

These protests culminated in the formation of a preparatory com-mittee to create the Association of Iranian Women. Several independ-ent women's organizations were also formed, and existing women's organizations were revitalized. The Revolutionary Union of Militant Women, more outwardly socialist in its goals, also demanded an end to the exploitation of the working class by the bourgeoisie.[11] The Women's Awakening Association condemned the mandatory veiling.[12] The National University Association (Sazman-i Milli Danishgahian) announced that women must not be subject to any discrimination and declared that the choice of dress is one of the most basic rights of any human being.[13] During these events a number of demonstrators actually wore the veil. In interviews with the popular newspaper *Ayandigan*, some of these women stated that they believed in the veil but that they did not believe it should be mandatory. One of them, a teacher, said, "We. . .wore the chador before the Revolution in order to fight the shah's regime, but it was our own decision. No one forced us. We do not want to be forced now either."[14] Women became more organized and articulated their goals and demands. They braved a heavy snow, mace, stones, bricks, broken bottles, chains, and knives on the eighth and ninth of March to express their opposition to the hijab code.

They chanted slogans such as "We fight against the hijab," "Long live freedom, mandatory veiling is the death shroud of freedom," "For freedom, we'll fight, we'll fight," and "Women must be freed from captivity."[15] These rallies and demonstrations eventually met with violent repression from the government agents and fundamentalist groups and resulted in injury and arrest. The weather did not deter the Islamic forces, including members of the Islamic Revolutionary Committees and fundamentalists, who attacked the women demonstrators. Groups of radical Muslim men, chanting slogans in favor of the dress code, attacked rallies at the University of Tehran, the Ministry of Justice, and the prime minister's palace, while government agents fired shots into the air, intensifying tension and fear.[16] Deep-rooted cultural discrimination against women, which had itself contributed to the rise of women's consciousness, surfaced during these events. In attacking women's demonstrations, counter slogans of the Hizbullah (Party of God), which organized the various supporters of the state, were "Unveiling propagates prostitution," "Women's unveiling means men's dishonor," and "Wear a scarf on your head or get a cuff on the head" (*ya ru sari, ya tu sari*).[17]

Violent encounters lasted for several days, and then the authorities recanted their stance on the veil: "The women's hijab is not obligatory."[18] Women, however, continued to hold public meetings, marches, and street discussions. A group of women, protesting the Radio and Television Organization's refusal to cover the news of their struggle, attacked and damaged the car of the organization's president while he was driving to work. Eventually the government further capitulated by announcing that women would share the same rights and privileges as men. This victory, however, was not a lasting one. Hizbullah forces soon established several Islamic women's associations to counter the oppositional women's movement and to present a rationale in support of the veil. They arranged for a demonstration to support the veiling code and to condemn the attack on the president of the Radio and Television Organization. Members of various Islamic women's associations violent extremist groups, and the police again began to enforce the veil. Women were, in the end, deprived of their freedom of dress. *Ayandigan*, which had covered the women's struggle most consistently, was the first newspaper to be closed down by the authorities. Women realized that the government's earlier retractions had been only tactical moves to prevent the expansion of dissent and women's activism to other sectors of society.

The leftist opposition, especially the larger organizations, did not officially support the women's movement. Both the Organization of Iranian People's Fada'i Guerrillas and the Organization of People's Mojahedin of Iran, which enjoyed wide public support, decided not only to keep quiet on the issue but on some occasions to condemn the women's demonstrations. On the occasion of International Women's Day, the OIPFG commended prerevolutionary heroic women who had fought against imperialism and dictatorship and asked for additional benefits for female workers, such as a decrease in their working hours. The organization did not, however, make any mention of the ongoing demonstrations. The OPMI, in its announcement, implicitly condemned these demonstrations, saying that they had helped antirevolutionaries. According to *Ittilaʿat* (March 14, 1979) and *Payam-i Khalq* (March 1979), the OPMI did not want people to make a "fuss" about the veil. A similar position was held by the OIPFG in their conferences.

These organizations did not want to get involved because they believed that feminism was associated with bourgeois ideology and that independent women's movements would jeopardize the sense of unity necessary for the struggle against imperialism. Ultimately, the unspoken reason behind their behavior was that they believed women should meticulously follow the policies of the organization in order to gain freedom. This is why, when speaking of the women's struggle, the OIPFG praised Marziyeh Ahmadi Osku'i or Fatimah Gharvi, two martyred guerrillas who had remained within the organization and sacrificed their lives in the struggle against the shah's regime.[19]

Suppressed by the Islamic forces and ignored by the left, the women's demonstrations ceased to expand. Since then, however, women have constantly had to deal with the question of the veil in their writings. Women activists published articles and reports on women's rights and the struggle over mandatory veiling immediately after the suppression of their demonstrations.[20] They criticized not only the political establishment, the fundamentalists, and the left (by which they were once influenced) but also patriarchal culture in general.[21] Emerging feminist writers criticized men who stood by silently as women's rights were restricted as well as men who actively promoted the new limitations.[22] Twenty years later, Muslim women are still locked in debate. These critical writings are so numerous that a professor at Al-Zahra University argues they have caused an increase in the divorce rate.[23] Today it is common for interviewers to ask an Iranian woman writer whether she is a feminist.[24] Although such questions were previously unheard of, there are now numerous publications engaged in debates over feminism and women's issues.[25]

Since the Revolution, the number of women writers has increased dramatically.[26] Their work, despite great diversity in literary value, commonly manifests an awareness of women's issues and gender relations. This work shows concern over problems of gender hierarchy and women's suffering and expresses it in a figurative language that transcends male-dominated literary discourse. Women's personal and private experiences become public. Women protest against sexual oppression and struggle for identity. This body of work contrasts sharply with the literary works produced by women in the decades preceding the Revolution. Women's literary paradigms before and after the Revolution represent different literary episodes, and the Iranian Revolution of 1979 appears to be the decisive historical event responsible for the shift.

In other words, what explains the increased significance of gender issues in women's literary works after the Revolution is the state's structuring role in social as well as literary movements and the attitudes of the left toward women's issues. This new political influence on literature and a "cultural revolution" that directly undermined women's freedom brought about changes in the themes, characters, and language used by women writers. Ironically, the Islamization of the country caused the emergence of unprecedented literary works by women.

From this burgeoning group of authors, I shall discuss the works of several prominent writers, including Shahrnush Parsipur, Muniru Ravanipur, and Shahin Hannanih. In addition, I shall compare the postrevolutionary works of Simin Bihbahani and Simin Danishvar with their earlier works to demonstrate further that a shift in women's literary discourse has indeed occurred. I shall also discuss the prevalence of feminist discourse among a new generation of women writers. Most literary critics who have been concerned with women's writing in Iran have so far limited themselves to discussions of the fact that women have actually participated in literary activities. I shall also address the way these authors represent the female in their literary community and in their works and how they approach gender issues within their texts. In reading these works, I keep in mind, as Jacques Derrida and Julia Kristeva have suggested, that "the limitation of male-female dichotomies" may hinder the full exploration of the texts.[27] For this reason, I go beyond the text to discover the forces that require individual creative responses.

Since the late 1980s literature has become a particularly important medium for women's self-expression because public space for discussion and debate has been extremely limited.[28] A survey of journal titles and the female names on their editorial boards shows that many recent periodicals are dedicated to women's issues, some of which are managed or edited by women.[29] These journals publish women's works in all genres, including literary criticism, translation, and scholarly writing. However, women writers still find it more difficult to have their work published than men because of the publishing industry's patriarchal nature. Lack of publishers—women more often appear as their own publishers—and the fear of being persecuted—Shahrnush Parsipur, for example, was imprisoned for publishing *Zanan Bidun-i Mardan* (Women Without Men) (1990)—are common problems. But women writers have found a voracious audience: other women. Literary critics such as Barahani, Takhayuri, and Imami confirm that ordinary women who are confined to their homes spend a great deal of time reading.[30] The presence of such a readership and the popularity of women authors are reflected in the frequent reprinting of these works.[31]

The themes of these works indicate that women are paying attention to all aspects of their social and private lives—poverty, patriarchy, marriage traditions, history, and politics for example. The unprecedented titles of their works demonstrate the feminist orientation of this women's literature, especially in the context of an Islamic society: *Women's Portraits, One Lonely Woman, Left Alone, Unfinished Woman,* "Life is My Sister," "The Sad Story of Love," *Women Without Men, Sorrow of Being a Woman, Above Love, That Man: My Fellow Man, The Princess of Fire, Women Searching for Freedom.*

Although the canons of the literary establishment have, to some extent, changed in the postrevolutionary period and although in the broader context of literary activities a decentralization has occurred in the literary establishment, women commonly manifest a strong tendency to present a more profound thematic and stylistic difference from the prerevolutionary women's work in their literary works. Their new literary discourse provides them with more space to explore deep-rooted sexual norms such as virginity, which is highly-valued in their society, and to disclose the related physical abuse and violence toward women. Their female protagonists tend to exemplify the political nature of the self, care for their historical sisters, promote womanhood, and express awareness of the political issues surrounding the female body and sexuality. This shift includes changes in literary form and style. In both fiction and poetry, these authors break away from the realism that was dominant in prerevolutionary writing. A new set of figures and metaphors in their language distinguishes them from both the prerevolutionary writers and postrevolutionary male authors. In their writings the symbols and metaphors turn into an ideological representation that does nothing short of usher in a new era. Previously silenced voices, sequestered actualities, hidden talents, and marginal literature have come to the fore. Major postrevolutionary writers who represent this new literary movement include Parsipur, Ravanipur, and Hannanih. In this period feminist themes have become central in the works of even Danishvar and Bihbahani.

Shahrnush Parsipur: Speaking the Taboo

Although Shahrnush Parsipur started publishing before the Revolution, she did not become a well-known writer until the late 1980s. Two of her novels, *Tuba va Mana-yi Shab* (Tuba and the Meaning of the Night)

(1989) and *Zanan Bidun-i Mardan* (Women Without Men) (1989), which were not only popular but also controversial, brought her fame. In these works Parsipur is concerned with the condition of women. Her female characters speak of women's sexual oppression throughout history, express their acceptance of their sexuality, ridicule chastity, and resist male-dominated culture.[32]

Born to a religious and relatively wealthy family at the turn of the century, young Tuba, the main character of *Tuba and the Meaning of the Night*, voluntarily marries a fifty-year-old man, thus embarking on a traditional life. The husband, Haji Mahmudkhan, soon comes to believe that there is a connection between the drought and Tuba's presence in his house:

> In the beginning, Tuba could not comprehend the significance of this accusation. She was not used to thinking of herself as a damned being. So she was neither sad nor disappointed because it began to rain. It brought happiness because during the four hard years of her unhappy married life, she had continuously borne the accusation that she was responsible for the drought. (11)

The Haji even blames other social ills on Tuba:

> The peace of the country was disturbed by uprisings demanding a constitutional monarchy. Haji was constantly thinking of the British and the Russians. There was famine everywhere. Like a good merchant, he filled all his storage spaces so there would be plenty of flour in the house. But the anxiety of being unable to predict the future drove him crazy. Rainfall was scarce. People were dying in multitudes from the plague, typhoid fever, and hunger, and it was all Tuba's fault. Why? Not even he himself knew the answer. He did know that women who are blesssed bring happiness and plenitude. With this woman had come famine and devastation. (36–37)

When in the meantime, she meets a man who is a spiritual leader and a member of parliament, however, her life begins to change. In their first meeting during a funeral procession, the mullah tells her:

> that hunger killed people, and that it was not good. He said that for thousands of years a man had toiled to solve this problem. People talked of predestination to account for hunger, but what they did not know—or want to know—was the law of hunger. Thousands of

years ago, man believed that he had conquered this pestilential law, but now it was killing him once more, for he no longer acknowledged its existence. The mullah said that ignorance was the cause of hunger, and not poverty.

Even though she likes what she hears from the spiritual mulla, she feels an urge to leave immediately:

While the man was talking, dusk spread her wings over the graves. In a moment of silence Tuba anxiously felt the need to depart, and without a word she headed homeward, guessing at a direction she thought might be right. Uncertain of her way, she stepped on rocks and gravel, trying to bypass the graves. Suddenly she came upon two men closing in on her. Their breath reeked of alcohol, and one of them walked unsteadily. Tottering, one of them grabbed the woman's arms and tried to pull away her face cover while the other one tugged at her veil from behind. As her veil slipped to the dusty earth of the cemetery, the man was better able to pull at the face cover. Tuba's hair was pulled along with it and she felt an agonizing pain, deep in her whole being. She was down on her knees struggling to free herself, when she heard the same voice she had heard by the graveside, but this time he was shouting forcefully, "Bastards!"— followed by the loud sound of a face being slapped. And then no one harassed her any longer. She heard the voice of one of the drunken men, trembling and surprised, saying, "Oh, Mr. Khiyabani!" [revolutionary leader of the Khiyabani Movement] then she heard the shuffle of his feet tripping over everything as he disappeared into the darkening graveyard. The second man reached down, picked up the woman's veil from the ground and tried to place it clumsily on her naked head. Mr. Khiyabani's loud cry resonated in the air, "Get the hell out of here!" and his fist came down heavily on the man's back. The second man also disappeared rapidly into the darkness. Mr. Khiyabani turned his back to Tuba and told her to cover herself. In total shock, she pulled her veil over her head and began to search for her face cover, but without success. The man, thinking that she was ready, told her to walk two steps ahead of him and that he would escort her home. He could see that she did not know her way well. The only words they exchanged the whole way back were about the direction in which to go. (42–44)

Later she shows more interest. She becomes interested in this man's liberal activities in the parliament, even though she fails to fully understand the ongoing social changes and political events that marked the end of Qajar era and the beginning of the modernization of the country. Several years later, her husband divorces her. She then marries a Qajar prince, who after the fall of the dynasty flees to Russia, leaving her behind to raise four children. After the prince, who has now returned and lives in Tabriz, marries a fourteen-year-old girl, she divorces him. Tuba's youngest daughter is also divorced from her husband, an older man. The daughter marries again and becomes pregnant. When her new husband is imprisoned for political activity, she feels forced to undergo an abortion, which injures her uterus. Years later, another young woman who had been adopted into her home joins the armed struggle against the Pahlavis' regime and is fatally wounded during a shoot-out with the police. The woman dies, and Tuba buries her under a pomegranate tree, where she had earlier buried another young girl, a victim of her uncle's religious fanaticism. Tuba survives these tragedies only to find herself finally alone beside the same pomegranate tree at the end of the story, where she seems to be struggling for sanity.

The narrative of *Tuba and the Meaning of the Night* portrays the main character's gradual realization of the reality of women's oppression as she endures experiences shared by many women. In the course of the novel, Tuba begins to realize that her difficulties are emanating from the fact that she is a woman. At the conclusion of her search for truth, she realizes that women have suffered throughout history mainly because they live in a world that does not belong to them, in a world where they do not even have a chance to "look for a while at a butterfly, or gaze at the beautiful wings of a cricket."[33] She realizes that women suffer from social upheaval, religion, tradition, marriage, and a lack of power over their own destiny.

Tuba and other women in the story play central roles and are markedly assertive about their womanhood.[34] Tuba is a woman who constantly seeks answers to the causes of women's misfortunes and resists her victimization by all possible means. Tuba ventures into orthodox religion, Sufism, nationalism, and other forms of thought only to find them futile. She and the other female characters represent traditional and intellectual women in Iran during a half century marked by rapid ideological and social change. They are brave characters: one breaks away from the Islamic seclusion of the home; one joins the armed struggle against the regime; another, Amniyah Khanom, simply yet persistently protests against her undesirable situation. Amniyah typifying many traditional female figures in the book, continues to live under the same conditions yet complains openly about her husband, who has confined himself in bed, smokes opium, and orders her around. She wants him to die (383). Amniyah's life exemplifies those of many other women who, as Parsipur tries to show, have been at a dead end for hundreds of years, captured in the closed circle of misfortune.

In addition to the content, the form of *Tuba and the Meaning of the Night* represents a break from the norms of prerevolutionary socialist realism. The story does not have a conventional realistic ending, and the shifts between reality and dreams transgress the rules of socialist realism. Time is not confined to the period of the story but, rather, includes the narration of mythical stories about the past, smoothly integrating a tale of medieval Iran into the present. The novel is also different from the prerevolutionary works by portraying the upper class and royalty neither negatively nor as elements of class conflict. Indeed, in many women's postrevolutionary writings, cultural issues have gained more importance than the class issue.

Parsipur is even more radical in *Women without Men*, a novel composed of interwoven stories about several women. Five women, all without men, from different times and spaces converge in a country garden in Karaj. Mahdokht, the first of them, deeply influenced by the patriarchal culture, is disgusted when she witnesses an act of licentious sex, resulting in the loss of a young servant's virginity. Confused and traumatized by the incident, she wishes to become a tree in a garden to escape the pressure. Later, in a different time, Mahdokht reappears as a tree, turns into seeds, and is carried all over the world by water.

Zarrinkolah is another woman who goes to the garden from another space and time. Now twenty-six years old, she is a vivacious prostitute who has been working in a brothel since her childhood. She started with three or four customers a day, but now serves twenty to thirty. One Sunday morning she is obliged to serve a customer:

> Zarrinkolah left her breakfast there, at least for the moment. She angrily went back to the bedroom, lay down on the bed and opened her legs. Then the customer came. It was a man without a head.

> Zarrinkolah didn't dare scream. The headless customer did his busi-
> ness and left. From that day on, all of the customers were headless.
> Zarrinkolah didn't dare say anything about it.[35]

She tries several ways to overcome the resulting fear, including singing
every night. But a musician (a tar [string] player) discourages her, saying, "You bitch, you don't even have a voice, you're giving everybody
a headache" (79). Zarrinkolah concludes that male domination is the
cause of her misfortune. She leaves the house for Karaj and ends up
in the same garden with Mahdokht and the others. This is quite different from the portrayal of prostitutes in prerevolutionary writings of
authors such as Bihbahani; this text does not reflect on the "ill-fated-
ness" of either party but instead expresses a more realistic, harsh portrayal of one woman's existence.

In another section of the novel, two other women, Munis and
Faezeh, have a discussion about the hymen before their journey to the
garden begins.

> "Virginity is a curtain, my mother says. If a girl jumps down from
>   a height she'll damage her virginity. It's a curtain, it can be
>   torn."
> "What are you talking about? It's a hole. However, it's narrow, and
>   then becomes wide.
> "Oh!"
> Munis turned pale. Faezeh looked at her and asked, "Is something
>   wrong?"
> "No, nothing. But it must be a curtain."
> "No. I read about it in a book. I read a lot. It's a hole." (32)

For twenty-eight years Munes had assumed that virginity was a cur-
tain. When eight years old, she was told that God would never forgive
a girl who had lost her virginity and for that reason she could not climb
a tree. Now, having been told that virginity is a hole, she feels broken
inside. Munes ends up having a miserable life; finally, because she
came home late one night, her brother stabs and buries her in the yard.
But she returns to life and now has the power to read minds. She
decides to move to Karaj with Faezeh, where they may live independently. While walking toward Karaj, wearing their chadors, a truck stops
beside them, and the driver asks the women where they are going.
They respond, "We are going to Karaj to find a job so that we will not
need a man to rule over us" (86). The driver and his helper then attack

and rape them. Munes's attempt to guard her hymen for the night of marriage, then, ends in its tragic loss.

Fifty-one years old, Farrokhlaqa regrets her past love and fantasizes about a European lifestyle but continues to endure living "with a bad-tempered, solitary" husband she has detested for thirty-two years. One day she causes him to lose his balance and fall down the terrace stairs to his death. Farrokhlaqa then buys the garden in Karaj, where Mah-dokht has planted herself and other women gather, hoping to find friends and turn her garden into a literary salon, "just like the French ladies in novels"(92).

The garden in Karaj becomes the ultimate destination, a sort of utopia and a place of congregation for women disenfranchised by society. There the presence of men is minimal, and women may live independently or choose to become trees. Karaj, its gardens, and its rivers, promise hope, freedom, and mobility. However, the realities of male-dominated society still disturb the garden or oppress the women as they travel to it. Once in the garden, they merge their lives with fairy tales because, apparently, such an utopia cannot so easily exist.

The intricate, multivocal narrative of the work challenges the traditional notions about gender relations. Surrealistic images help to express the issues related to virginity that are otherwise taboo, the boldness of her writing is provocative, and the novel's nonlinear time suggests a historical relevance of its message. Even in the surrealistic images, the protagonists' dialogue demonstrates their limited social space and makes situations realistic. The novel shows how the normative sexual morality surrounding female virginity shapes the feelings, aspirations, and internal conflicts of women. It disputes those norms that have justified violence against women and often have led to a sympathy for the violator. Parsipur demystifies sexuality, virginity, and rape by speaking frankly about them.

This novel, like *Tuba and the Meaning of the Night*, presents a stark, bold depiction of the male-dominated culture. This surfaces in every encounter with men, such as the headless customer, the violent brother, and the cursory character of the tar player. Parsipur's newer works, such as *Adab-i Sarf-i Chai Dar Huzur-i Gurg* (Tea Ceremony in the Presence of a Wolf) (1993) and *Khatirat-i Zindan* (Prison Memoirs) (1997), which she has published in exile, also indicate her commitment to the cause of Iranian women. *Tea Ceremony in the Presence of a Wolf* contains several short stories and articles that together intriguingly express the author's views on social and cultural issues. Written in rather simple but witty language, the short stories sometimes portray her own experience and sometimes depict the minds of alienated men and women who seem stuck between two worlds: traditional and modern, old and new, determined and free. In her *Prison Memoirs*, Parsipur takes the opportunity to recount some of her keen observations about questions related to sexuality, male-female relationships, and the oppression of women. She exposes the political conditions in which Iranian women writers must struggle in order to continue their literary work. According to her account, she was never charged with any crime, although she was incarcerated in several prisons for four years. Through an insightful portrayal of prison conditions, Parsipur reveals rampant ideological and political rivalry among political prisoners, sadistic relationships among nonpolitical prisoners, and the social, cultural, and personal differences among prisoners and guards. Then the characters break out of these restrictive roles, highlighting the contrast between them and fulfilling lives. Both works challenge state ideology and vividly depict the agony of living under an institutionalized form of male supremacy.

Muniru Ravanipur: Literary Advocate of Women's Rights

Feminist themes predominate in the works of Muniru Ravanipur, a leading postrevolutionary woman writer, whose books, like Shahrnush Parsipur's, enjoy wide circulation and frequent reprinting. Ravanipur explicitly addresses issues related to women's social conditions and gender relations by emphasizing the importance of women's literary activities. In an interview, she states, "No one takes us seriously before we publish a work. Until then we are lonely women . . . and then they say, 'Oh, a woman is writing!' As if they are saying a disabled person is writing. And then everybody wants to help as if a blind person is crossing the street. Yes! A woman is writing, someone who was supposed to keep her mouth shut."[36] Ravanipur asserts, "My life involves struggle and resistance for the sake of the women of my country and my heroines will therefore face suffering and struggle as well as good fortune and happiness."[37] Promoting the image of the women who "shout" their "suffering," Ravanipur adheres to a feminist notion of literature that portrays women not as helpless victims but rather as rebels.

Ravanipur's short story "Qisah-i Ghamangiz-i Ishq" (The Sad Story of Love), from the collection *Sangha-yi Shaytan* (Satan's Stones) (1990), explores these issues through an unusual yet compelling narrative and deep insight into the conflict between female and male characters.[38] An extensive analysis of this very short story may illustrate how Ravanipur and other women writers evade censorship through the use of metaphors and by leaving gaps in the narrative. The story recounts the experiences of a woman who works in a publishing firm, where she writes fiction under the supervision of a male editor. Neither character has a name; they are simply "the woman" *(zan)* and "the man" *(mard)*. Versed in the art of writing fiction, the man decides to make a writer out of the woman, treating her like raw material that can be molded to perfection. Meanwhile the woman attempts to attract his attention as a woman, not as commercial property. Her love for him and her desire to please him drive her to become a famous writer. But even so, her love is thwarted: in the final scene she ceases to exist in human form, turning into words.

The problematic situation begins when the woman falls in love with the man. The man thinks only of the pragmatic aspects of her writing career, looking forward to the publication of her novels. The woman does not refrain from expressing her feelings. When she notices that their relationship is not progressing, she decides to write more and more in order to bridge the professional gap between herself and the man. When her works are published in great numbers, she becomes famous. The man, wishing to discuss her writing, invites her for a walk; but she declines, saying meekly, with a faraway look on her face, "I cannot. I am busy." This response marks a turning point in the evolution of her character. She no longer resembles the lively woman of the beginning of the story but is consumed by her work and does nothing but write.

The underlying notion of the story is that there is a difference between the woman, who is not concerned about anything but love, and the man, who is represented as just a manipulative, market-oriented superior. A woman writer confronts a man incapable of understanding her passion. This confrontation results in her self-alienation. Ravanipur grapples with these thoughts in depicting the distinct patterns of behavior in the male and female characters of the story. Throughout the story the man and woman are held up as opposites. The sincerity of the woman sharply contrasts with the man's pretentious professionalism. In response to the woman's desire to hold his hand, the man replies, "Save it for when you are a writer," whereas the woman "does not see any difference between a moment or a year," between now and the future, and therefore does not understand why she has to wait. Moreover, in response to the woman's frequent overtures of friendship and love, such as "you are nice, let's be friends . . . I am lonely," the man only smiles and does not answer her directly. And, when the woman asks again for his hand, stating "I want you to caress my head with your hand," the man refuses. When the woman begins to work very hard, it is the man who is "satisfied with his job" (the fact that he has succeeded in making her an author). The main difference between the character of the woman and that of the man is the fact that the woman has an integrated personality and less dissonance about her feelings, but the man's feelings are inconsistent.

> The man had read the woman's short stories and pretended to be interested in them, began to speak about the things that he was supposed to mention without uttering a word about love. The woman concluded that if she wrote good stories, the man would be hers. The days passed and the man maintained the silent smile on his lips and left everything conditional and hanging in the air. The woman was as she had always been. She would pace the room, search the books and the shelves, organize the papers on the desk, spread them out, and reorganize them again. . . . The woman was impatient in every step she took and in every word she uttered and one day after she had messed up things all over the place, she sat in front of the man and said, "Give me your hand, I want to tell your fortune." (31)

Moreover, "The time was never important in woman's life," an observation that contrasts with the man's timely schedule and his frequent question, "How far has the work progressed?" The man begins to pay attention to her only after "the woman's books were published one after another," while for the woman, love and a passionate relationship are more meaningful, regardless of her success. She repeatedly asks him, "Do you love me?" but receives in response only smiles and the question, "How far has the work progressed?"

The concept of wholeness, another allusion to the integration of the woman's personality, surfaces several times in various ways. In fact, the story has what amounts to a refrain: "The woman was simple.

There was no distance between her mind, her tongue, and her heart. What she said was the same as her thoughts and her feelings." With the repetition of these few sentences, the author drives home her message: Women may possess more unified and integrated personalities.

The question of wholeness and integration in the woman's character is emphasized to such an extent that it affects the structure of the story. At one point the narrator, the protagonist, and the author become one. The story is narrated from an omniscient point of view, yet the author speaks at one point in the first person, "I am writing this story very quickly because I am afraid someone may come in and sit by that window and look at me and ask, How far has the work progressed? I am writing this story far from people's eyes because I don't like anyone to read it while it is not finished yet"(29). Then, in the next paragraph, the narrator refers to the woman of the story in the third person, stating that "time, for a woman like her who was after someone to love her, meant only time." Time for the woman was not deadlines or anything that was important to the male character. This appearance of the author, speaking on behalf of the protagonist, again illustrates the wholeness of the personality; that is, this love story can be narrated by an author, a narrator, or a protagonist anytime, in the same way, provided she is a woman.

In not naming the characters, the author implies that they are to be interpreted as gender categories rather than as individual personalities. Ravanipur thus controls the theme and emphasizes the most important aspect of the story, the universality of the question of relationships between men and women. In fact, Ravanipur makes it very clear from the outset that each of these no-name characters represents her or his gender, commenting in the second paragraph that "Many know the woman now, for this very short story is about the woman who would write herself in the stories, and to name her doesn't change anything. And there is the man whose being or absence is the same since no one knows him"(29). She retains control of the theme also through her repetition of the words "man" and "woman." In this short story, which consists of just over 1,400 words, the word "woman" (zan) appears 42 times and the word "man" (mard) 35 times, together more than 5 percent of the text's entire word count. One cannot avoid thinking of the question of male-female relationships, if only because these two words are repeated so many times. By not naming the characters, the author reemphasizes this theme as universal, a situation in which the main conflict is women versus men, regardless of time and place. This story transcends individuals, time, and setting.

Although there are only two characters and one theme, a significant amount of time must pass for the events to occur. The plot involves a long process in which a novice writer becomes a successful author. She publishes several books, obtains fame, and is finally transformed into words at the peak of her career. Yet there is no indication of culmination—only an urgency and acceleration. Ravanipur deemphasizes the importance of other events that may have occurred during the time span of the story. Events occur so quickly that the reader must contribute to the story by imagining some of the changes in the lives of the characters. For example, when the woman becomes a famous writer, and the man buys her flowers, the gesture is portrayed as hollow rather than romantic. The man is only rewarding the woman for her marketable qualities. Had she not published, he would not have bought flowers. But Ravanipur does not allow the flowers to reach the woman. The woman would have appreciated them, had they been given before she became so successful.

In the story's ambiguity as well as in the central character's metamorphosis, Ravanipur's "Sad Story of Love" bears some resemblance to Parsipur's novella *Women Without Men* (discussed earlier in this chapter), in which Mahdokht turns into seeds. The female protagonist, Mahdokht, reappears as a tree to be turned into seeds and to be carried all over the world in water.[39] There, Parsipur writes:

> She was finally finished. The tree turned [shudeh bud] entirely into seeds. A mountain of seeds. The wind blew. A brisk wind blew. It carried Mahdokht's seeds into the water. Mahdokht traveled with the water. She traveled in water. She became a guest of the world. She had gone to the whole world.[40]

Seeds and words have one thing in common—they are sources of production, one in nature and the other in text. Both are represented here as universal. This universality transcends women's role in domestic production, reproduction, and economic stability. The difference is that now these women do not stay at home to raise children or produce value for men but are free to travel all over the world, which has been recreated anew by them. Similar to the passage above from *Women Without Men* is the end of the "The Sad Story of Love":

The woman was not a woman any more. She had turned into a fossil [*sangvarih*] of words, and when the man touched her on the shoulder thousands of words spread on the ground all of a sudden and among all those thousands of words the man saw these words: you are nice . . . let's be friends . . . I am very lonely.[41]

The metaphors of seeds and words both suggest female creation and productivity.

The woman dies or, rather, is transformed into words. Again, like Parsipur, Ravanipur uses a quick symbolic "death" to complete the narrative. Except for the beginning of the story, where the author writes an allegorical prelude about time and love, and the ending, with its strange metamorphosis, this short story is written as a realistic interaction between the characters. Although the woman sometimes sounds too assertive and too naive, the story serves as an illustration of women's lucidity and clarity in their relationships with men. The story's form and its diction—the fast-paced, rhythmic prose—complement each other, as the author narrates the events in quick succession through to an end in which a sudden death signals both the climax and the conclusion of the story.

Ravanipur creates a concise syntax through an economy of words. When she refers to "the woman hero of her stories, whose eyes were shining" (*qahraman-e zan-e qeseh'ha-yash cheshmanash midarakhshid*), she is implying that the protagonist of the woman's stories is a brave female, reflecting on the way she violates the female conventional role. The phrase "feeling skin and blood," which makes use of an old political cliché usually reserved for male political heroes, is applied here to a woman: "she was a woman who felt her skin and blood in her stories," implying that she does not fear being punished for expressing her feelings.

In order to convey her message, Ravanipur has employed some mystical elements, but in a secular sense. These elements are more easily distinguished in the monologue at the beginning of the story. There, while talking about the seeds of love, the author presents her own concept of time. Time is irrelevant: the moment is all that matters. Moreover, man and woman can reach the stage of oneness only after the seeds of love spread all over the world—and as far as eternity. Without oneness, love is incomplete; and without love there is no happiness. In the opening paragraph, Ravanipur presents the notion that the explosion of time on a larger scale will create change in the world:

> Time will perhaps explode from within because of these sad stories which repeat and fill it to capacity. When time fills with love, over-flows with feeling, and chokes with tears and shouted loneliness, its crystal walls will break. But every love story will make a home in the particles of this broken sphere and will, itself, make a new "time." And perhaps a day will come when eternity and everything that has been created and everything that has not been created will be noth-ing but crystal particles which have in their heart a seed of love, a seed of the sad story of love. Then, time will be a woman and a man sleeping in a bubble of time . . . stories with endings not quite the same. (29)

This imagery of the explosion or moment of ascendance resembles very much the *fana* stage in Sufism, though in an even more symbolic sense. In the *fana* stage, one becomes free of earthly bonds, free of self (*nafs*) to begin the long process of enlightenment, perfection of love, and union with the absolute.[42] *Fana*, therefore, means "to cease to exist, in order to achieve the complete denial of self and the union with God." In this story God is replaced with the beloved. The protagonist, losing herself in the love in order to gain a permanent coexistence with the beloved, reaches the stage of *fana* and is reborn as seeds or words. But the woman first becomes one with her work of writing, so that her transformation can serve to confirm this oneness. In having the frag-ments of the woman's body form the final sentence of the story, Rava-nipur is alluding to the story of Mansur Hallaj, told in *Mantiq al-Tayr*, whose blood formed on the ground the sentence "I am God."[43] The dif-ference here is that Ravanipur's mysticism is secular.

Furthermore, the woman displays her spiritual superiority by avoiding any expression of hate or criticism when the man does not respond to her advances. Even after the final explosion in which the woman turns into clusters of words, those words are expressions of "Let's be friends." Although this phraseology represents a mystical attitude, its message is the rebirth of an identity in a different form. In this discourse, love plays a role similar to that of God in mysticism: both can be found in everything. Thus, an old mystical concept has appeared here but in modern language and with new imagery.

The man's response to the woman's overture of love is conditional, and the woman's incapability to understand this incites a mystical sus-ceptibility that, because of its object, an earthly love, differentiates it from the classical religious inclinations. In a society that dictates that she must not even reveal her hair to strangers, the woman takes a risk when she expresses her feelings and is willing to touch the man, although she is unsure of his reaction. Her feelings for him are portrayed in a way that leaves no doubt that she is offering a love that is not simply physical. And this higher, more devout, unconditional love again links the theme of the story to mysticism.

"The Sad Story of Love" is brief, and the reader is forced to fill in the gaps in the chronology. In that limited space, however, the author provides her readers with many windows from which to view exterior scenes. In all of these scenes, a woman and a man are present; but a relationship based on love is absent. Neither the language of the story nor its form is solely responsible for creating its effect. The theme of the story and the idea behind the title serve as possibly the most important devices in controlling the progress of the events, since they dictate every sentence and turn of phrase. The story also indicates that, in relationships between men and women, men are preoccupied with market value and women have the choice of submitting themselves to a patriarchal order or sacrificing love. The story leaves the reader with the vague hope that women, described as having an innate affinity for productivity and friendship, can sustain love in the face of great adversity. Yet the author acknowledges the fact that women must often sacrifice themselves for the sake of love.

The similarity of "The Sad Story of Love" and Shahrnush Parsipur's "Mahdukht" in *Women Without Men*, lies in the similarity of their ideology of representation. Each of these works uses the quick symbolic death in which an unveiled woman is transformed at the completion of her narrative. Each ending, moreover, portrays a situation in which the woman reacts mysteriously or relies upon some solution that may even appear irrational. In each work the final scene implies that the character cannot reconcile herself to an unbearable fate and so changes herself into a creative entity—seeds in nature or words in culture—whose images draw on the reproductive capacity of the female body. This act of transformation represents women as having the power to escape the constraints of domestic life and reproduction and to become productive and mobile in the outside world or perhaps in a new world. Procreation is replaced by public creativity. Both Ravanipur and Parispur developed a great appreciation for magical realism through their appreciation of Garcia Marquez's *One Hundred Years of Solitude*. This was not simply because this influential work came from a third world country but also because these women found in that book a genre that could best express issues related to women. They found magical realism to be an accommodating genre that could convey realities that otherwise evaded expression within any satisfactory realm of rationality. Thus their texts combine realism and irrationalities resulting in a fantastic but believable portrayal of the agony of women's lives in their culture.

Other short stories in *Satan's Stones* also explore women's issues through an unabashed narrative and keen insight into men-women relationships. They all recount the difficult experiences of women within traditional culture. "Satan's Stones," the title story, portrays a woman from a remote village whose move to the city of Shiraz to pursue a medical degree raises suspicions of promiscuity. According to the old superstitions circulating in the village, if she has committed adultery or lost her virginity, she could be turned into a stone—one of Satan's stones. When she returns home for vacation, the old woman of the village examines her only to find out that she is still a virgin, hence the family's name is untarnished. Another story, "My Blue Bird Is Dead" symbolically recounts a woman's frustration in two experiences with men. She is self-destructively drawn to men who are mentally unstable. Repeated attempts at formulating stable relationships are all in vain. "We Only Fear the Future" portrays moments in the lives of aspiring intellectuals who realize they fear the future as they get to know themselves better through their encounter with a woman artist, who symbolizes change in society. The story touches upon the issues of shallow intellectualism, thwarted and socially repressed youthful love, and male-centered viewpoints of women. "Jeyran" focuses on the life of a dancer who is depressed because of her circumstances. Dancing mainly at weddings and other festive occasions, she is always the entertainer and never the cause for the celebration (i.e., the bride). Even though she is aging and her consciousness of this, her loneliness, and facing a dismal future, she must conceal her unhappiness when she performs at these joyous occasions because her job is to provide entertainment. At the end of the story, her lover leaves her to marry another woman. "Haros" portrays a lonely Armenian mother whose family has been torn apart by the Iran-Iraq war. The story touches upon the alienation of the regional issues and the religious minority. "Play" is a brief tale of young, aspiring actresses who sleep with the director and hang on his every word, especially his criticism—in turn, encouraged or devastated by his pronouncements. "Another Version" is an account of an unfortunate woman who at her birth disappointed her family, who anticipated a "roaring male lion." Her crippled, disappointing life ends with her sad death amid quarreling kin and hired mourners. Finally, "Three Pictures" is a cross-section of the life of a war widow who is having to deal not only with her grief but also with financial difficulties. Having lost her husband in the Iran-Iraq war, she now regularly visits his grave, witnessing the grief of others while she mourns her own loss.[44]

Although these stories render a wide range of themes and issues in a variety of contexts, they are connected through their exploration of women's frustration in relation to men and traditional culture. These stories vividly represent struggling Iranian women who resist succumbing to the dominant conditions.

Ravanipur's novel *Dil-i Fulad* (Heart of Steel) relates the story of a young woman writer, Afsanah, the victim of an abusive husband. At one point she feels that she has no choice but to leave her marriage. She looks for a place to live: "a room of her own" where she can live and write a historical story, her own version of history.[45] Released from the bonds of wedlock, the woman finds a private space and a new voice and eventually begins to write. She intends to claim that historical oppression throughout time has caused individuals to become dictators in their relations with each other. She feels that male domination has blurred historical facts. She looks for a room to write about these issues; however, she still finds herself struggling between "male professionalism that requires writing and womanly caring [for other people]." In her new residence she becomes involved with the addicted landlord's son, a drug addict who has created many problems for himself and his family. Trying to help him distracts her from reorganizing her own life and writing her history. After her thwarted romance with this landlord's son, she finds herself looking for a room of her own once again.

Afsaneh surmises that the only way to rewrite history (to write an/other history) and to remain a human is to give space to female consciousness. Her personal fulfillment can be achieved only when she renounces the traits that have been forced upon her by society—such as her tendency to favor autocracy or even her womanliness—in favor of the self.[46]

Ravanipur's poignant short stories "Kanizu" and "A Long Night" explore first encounters between child brides with their much older

and unfamiliar husbands. The experience of young Kanizu, for example, is made analogous to the situation of a goldfish chased by a shark:
"The shark's mouth moves all the time, it is bloody all the time. The fat
man kissed Kanizu. His chin was moving and his open eyes showed
everything."[47] The author forces the reader to imagine everything—
from luring to lurid, forceful to fierce, greedy to gross—that may
appear in a man's eyes as he rapes a young girl. No other writer has
produced so horrifying an image as the defenseless goldfish and the
bloodthirsty shark. The vivid images give the story an edge that similar imagery in the prerevolutionary period lacks. In prerevolutionary
writing, a fish could, as in Bihrangi's famous story "The Little Black
Fish," symbolize an avant-garde revolutionary who knows how to
solve antagonism between "people" and "anti-people" in social conflicts. In contrast, the fish in Ravanipur's work simply tries to survive;
it does not symbolize a revolutionary but simply a weak, helpless
human.

This diversity in Ravanipur's works has made them more appealing and helped her achieve her goal of furthering "the cause of all
oppressed Iranian women." She uses a wide variety of settings in presenting her characters and themes. While *Heart of Steel* describes modern yet frustrating urban life, "Kanizu," portrays life in a southern
coastal area (from which the author hails), and is in fact a journey into
time and into the darkness of superstitious aspects of beliefs that have
long doomed women's lives in this region. The collection *Satan's Stones*,
discussed earlier, depicts women's exhausting lives in both rural and
urban areas.[48] Ravanipur's multiple interests, her southern experience
and background, and her deep involvement in women's issues have
caused the meanings of her stories to be overwhelmingly appealing,
a fact that has forced literary critics to recognize the importance of her
work.[49]

Simin Danishvar and Simin Bihbahani: A New Presence

The new literary discourse produced by postrevolutionary women
authors may have been affected by generational factors. Many of these
authors are younger than the ones who began their careers in the prerevolutionary period. It may also be true that the new generation has
been influenced by feminist ideas in vogue in the West since the late
sixties or by the rise of feminist movements in other parts of the Mid-

dle East.[50] These factors, while important, do not question the significance of the political conditioning brought by the 1979 Revolution. Just as the Pahlavis' dictatorial policies and the promotion of "feminism" from above structured literary discourse, the Islamic Republic's unequivocal attack on what it considered the influence of "Western decadence" on women provided a new discursive context for literary production. Themes related to the situation of women and feminist consciousness predominate in postrevolutionary women's literature, even in the recent works of Simin Bihbahani and Simin Danishvar. In their postrevolutionary writings, the personal has gained a new level of significance, and neither writer maintains her loyalty to the old forms and themes.

Danishvar's postrevolutionary works speak of feminism, men abusing women, the general problem of the treatment of women, and opposition to traditional marriage. In a 1987 interview, Danishvar stated that she had been a feminist throughout her career.[51] One should not doubt that Danishvar was sympathetic toward women's causes before the Revolution. Nevertheless, any feminist convictions she may have held were not manifested in her prerevolutionary writings and activities. Feminist themes became explicit in her works in the postrevolutionary period because, in all likelihood, the new discursive context allowed her to translate into literary works what she had always had in her heart. Several facts attest to this assertion. First, in "A Letter to Readers," published along with the translation entitled Danishvar's "Playhouse," Danishvar categorizes prerevolutionary writers according to their political orientations, placing herself among those who belong to the political opposition.[52] Second, her account of her own life and literary works indicates a shift in her ideological perspective during the postrevolutionary period: "As an Iranian woman, I have suffered from the despotism of the regime, the exploitation of East and West, the limitations of a male-dominated culture, and a patriarchal system."[53] The juxtaposition of the subjects mentioned in this statement not only corresponds chronologically with her presentation of these topics in her fiction but also is in accordance with the discourse prevalent in each literary episode. In the prerevolutionary period, she was preoccupied chiefly with political and social problems in Atash-i Khamush (The Quenched Fire) (1949) and Surat Khanih (The Playhouse) (1961), and with the "exploitation of the East by the West" in Savushun (1969) and Shahri Chun Bihisht (A City Like Paradise) (1961). In the postrevolutionary period she confronts women's issues. In this period she specifically acknowledges the gender of the authors to whom she speaks: "Then women writers came to my rescue, none of whom I had ever met before."[54]

Danishvar uses diaries, biography, and letters as forms of literature in the presentation of these issues. The mode of expression, the tone, and the pauses in *Ghurub-i Jalal* (Jalal's Sunset) (1982), a biographical account of her relationship with her late husband, Jalal Al-i Ahmad, reveal a great deal of its meaning that is associated with her new feminist representation. Behind each of the phrases in the book, the reader finds a woman torn between the love for her husband and the hardships of a male-dominated family structure that she feels she is obliged to endure. Danishvar constantly reminds herself of her love for him, but ironically her language reveals the unpleasant condition that it is trying to cover up. Recalling her fourteen years of marriage to Al-i Ahmad, Danishvar describes her husband as "a man with little patience . . . [who] is afraid of a wealthy and rich life. . . . Jalal, in his private life, is docile only if nobody steps on his tail." She eventually brings herself to ask, "Are all men a bundle of contradictions, or was it only Jalal?" and continues:

> If you provide him with an excuse, he becomes a bully, growing indignant, and transforming into a ball of nerves. In such a physical and emotional situation, for a minor mistake such as the lack of concession or untimely talk, he loses his temper so that he begins to rant and rave and utter such words that when you hear them you grow horns. After calming down, he himself does not believe what has happened. He may therefore lecture in favor of free love and reject family life, or, on the contrary, speak approvingly of polygamy and talk about the paradise described for the Muslim man, his concubines, his permanent wives, his houris of paradise, and his excitements. At such moments heaven save you if, being cheerful, you laugh at him. Then you must face the consequences.[55]

If Zari, the protagonist of *Savushun*, celebrated only the courage of her husband, the woman's voice in *Jalal's Sunset* unmasks the husband to show the real man behind the political activist. Zari's voice did not cross the boundaries of communication of that time because she was most probably concerned with what Danishvar now refers to as the "consequences."

Danishvar has revised some of her former works in the years after the Revolution, further indicating a shift in her approach to the representation of gender issues. For example, she added a new passage to the story, "Bih Ki Salam Kunan" (To Whom Can I Say Hello), which reads, "The school headmistress would say 'Mirza Riza's grandmother had gone to Ayn u-Dawlah [the prime minister], taken off her head scarf [*lachak*, a derogatory term], and put it on his head and tied it under his chin. . . .' I want to go and buy all the cloth in the fabric stores, make them into scarves and put them on every single coward's [*na mard's*] head." Then the narrator reemphasizes her overt contempt for cowardly men by expressing her admiration for the headmistress: "All the light that pours on your grave is not enough, headmistress. You were right that women have a hundred times the honor of . . . [men]."[56] Moreover, in the older version, Kawkab, the story's central character, at one point says, "I begged him [her grandson] to let me kiss him; he brought his face to my lips." In the later version, she says, "I begged him to let me kiss him. He said 'Buy me a pack of gum, then I will let you.'"[57] These changes assign to female characters more active roles and to males negative attributes.

Feminist themes and ideas have also emerged in the recent works of Simin Bihbahani. She portrays the lives of women who are expected to endure untold daily burdens, such as bargaining for food in crowded markets and waiting in long lines for rationed foods, and all the while perform their roles as mothers, giving birth to children and raising them. She has written a poem about a woman who actually gives birth while waiting in line to buy food. Its exposure of the female body contravenes both traditional conventions and state ideology, which contend that a woman's body is a private possession and not to be put on public display. The lines "A man is pressing me / say nothing, ignore him / he wants you to perceive / what the pressure of the grave is"[58] may read on a literal level as a description of a sexual relationship between a particular man and woman but they are also an allusion to men's daily pressure on women, who must simultaneously withstand economic, political, and private pressures.

Bihbahani also challenges masculine power by portraying an autonomous woman who freely transgresses traditional boundaries. The main character of *An Mard, Mard-i Hamraham* (That Man, My Fellow Companion) (1990), a combination of poetic prose and poetry about herself and her husband, usurps the central position from the male characters. The female protagonist of this book is the grammatical and thematic subject, the man is consistently the object, the subordinate. Through stream of consciousness, the author reconstructs in symbolic language the process by which leftist discourse rose in the prerevolutionary period and fell after the Revolution because of massive attacks by government forces. Losing her husband, on the one hand, and being hurt from leftist political activism on the other, the protagonist continues to live and meet the challenges of life. The advice she gives her daughter is: "Man! Man! What can a man do that I cannot?"[59]

This book is perhaps complemented by "Finjan-i Shikastih" (The Broken Cup) (1995), a short story that portrays a woman who regrets sacrificing love for the sake of the revolutionary movement.[60] As it was common among the intellectuals in the decades before the 1979 Revolution, this woman devotes her life to the political movement for freedom and "sacrifices everything," including her love, for its sake. She advocates the dominant leftist/Marxist ideology of the early 1950s and then becomes more radical after the 1953 coup d'état against Mossadeq's government. As it "was suitable according to moralists and others" (72) in that time, she too believed that it was

> a great sin to fall in love when inequality, suppression, and profiteering have exhausted society. Is it possible to be in love when others are on fire? To get a wife, to get a husband, to think of a small unit of your own, this is a mistake when one has to think of society as a whole. Those who have wives, or husbands, or children, those in love, are not able to completely devote themselves to sacred ideals. One must be free of any constraining ties and love.(72)

Forty years later, however, as she is prepared to see the man whom she once rejected for the sake of the revolutionary movement, she expresses her regrets for sacrificing her love. She now realizes that she is so full of love that she sees "nothing else"(72). She now believes that "a house; a kind man; an affectionate gaze; a heart full of kindness; a kitchen; a table; a single rose; nights of excitement, happiness and laughter; healthy, sweet children, and . . . a life of mutual commitment"(72) are also significant aspects of a woman's life. She writes, "I wanted to have said something. This way I could express my sorrow better for wasting my life and that's what I wished to do. I wanted to say, 'All humans, and their fairy tales, are proof of love's presence.' I wanted to say that I had always loved him"(73). Not only the timing of the events in the story and the political orientation of the main character but also references to the man as an alert and intelligent *Hushyar* (the last name of Bihbahani's husband) suggest that the protagonist figure is indeed the author herself.

In *That Man, My Fellow Companion* and "Broken Cup," Bihbahani uses a well-constructed, classically eloquent, and rhythmic narrative that differs from the prose of Committed Literature. She also employs this style in the introduction to *Guzidih-i Ash*ʿ*ar* (Selected Poems) (1989), in which she states that her ideas cannot be expressed in traditional forms such as the ghazal: "The ghazal is for beautiful thoughts, so how, then, can I beautifully allude to what the women of my society have suffered throughout history, such as the 'bringing of the severed head of Zuhreh to the party of Khan,' the bloody loss of virginity of girls to Ginghiz, hanging the cut hand of a gypsy from a branch, the aiming of an arrow of Timur at the pupil of a woman's eye?"[61] Such fiery utterances are the result of author's adherence to the new notion that shapes her ideology of representation in this period. She asks again, "How can I place any of these in the old meter of the ghazal so that it rhymes harmoniously and does not sound strange?" (29). Her most recent works, however, attest to a powerful return to the ghazal, through which she has, after all, found a way to express new concerns and concepts. In her collection of ghazals, *Yik Darichih-i Azadi* (A Window for Freedom), she shows such maturity that it would be hard for anyone from any background to question the beauty of her poetry. She has used the classical prosody, but she has opened a "window" from the beauty of the old poetry to the relevance of contemporary issues: "Qasam beh anjir o zaytun, kinayat-i asmani / keh bagh misuzad az tab o, faghan az in baghbani![62] [To the fig and olive, these heavenly metaphors, swear / that the garden is burning in fever, O you gardener]. With this, Bihbahani will possibly put an end to the exhausted debate over form.

Women Respond: Hannanih's Talk with Artists' Spouses

Shahin Hannanih's interviews with artists' wives, *Pusht-i Darichah-ha: Guftgu Ba Hamsaran-i Hunarmandan* (Behind the Windows: A Conversation with Artists' Spouses) (1992), resembles Danishvar's postrevolutionary memoirs in that such narratives would hardly be welcomed by a prerevolutionary audience for whom Al-i Ahmad, for example, had been a literary and political icon. Women's memoirs and autobiographies, especially those of women married to famous men, have become popular genres in Iran.[63] These works appeal especially to those readers who want to know the peculiarities of these people's lives. These genres strengthen women's position in their ongoing struggle against seclusion and oppression, because such works expose private family matters and thereby open women's lives to public judgment. Making women's dilemmas public may, as a consequence, provide some protection for them against domestic abuse. This type of communication works against the secrecy and privacy of the home, which have traditionally helped men suppress women.

In *Behind the Windows: A Talk with Artists' Spouses,* women describe their domineering husbands with deep affection as they answer simple questions.[64] Of the thirty-one interviews in the books, all but one are with women. The author, Shahin Hannanih, herself wonders why only one man is interviewed and asks, "Does an Iranian man really have the patience to live with a woman artist or not?"[65] She continues, "Iranian and in general Eastern men do not recognize a woman's identity as independent from a man" (5). The author then tries to support this generalization throughout the interviews. In short, the book is an attempt to uncover male-female relationships in the Iranian intellectual community in terms of power relations. It suggests that even though most of these wives were deprived of the public attention their husbands enjoyed, they should be able to speak out even if they have to do it from behind their windows.

Behind the Windows can also be considered the readers' response to the rise of feminist consciousness in literary activities. The book weaves together the words of women married to prominent contemporary Iranian artists, who now, because of the new discourse, find an interested audience or at least a need to speak out. These women are now willing to talk about themselves and, in doing so, disclose information about their relationships with their spouses. Although they try to avoid direct criticism of their husbands, their responses reveal a hidden tension. Their disclosures are concerned primarily with their private, individual relationships with their husbands or with cultural issues rather than with the political system or with the need for political change, fashionable topics in the prerevolutionary period.

The reader of this book soon notices that the dichotomy between

East and West often presented in prerevolutionary Committed Literature has been replaced with a new pattern. The East now takes the
position of the West, formerly portrayed as the exploiter of the East,
in being an exploiter of its own women. To show the relationship
between Eastern men and women, Hannanih follows a simple format:
Before each interview she describes the artist's house or apartment and
the wife's appearance, creating a visual context, and then asks each
woman a few questions. In general, the women's answers are very
informative responses regarding the private lives of Iranian writers,
painters, and musicians. These wives usually express their love and
support for their husbands but do not hesitate to exhibit their feelings
about the negative aspects of their lives with them and at times expand
their criticism to all men. Many of them have traveled to Western countries and refer to these experiences as positive and joyful. In their narratives they do not discuss exploitation by the West.

Some of these women express their grief as they criticize their situation. These articulations of sorrow and dissatisfaction with men reveal
the scope of awareness and assertiveness among these women. For
example, a painter's wife maintains, "An Iranian man, in any case,
likes his wife, before anything else, to be a housewife. He likes a traditional woman, a woman like his mother" (11). Complaining about
her unfulfilled life, a widow of a musician states, "I used to make him
cappuccino two or three times a day for twenty-seven years. I am so
used to doing this that I sometimes find myself mixing sugar and coffee unconsciously" (18).

Many of these celebrities' wives declare that they sacrificed their
lives for the sake of their husbands. It is thus not surprising to find that
a sense of lack of personal accomplishment, fulfillment, and satisfac-
tion is rather common among the interviewees. A poet's talented wife
who had to give up playing the piano, painting, and ballet dancing two
months after getting married complains, "I became so involved with
the difficulties of daily life that I decided to be a supporter of the arts"
(20). What she protests most against, however, is the division of work
between her husband and herself; she dislikes the fact that she, like
many other women, performs all the routine household jobs and that
her husband performs the artistic tasks. Her only achievement, she
believes, is supporting someone else's (her husband's) art. Another talented woman, an actor's wife who has beautiful voice, reveals that
"after our wedding he told me, 'You must not even sing at private par-

ties' [let alone in public] and I who was in love with music had to be happy with listening to music and humming at home. I was a bird singing in a cage rather than in a garden of flowers" (288). Other women, reflecting upon their pasts, express honest doubts about whether they have been appreciated at all for their contributions to, and support of, their husbands' careers. A painter's wife puts it eloquently: "[It is] twenty-seven years that I have been living this life. I spent my time and youth for him to be comfortable and draw. Now where is my place in these paintings? God knows. Maybe behind those poplar trees. I sometimes see the shadow of my tired hands above those naked branches and on the top of those tile roofs" (281). In whatever way these women choose to confront and analyze their lives, it is significant to note that such openness, such bravery in speech and the written word, is unprecedented in Iranian women's writing.

Some women go beyond their complaints and criticisms to offer insights into the problems that they face, and a few seem to have arrived at a solution. A novelist's wife remarks, "I am not for the idea of sacrificing [myself for him]. Sacrificing has a negative effect on our common life" (268). Another writer's wife explains, "I am principally a person who does not bear the burden of force or unfairness. . . . For this reason, we frequently argue" (56). A third woman warns, "Yes, I am in love with my husband but I am very, very tired. . . . He is a very kind man but like all Iranian men when coming home he likes everything to be ready. . . . We have to accept that the Iranian woman has a long road in front of her before she saves herself from this situation and from this patriarchy" (149, 151). In this last statement the conjunction "but" *(amma)* is quite emphatic. The clauses before these conjunctions are short, whereas the phrases after them are long and emotionally loaded. For example, "Yes, I am in love with my husband, but I am very, very tired, don't tell me, now, how can I be tired if I am in love— a lover doesn't get tired" (149). In other words, her love does not justify exploitation anymore. In addition, the word "tired," often repeated in the interviews, has a significant meaning: It announces the approaching end of an era in Iranian society—an end that is perhaps long, but inevitable, in coming.

Both the author's comments and the women precise, frank language in their recollections expose uneasy conditions that extend beyond their private lives. Hesitant, yet straightforward, they open their hearts about the nature of their relationship with men in an effort to reassert the social significance of their male-female relationship, a significance that has been ignored for so long. This presentation of self is also impressive because it is so honest and vivid. No matter how much these women emphasize their love for their husbands, they cannot avoid alluding to the reality of the patriarchal system that encompasses them. Although the interviews with these women present their points well, readers cannot discern the facial expressions and the body language behind them. But after observing, listening to, and sympathizing with these women, Hannanih seems to be confident in concluding that the husbands do not recognize the independent identities of their wives.

The readers, however, can conclude that these women are determined to change their condition; increasingly outspoken about their discontent, they are beginning to express their desire for change. A change in the situation of women means a change in the political order as well, since, according to Islamic standards, the position and treatment of women symbolizes the degree of a society's religiosity. For example, the Islamic Punishment Law, which oversees and regulates relationships between men and women, is inspired by Islamic traditions and the Qur'an. Any modification of this law requires a revision of religious principles, an action that could be accomplished only through cultural and political change.

Behind the Windows was not well received by a few critics who still advocate the Committed Literature in *Adinih*, a popular and influential cultural and literary magazine. According to the conventional criteria of the journal's reviewer, the language and themes of the book seemed deficient. Clearly the unsigned negative review reflects the concern that exposure of the tensions described in the book is either harmful to the cause of Committed art or frivolous because it is too personal.[66] Another critic, Layla Gulistan, an advocate of Committed Literature, does not see this book as even worthy of criticism.[67] However, she does not present a strong argument against it. Her most significant point is that topics such as the relationships of these women with their mothers-in-law and the description of their houses do not benefit the readers. By belittling the book, such criticism refuses to accept the fact that these women are entitled to speak about their lives and the lives of their artist husbands. It is interesting to note that *Adinih* itself had published a translation of Chekhov's short story "Artists' Wives," which has a similar theme, in an earlier issue.[68]

Contrary to what the critics claim, the book discloses women's daily concerns and emotions. In it, women speak of love, relationships with their husbands, children, the realities of artists' lives, and, most important, the oppression that they suffer. By raising their voices, these women have challenged the existing male-dominated order, particularly among the intellectual community. These voices also challenge the left's socially oriented perspectives toward art and women's issues. Although she relies heavily on generalizations, the interviewer cleverly approaches this topic.

Women Writers in Profusion

A whole wave of younger women writers has now joined the established writers discussed earlier in this chapter in criticizing the traditional, patriarchal aspects of Iranian culture. In recent years these young authors seem to have moved the course of literary activity to a new level of cultural significance. They have expanded their readership; novels such as those of Faridih Gulbu and Nasrin Samani have set records in their number of printings.[69] Their themes often involve love. These authors produce works that on the surface seem to be romances, but indeed they address serious cultural issues—and their technique of unobtrusively working these issues into their narratives has become very popular. The baby boy versus baby girl issue is a key theme in many recent short stories. In *Dukhtar-i Haji Aqha* (Daughter of Haji Agha) (1991) by Zahra Kadkhudaiyan, a young girl witnesses her grandmother playing a trick on her father by telling him that a baby girl has been born to her mother instead of a baby boy. The father is visibly upset when he receives the news, but soon the grandmother reveals the truth by displaying the naked baby boy. The father's mood changes: "The light of happiness glows in his eyes. He grabs the child from the grandmother's hands and says, 'It is a boy . . . you had fooled me. It is a boy, it is a boy.'"[70] As the sister, now a woman, tells of this event, she implies that it has had a great effect upon her personality. She asserts, "I was right to think that my father did not love me or at least he did not love me the way he should" (171). Similarly, Tahirah Aybud in her story "Bih Rang-i Khatistar (In the Color of Ashes) describes a woman giving birth to a baby, afraid that it might not be a boy. Through her depiction of a traditional family, Aybud maintains that the sexual oppression of women starts very early, at birth.[71]

Although Simone de Beauvoir is right when she states that "one is not born a woman; one becomes one," in postrevolutionary Iranian women's writing this process of subjective orientation and identity formation is portrayed as transpiring so early in life that it appears as if one is indeed born a woman.

Other themes in these authors' works revolve around women who are forced to depend on men, even on married men, for a living under the severe economic crisis that has disturbed Iran since the Revolution.[72] Mansurah Sharifzadih, in her collection of short stories, *Mawlud-i Shishum* (The Sixth Birth), portrays women whose relationships with their husbands or brothers reflect this financial dependence. The men she portrays take advantage of the situation and exploit women as sex objects. One beats his wife to death; another cheats on her; a third marries another woman and kicks his first wife out; and yet another demands of his wife that their sixth child be a boy because they already have five girls. These narratives bring together the topics of economic problems, cultural rigidity, and the domestic violence that result from them.

Poets, too, capture the grief and disappointment of women caused by their oppression, as well as their struggle and defiance. In her collection of poetry *Anduh-i Zan Budan* (The Sorrow of Being a Woman) (1992), Khatirih Hijazi writes,

Nah zibatarin zinat-ha
nah khoshbutarin gol-ha
va nah hatta boseha-ye to.
Hich
mara az anduh-e zan budan raha nakhahad kard
. . . .
Vaqti in anduh garibanam ra migirad
ehsas mikonam:
tanha shahed-e yek jenayatam
va zabanam ra nasl dar nasl boridehand.[73]

[Not the prettiest ornaments,
not the best smelling flowers,
and not even your kisses
nothing
will release me from the sorrow of being a woman
. . . .

When I deal with this sorrow
I feel: I am alone witnessing crime,
they have cut out my tongue generation after generation.]

Throughout her book, Hijazi alludes to the long history of oppression and states that she, as a woman, is held captive by her culture.

Firishtih Sari, who is more optimistic, challenges the darkness of oppression with the light of her pen. In the poem "Lahzih" (The Moment), from *Pizhvak-i Sukut* (The Echo of Silence) (1989), she writes:

Inak Chonanam
keh mitavanam
khurshid ra chun anari beshkafam
va ꜥusareh-ʾe foruzanash ra johar-e kelkam sazam.
Inak mitavanam
khafiyehgah-e aftab ra dar shab efsha konam
hata mitavanam
shab ra
chun tumar-e farsudeh-ʾi fru picham
va beh gusheh-ʾe anbari begozaram.[74]

[Now I am in a manner that I can
split the sun, like a pomegranate
and from its shining juice
make my pen's ink
I can now reveal the hiding place of the sun at night.
I can even
roll away the night
like a tattered scroll
and store it away in a corner.]

The image of the pomegranate, a classical Persian symbol of femininity, here suggests female rebellion, hope, and creative production.[75]

The present upsurge in women's writings includes an enormous number of essays, articles, and books on women's issues that further demonstrate the depth of the new feminist discourse.[76] Banafshih Hijazi in her book *Zan bih Zann-i Tarikh: Jaygah-i Zan dar Iran-i Bastan* (Women According to History: The Place of Women in Ancient Iran) (1991) describes women's situation in ancient Iran and compares it to that of the contemporary period.[77] An obstacle to feminist expression under the present political conditions is censorship, which leaves little room for free debate. Yet in spite of these limitations and the hindrances that the state ideology places before them, an increasing number of women are digging deeply into traditional life. To minimize the restrictions placed upon them, some women writers and researchers try to convince the authorities that their criticisms originate not from the West nor from the left but rather from their own experiences.[78]

These writers use history in order to denounce contemporary problems and uncover the forces behind their victimization. By reinterpreting history and presenting their own perspectives on social conditions, they attempt to identify the barriers that prevent them from fulfilling their potential in society. In recent years, writing has been the most direct manifestation of these authors' desire for the abolition of socially institutionalized gender roles. These themes clearly indicate that the authors resist the attempts to silence them, the reinforcement of tradition, and compulsory veiling. They associate the veil with the traditional victimization of women and oppose it by unveiling their protagonists.

Like other episodes of Persian literary history, this episode and its figurative language came into existence as a result of particular social changes and in turn this literary episode began to influence the process of cultural and political change. In recent political campaigns candidates identified the situation of women as a central issue. Many in the higher echelons of the government were influenced enough to take the women's movement more seriously—to the extent that they now support the publication of exclusively women's journals.[79] These developments may be regarded as ways of subverting women's discourse (or to be more optimistic, a way of appropriating it) but they do stand in contrast to what was originally enforced by the state discourse and thus point to the growing power of this cultural episode. This is precisely why the aggressive social participation of women has created fear within the fundamentalist camp.

In sum, the 1979 Revolution, the subsequent sociopolitical changes, the rise of Islamic literature, the compulsory dress code, and the women's demonstrations in March 1979, provided the context for and explain the shift in women's literary enunciations and subsequently the creation of a feminist episode. After the Revolution the ideology of the ruling clerics stressed religion as the most important organizing principle of society. Much of the modernization by the Pahlavis in regard to women was undone when the new regime began to impose its own view of womanhood on society. The veil became the symbol of the new regime's gender policy. The new rulers increased social and religious pressures, using all means—including literature—to achieve their objectives. Consequently—and as a reaction to the state ideology—intellectual women, especially those in the opposition, began to speak out on all aspects of gender issues, beginning with organized resistance to mandatory veiling, while simultaneously breaking away from the left, which remained indifferent to their cause. This situation gave rise to feminism as a new oppositional ideology among women and as an ideology of representation in women's literature.[80] In this new literary movement, women use new forms, write in a new style, suggest creative approaches to social problems, and address taboo subjects. Their activities and works continually influence the course of culture production.

6

Conclusion: Applicability of Episodic Literary Movement in Arabic and Turkish Literature

Persian literary history is a combination of several episodic literary movements. It is definitely and curiously spiral. As every great event—whether the Constitutional Revolution, the 1954 coup d'état, or the 1979 Revolution—reverberated through the country, metaphors too spun into new modes of literary production and new episodes emerged. In each of these episodic literary movements, a dominant ideology influenced representation, and representation in turn influenced social movements. The themes, characterization, and figurative language of literary works in each of these discontinuous episodes point to a certain approach toward social issues and literature itself. In each episode, literature is at once ideologically conditioned and socially influential.

I have described the concept of *episodic literary movement* through the analysis of several key concepts—episode, ideology, literary movement, and metaphor—and based my analysis on an understanding of the pattern of literary change in Iran. I define a *literary episode* as a cluster of aesthetically significant literary texts that delineate the literary history of a society. *Ideology* is a discursive element that is determined according to the syntagmatic and paradigmatic rules of expression. Ideology is related to literature because one is often embedded in the other and because they can both share a particular set of metaphors through which they communicate. A *literary movement* is defined by its ideology of representation. In that regard, literary movements demonstrate a close affinity with other social movements, because all inevitably display a discursive quality, and they are all related to the social, political, and historical events. *Metaphor*, a binding element in all of these concepts, is taken to be both a linguistic feature and a mode in which things and signs are perceived in terms of other things and other signs. Metaphors in each episode establish an implicit (and sometimes also an explicit) parallel with ideology. They not only help the reader decipher the meaning of the text but also assist in defining the heralded ideology.

Ideology may be best conceptualized, then, as a set of somewhat structured metaphors that function as open-ended discourse and conjoin people's activities with their ideals, explaining one in terms of the other. The conceptualization of ideology as a loose system of metaphors helps to elucidate the relation between the episodic literary movement and the sociopolitical context. Metaphors, as they represent ideology in literary texts, are both agents of political change and consequences of that change. And it is not the same set of metaphors or the same type of ideology that initiates each and every change. To assume that one ideology is responsible for the rise and historical development of a literary history and that the literary history of one particular society is the product of one particular culture is to ignore the dialectical relationship between a literary work and the cultural movement of the period and the place in which the work is produced.

Ideology plays a specific role in the interpretation of literature, and consequently reading becomes problematic. Iranian readers and critics, for example, must scrutinize the figures and metaphors presented in an ambiguous text. They must interpret the full range of the implications of the syntactical and grammatical features and consider not only the implicit and explicit messages but also the unintended and intended meanings contained therein. The dominant discourse often colors such a reading and involves the reader in what can be conceptualized as discursive interpretation. By communicating their ideas, modern authors, their critics, and their readers participate in a collective action to promote a certain type of ideology. It is here that literary and ideological paradigms have the most contact.

In the nineteenth and twentieth centuries, literary activities in Iran grew increasingly political and socially powerful as the content of literary works and their corresponding ideal readers changed. This literature has since represented a fabric of national, anti-Western, or egalitarian values for its readers. The emergence of a new set of literary values or new canons changes the way writers and readers perceive literary activity. In the modern period, writers and their loyal readers have moved through the roles of Persianist, socialist, Muslim, and feminist as the literary transformation and social need warranted each movement. As the author plays the role of a cultural leader, the reader remains a sympathizer or a constituent. Literature is therefore written, read, and interpreted by individuals whose literary decisions affect their social identities.

Such communal literary activities contribute in several ways to the dialectical movement of literary change and the construction of new literary values. Each episode disseminates particular ideas about social issues by problematizing them and thus making them popular topics of discussion. At the same time, by engaging the works of other authors, a community of authors facilitates the formation of a new canon. In doing so, the authors both borrow from each other and recontextualize older literary works. When old works are cited frequently enough in current contexts, they cease to be of only historical relevance and can become instead a vehicle for debate about current politics. This process of becoming involved in imaginative social activities defines both literature and its reading as a commonality among intellectual elites. That is, a new social role for literary activists develops through the collective acts of writers and readers. Literature becomes a means of communication, an arena of cultural and political debate as well as a means of entertainment for those intellectuals who are not satisfied by the increase in the imitation of Western cultural production and instead appreciate a "serious" art. That is how each episode can thus be overlaid with a specific ideological issue, such as cultural change, social revolution, gender equality, or religion. Metaphor seems to be the dynamic entity that can continually change its meaning in order to articulate new concerns as a new episode emerges. Ideological representation through metaphor has therefore been a dominant and constitutive feature of literary works in every period.

Literature goes beyond the aesthetics of self-expression to serve as a powerful social and collective reaction to prevailing social conditions. Each episode seems to have renounced a certain set of meanings and forms while giving prominence to others. When literature is the subject to state control, literature becomes a revolutionary force that propagates social change. Following change and being affected by it, literature devotes itself to a different goal. Iranian women's literature in the pre- and postrevolutionary periods, for example, reflects this powerful devotion to bring about change. In the prerevolutionary period it sought to convert the political arrangement; in the postrevolutionary period, it explores cultural change. Dialogue is a part of a dominant discourse that, as Bakhtin indicates, connects the writers as a system.[1] Each writer seems to be a member of a collective whole, contributing, whether consciously or not, to a collective voice.

The unitary sets of meanings (such as those produced by Iranian authors), which often develop into an episodic literary movement with a specific ideological orientation, have all the particularities of a sign system. These meanings and signs, communicated through theme, character, and style, can occasionally transcend their historical time and place; but they always remain reflective of the dominant ideological movement of their period. Accordingly, modern Persian literary products, when being deciphered, need to be viewed within their discursive context in order to convey their full meanings and signs.

Further Applicability: Episodic Literary Movement in Arabic and Turkish Literature

A pattern of literary change similar to that in Persian literature may also be found in Arabic and Turkish literatures. These three literatures not only have certain ancient or medieval traditions in common, but also have been simultaneously influenced by Western modernity. Moreover, their social, historical, and political contexts show remarkable likenesses.

The concept of episodic literary movement, here applied to Persian literature, may help in understanding these other literatures as well. Literary movements similar to Persianism appeared in Egypt and other Arab countries and in Turkey in the nineteenth and early twentieth centuries. Arabs and Turks enthusiastically admired Europe even as they promoted pan-Arabic and pan-Turkish sentiments that sought to remove European controls. What they desired was an identity steeped in the pre-Islamic past but progressing along modern lines—hence the ideologies of what I may as well call Arabism and Turkism, which demonstrate a strong affinity with Persianism.[2]

Nationalist movements demanding the expulsion of British troops in Egypt and the Levant, as well as the broader Pan-Arab movement in other Arab countries, played a constructive role in giving rise to Arabism.[3] The revolutions and uprisings that occurred almost simultaneously between 1919 and 1922 in Egypt, Iraq, Palestine, and Syria provided a context for the development of Arabism in these societies.[4] Arab writers who seemed to be fascinated by Western democracy accordingly advocated modern ideology whose basis was independence and which glorified the Arabic language as a foundation for Arab indentity. Charles Smith observes in *Islam and the Search for Social Order* that M. H. Haykal believed (and stated in 1925) that Arabic and Islam were both foreign elements to Egypt (90).The new generation of Arab intellectuals was impressed by the scientific and technological achievements of the West and came to believe that by finding a true Arab identity (and with further unification), the Arab world could have its own Enlightenment and advance and evolve. The Egyptian writer, Mahmud Taymur (1894–1973), known as the father of short story writing, typifies such ideology in his work *The Enemy* (1965). Through the promotion of an indigenous culture and a national language and the separation of Islam and governmental policies, Egyptian writers struggled to promote the idea of a secular national state. In Egypt the Arabic language became so central to the Egyptians' cause that Christian and Muslim activists cooperated closely in a literary movement for the modernization of their language. Jurji Zaydan (d. 1914), a Christian Lebanese author living in Egypt, Shakib Arslan (d. 1946), of Druze origin, and Muhammed Kurd ʿAli (d. 1953) worked in the same direction in the development of Arabism. The emergence of literary forms such as the novel and drama, the proliferation of the press, and the campaign of the modernists against the highly ornate style of past centuries all contributed to the emergence of a simpler and more direct style of Arabic that called for the modernization of their societies and at the same time appealed to a wider reading public. In more than twenty novels, Zaydan rewrote history in order to educate Arabs about their glorious past. And like Jamalzadih, Muhammad Husayn Haykal (1888–1956) used spoken Arabic in his groundbreaking novel *Zaynab* (1913) to effect a stronger realism.[5] The works of Ahmad Faris al-Shadyaq (*al-Saf ala-Saf*), Amin al-Rayhani (*Muluk al-Arab*), and Jubran Khalil Jubran (his earlier works) reflected Arabism. Literary journals, such as *al-Adib* and later *al-Adab*, published numerous articles and literary works that helped in the formation of this movement.[6]

In Turkey, the process of modernism began with a reformist movement known as Tanzimat, which influenced a series of reforms carried out in the Ottoman Empire between 1839 and 1876. The purification of the Turkish language through the elimination or modification of Arabic and Persian words and a broader Pan-Turkish movement gave rise to a literary movement similar to Persianism. Young Turks (a revolutionary group whose revolution succeeded in 1908) and later Kemal

Ataturk, the founder of modern Turkey, searched the Turkic past in Anatolia and Central Asia to formulate an ideology of Turkism. Ataturk, who indeed influenced Reza Shah, adamantly promoted Westernization, modernization, and secularism in his newly created republic. Turkism promoted a Turkish identity independent from Islam and its symbols, such as the veil. Another decisive change occurred in the area of modern Turkish language development when the new ruling elite replaced the Arabic script with the Roman one. Such changes and reforms had a great impact on the processes of literary creativity. The Tanzimat authors such as Ibrahim Sinasi (1826–1871), Namik Kemal (1810–1888), Zia Pasa (1826–1880) introduced new topics, fresh ideas, and new literary forms into literature. Namik Kemal's "Ode to Freedom" is representative of this group of works. H. El Adivar in "Zeyneb, My Zeyneb," Huseyin Rifat in "Who is this Woman?," and M. E. Yurdakul in "Anatolia" and "On the Way to War" embody a secular movement supporting a rejuvenated homeland and its shift away from Islam. This literary episode promoted the dominant state ideology.[7]

Social and political conditions similar to those of prerevolutionary Iran gave rise to Committed Literature both in Arab countries and Turkey. In Egypt, Marxism had a powerful influence on Arabic literature in the 1950s and 1960s. In the Levant and Iraq, leftist trends in literature matured in the late 1940s under the influence of the growing communist and Ba'sthist parties and remained strong in the post–World War II period.[8] Abd al-Rahman Sharqawi in, for example, *Al-Ard*, (Egyptian Earth) and Yusuf Idris in *Arkhas Layali* (The Cheapest Nights)—both published in the mid 1950s in Egypt—and the Palestinian Ghassan Kanafani in the *Little Cake Vendor* (reminiscent of Samad Bihrangi's "Little Sugar Beet Vendor"), and Halim Barakat in *Awdat al-Tair ila al-Bahr* (Days of Dust) represent the dominant trend of socialist realism of this period. The two Arabic novels *Days of Dust* and *Egyptian Earth* represent the literary works of the 1940s through the 1970s, a period dominated by socialist realism. These novels have in common a critical view of the dominant social system. They likewise advocate revolutionary social change and views that are influenced by Mao Tse-tung's ideas and his Cultural Revolution. Other writers who belong to this literary movement include Hann Mina (in *Fragments of Memory*), Emil Habibi, Illias Khuri, Jabra Ibrahim Jibra, Abd al-Rahman Munif, and to some extent Najib Mahfuz.

During nearly the same decades, a Committed literary movement also gained dominance in Turkey. The main concern of this movement were workers, petit bourgeois, and especially peasants. Turkish Committed authors of this period include Sait Faik ("Sivriada Nights," "Love Letter," and "The Man Who Doesn't Know What a Tooth or a Toothache Is"), Nazim Hikmat ("The Epic of Sheyh Bedreddin," "Saco and Vanzetti," and "Paul Robeson"), Aziz Nesin ("Civilization's Spare Part"), Yashar Kemal (Murder in the Ironsmith's Market) and Kemal Tahir (Esir Sehrin Insanlari). The writings of Mahmut Makal and Fazil Husnu Daglarca, especially, dealt with the wretched conditions in which the peasants lived. Yashar Kemal, is perhaps the most acclaimed author in this genre, uses a realistic style in *The Lords of Akchasaz* to portray the changes in the socioeconomic conditions on the Chukurova Plain; his novel *Seagull* represents the self-alienation of people living in a town that is rapidly approaching the end of the process of modernization.[9] Volumes of literary criticism inspired by Stalinism or by the kind of Marxist ideas in vogue in Europe in the 1930s were published in Persian, Arabic, and Turkish to accompany the works of Committed authors in these countries in the 1950s through 1970s. Even when in the 1970s a mixture of Marxism and existentialism (in Lebanon especially) began to replace the earlier, stricter Marxism, literary criticism continued to support of Marxist notions of commitment.

As a result of the vigorous revival of fundamentalism in the 1980s, an Islamic literary episode also developed in most Arab countries and in Turkey. Islamic fundamentalism gained prominence from the particular context of post–World War I conditions in particular societies. The transnationality of fundamentalist discourse attests to the fact that these movements did not occur in isolation. The fundamentalist movement is not perceived by its advocates as purely nationalist but rather as a universal ideology that seeks to establish the rule of Islam in all traditionally Muslim areas throughout the globe. As Sayyid Qutb states, "Patriotism should consist of bonds to the Faith, not to a piece of land. The present, territorial, sense given to this term should thus be greatly stretched."[10] In recent decades in addition to Iran, many countries from North Africa to East Asia have experienced one form or another of vigorous revival of fundamentalism. Like their Iranian counterparts, Arab and Turkish fundamentalists categorically reject secularism and Western literary influence. In Arab countries Committed Literature lost a great deal of its dominant position after the defeat of Arab forces by Israel in 1967 and the decline of the socialist move-

ment. Furthermore, a distinctive feature of the Islamic literary movement is its political nature, which benefits the broader Islamic fundamentalist movement. Literature of this nature is rooted in the writings
of Muhammad Ghazali, Sayyid Qutb, and Hasan al-Banna, who
founded the fundamentalist movement of Muslim Brothers in Egypt
in 1928, and in other religious texts. In recent years writing that supports the Muslim Brotherhood movement in Egypt and Jordan, Hamas
in Palestine, and the Refah party in Turkey has increased. Works such
as Azizah al-Ibrashi's *Islah: An Egyptian Tale* should also be mentioned
in conjunction with the promotion of Islamic culture in response to the
discourse of a secular state.

In Turkey growing Islamist literary activities emerged in response
to the secular ruling elite as well. Ismet Ozel, Sezai Karakoc, Suleyman
Cobanoglu, and Cahit Zarifoglu represent the modern Islamic literary
movement in Turkey. A group called "Muslim Poets" derived their
imagery from Islam and religious values. Turan Koc, Mevlut Ceylan,
Sezai Karakoc, Cahit Zarifoglu, and Afif Ary are among the members
of this group. This literary episode flourished during the campaign of
Erbikan and his Islamic Refah party's push for power in the early
1990s. However, because Turkey did not experience an overwhelming
Islamic revolution and the Islamic literary movement there lacks state
support, this movement differs in its scope from that in Iran.

Feminism in Arab countries and Turkey was more visible than ever
before in the late 1980s, when feminist activities contributed to a new
feminist literary movement. Examples of writing from this episode in
Arabic literature include Hanan al-Shaykh's *Hikayat Zahra* (Story of
Zahra) and *Misk al-Ghazal* (Women of Sand and Myrrh) and Huda
Barakat's *Hajar al-Dahkk* (Stone of Laughter), as well as other works
produced after the civil war in Lebanon such as Ghada Samman's
Bayrut 75 (Beirut 75).[11] Although women had been writing for more one
hundred years on issues related to women, it was only in the 1980s that
an indigenous feminist movement prominently appeared. Feminist
women in the Arab world in the previous decades were in one way or
another an extention of the western feminist discourse, which was
reflected here and there in the Arab countries. As in the *Story of Zehra*,
the Lebanese war provided a new space for women to physically
maneuver, the reality outside also facilitated a similar mobility in radical writing. The movement spread throughout the Arab world and
"by the 1980s and 1990s, there was a literary renaissance occurring
even in Saudi Arabia. Saudi women writers emerged to such an extent

that a casual observer of any newspaper or magazine could comment on the predominance of women's names."[12]

Modern Turkey has a long tradition of women's literary activities reaching back to last decades of Ottoman rule. Early writers (1870–1930) include Fatam Hanim, Halide Edib, and Nigar Hanim.[13] In the 1960s and 1970s, there was an upsurge of women's writing in Turkey, but, mainly to capture the national politics of the times. During this period it was social turmoil, military takeovers, and leftist politics that conditioned women's writing. Turkish women raised their voices in a variety of ways during the 1980s and since then, feminism has gained prominence. As mentioned, the recent women's movement developed in opposition to Kemalist feminism.[14] Kemalism, according to which women were supposed to enjoy equal rights with men, helped women's emancipation and brought women's issues to public discourse.[15] However, this discourse indirectly caused the rise of a radical feminism in 1980s.[16] Whatever the reason, it was during this decade of modern Turkish literature that works such as Latife Tekin's *Berji Kristin: Tales from the Garbage Hills* emerged.[17] Tekin, according to Nilufer Reddy, "has created a new language which has been one of the most stirring literary events of the 1980s."[18] Nazil Eray's "Monte Kristo" and the radical feminist literary works that were produced to support this movement best represent the feminist movement's effects upon Turkish literature. Turkish women who are active writing poetry include Gulten Akin ("Song to an Ageless Women"), Sennur Sezer ("My Name"), and Melisa Gurpina *(Summer Sequence)*.[19]

The meanings produced by Arab and Turkish authors can also be perceived in terms of the episodic literary movements that were influenced by and affected the broader ideological movements in vogue within the societies. These sets of meanings and sign systems were also communicated through theme, character, and style, which reflected the historical context and the dominant cultural tendencies of their period. A full understanding of the meanings and signs of these literatures draws attention to their discursive context. Therefore, an analysis of the formation of literary movements in these societies may very well help to further understand the way ideology influences and promotes representation and certain modes of reading. In these societies, too, changes in the social contexts have both caused and been influenced by literary shifts in an episodic fashion; often the state ideology, international trends, and political opposition have played a determining role in shaping episodic literary movements thereafter.

Notes
Bibliography
Index

Notes

1. Introduction: Episodic Literary Movement—A Model for Understanding Literary History

1. See, for example; Mark Jeffreys, "Ideologies of Lyric: A Problem of Genre in Contemporary Anglophone Poetics," *PMLA* 110, no. 2, (Mar. 1995): 196–205; Audrey Jaffe, "Spectacular Sympathy: Visuality and Ideology in Dickens's *A Christmas Carol*," *PMLA* 109, no. 2, (Mar. 1994): 254–65; Hélène Cixous, "The Laugh of the Medusa," in *New French Feminisms*, eds. Elaine Marks and Isabelle de Courtivron. (New York: Schocken, 1981): 245–64; Edward W. Said, "Opponents, Audiences, Constituencies, and Communities," *Critical Inquiry* 9 (Sept. 1982): 1–26; Gayatri Chakravorty Spivak, "The Politics of Interpretations," *Critical Inquiry* 9 (Sept. 1982): 259–78, 263; and Forrest G. Robinson, "The New Historicism and the Old West," *Western American Literature* 25, no. 2, (Aug. 1990): 103–23.

2. Gayatri Chakravorty Spivak, "The Politics of Interpretations." *Critical Inquiry* 9 (Sept. 1982): 259–78.

3. Alan Sinfield, *Faultlines: Cultural Materialism and the Politics of Dissident Reading* (Berkeley: Univ. of California Press, 1992), 32.

4. Terry Eagleton, *The Ideology of the Aesthetic* (Oxford, England: Basil Blackwell, 1991), 3.

5. For a discussion of censorship in Iran, see Ahmad Karimi-Hakkak, "Censorship," in *Encyclopaedia Iranica*, vol. 5, ed. Ehsan Yarshater (Costa Mesa, Calif.: Mazda Publishers), 135–42.

6. James Kritzeck, *Modern Islamic Literature* (New York: Holt, Rinehart & Winston, 1970) and *Anthology of Islamic Literature* (New York: Holt, Rinehart & Winston, 1964), and Muhammad Riza Hakimi, *Adabiyat va Taʿahud dar Islam* (Literature and Commitment in Islam) (Tehran: Daftar-i Nashr-i Farhang-i Islami, 1979). Others with the same approach include Claude Field, *Persian Literature* (London: Herbert & Daniel, 1912); Edward G. Browne, *The Press and Poetry of Modern Persia* (Los Angeles: Kalimat, 1983); Muhammad Taqi Jaʿfari, *Nigahi Bih Falsafah-ʾi Hunar Az Didgah-i Islami* (A Look at Art Philosophy from

the Islamic Viewpoint) (Tehran: Intisharat-i Nur, 1982); Ali Haʾiri, *Zahniyat Va Zaviyah-i Did Dar Naqd Va Naqd-i Adabiyat-i Dastani: Naqdi Bar, Sad Sal Dastan Nivisi-i Iran* (Tehran: Kubah, 1990); Musa Mudaris, "Risalat-i Hunar," *Mahnamah-i Pasdar-i Islam* 164 (Aug.–Sept. 1995): 16–20.

7. Muhammad Ali Sipanlu, *Baz Afarini-i Vaqiiyat: bist u haft qisah az bist u haft nivisandah muasir-i Iran* (The Interpretation of the Reality: Twenty-Seven Short Stories by Twenty-Seven Contemporary Iranian Writers) (Tehran: Nigah, 1988); Khusraw Gulsurkhy, *Nawgiraʾi Va Haqiqat-i Khaki* (Tehran: Morvarid, 1979), 1; Said Sultanpur, *Nuʿi az Hunar, Nuʿi az Andishih* (A Type of Art, a Type of Thinking) (Tehran: n.p., 1960); Mahmud Dawlatabadi, *Ma Niz Mardumi Hastim* (We Are People Too) (Tehran: Nashr-i Parsi, 1989); Muhammad Huquqi, ed., *Shiʿr-i Naw az Aghaz ta Imruz* (New Poetry from Beginning to Present) (Tehran: Ravayat, 1992).

8. Muhammad Ali Sipanlu, *Baz Afarini-i Vaqiiyat,* introduction.

9. In this book, the distinction between social-political, gender, and religious issues is an empirical one. These issues are distinguished and discussed according to their prevalence in each episode.

10. See Ervand Abrahamian, *Iran Between Two Revolutions* (Princeton, N.J.: Princeton Univ. Press, 1982); Janet Afary, *The Iranian Constitutional Revolution, 1906–11* (New York.: Columbia Univ. Press, 1996); and Arthur Goldschmidt. *A Concise History of the Middle East* (Boulder, Colo.: Westview, 1983).

11. Jean-Paul Sartre in *What Is Literature?* offers a conception of this approach to literary activity as *literature engagé,* a term translated into Persian as *adabiyat-i mutiʿahid.*

12. Several scholars have shed light on different aspects of the commitment and of Committed Literature in Iran. See Rivanne Sandler, "Literary Developments in Iran in the 1960s and the 1970s Prior to the 1979 Revolution," *World Literature Today* 60, no. 2 (spring 1986): 246–51; Hamid Dabashi, "The Poetics of Politics: Commitment in Modern Persian Literature," *Iranian Studies* 18, nos. 2–4 (spring–autumn 1985): 147–88; Ahmad Karimi-Hakkak, "Poetry Against Piety: The Literary Response to the Iranian Revolution," *World Literature Today* 60, no. 2 (spring 1986): 251–56; Reza Baraheni, *Tala Dar Mis* (Tehran: Nashr-i Zaman, 1968). Ali Gheissari explains the ideological commitment in the Islamic literature of the postrevolutionary period in "Naqd-i Adab-i Idiulugik," (A Review of Ideological Literature) *Iran Nameh* 12 (spring 1994): 233–58.

13. Kamran Talattof, "Iranian Women's Literature: From Pre-revolutionary Social Discourse to Postrevolutionary Feminism," *International Journal of Middle East Studies* 29, no. 4 (Nov. 1997): 531–58.

14. Michel Foucault, *The Order of Things: An Archeology of the Human Sciences* (New York: Vintage, 1973), 246–48, 364–65.

15. Mansoor Moaddel, "The Social Bases and Discursive Context of the Rise of Islamic Fundamentalism: The Case of Iran and Syria" *Sociological Inquiry* 66 (Aug. 1996).

16. Mansoor Moaddel, "Ideology as Episodic Discourse: The Case of the Iranian Revolution," *American Sociological Review* 57 (June 1992): 353–79.

17. Ferdinand de Saussure, *Course in General Linguistics* (New York: McGraw-Hill, 1964), 9–17.

18. Jacques Derrida, *Grammatology*, trans. G. Spivak (Baltimore: Johns Hopkins Univ. Press, 1976).

19. Michael Holquist, introduction to *The Dialogic Imagination: Four Essays by M. M. Bakhtin*, ed. Michael Holquist. (Austin: Univ. of Texas Press, 1992), xviii–xxi, 188–295.

20. Mikhail Bakhtin, *Problems of Dostoevsky's Poetics*, ed. and trans. by Caryl Emerson (Minneapolis: Univ. of Minnesota Press, 1984).

21. Caryl Emerson, introduction to *Bakhtin in Contexts: Across the Disciplines*, ed. Amy Mandelker (Evanston, Ill.: Northwestern Univ. Press, 1995), 2–3. See also Mikhail Bakhtin, "Toward a Methodology for the Human Sciences," in *Speech Genres and Other Late Essays*, trans. V. McGee, ed. Caryl Emerson and Michael Holquist (Austin: Univ. of Texas Press, 1986).

22. Anne Herrmann, *The Dialogic and Difference: "An/other Woman" in Virginia Woolf and Christa Wolf* (New York: Columbia Univ. Press, 1989), 12.

23. Caryl Emerson, introduction to *Bakhtin in Context*, 2–6.

24. Let us not forget how quickly even a nonpolitical ideology, such as that advocated by a peaceful religious group, can become a matter of politics.

25. Moaddel, "Ideology as Episodic Discourse in *American Sociological Review*.

26. Terry Eagleton, *Ideology: An Introduction*. (London: Verso, 1991), 221.

27. For a discussion of metaphor, see James Bono, "Science, Discourse, and Literature: The Role/Rule of Metaphor in Science" in *Literature and Science*, ed. Stuart Peterfreund (Boston: Northeastern Univ. Press, 1990), 61–62, and Clifford Geertz, *The Interpretation of Cultures* (New York: Basic Books, 1973).

28. According to Jakobson, some literary works, such as romantic and modernist ones, use metaphor and others, such as realistic writings, use more metonymy. See Roman Jakobson and Morris Halle, *Fundamentals of Language, Two Aspects of Language and Two Types of Aphasic Disturbances* (The Hague: Mouton, 1956).

29. The exploration of the metaphorical conjuncture between life and its representation dates back to antiquity. Plato, for example, does not allow poets into his ideal city unless their poems can serve educational purposes, especially for the younger generations: "What the poet mustn't say is that God did it, and the victims were wretched. It is all right to explain that the wicked were wretched because they needed punishment, and profited from receiving that punishment at the god's hands." See *Classical Literary Criticism*, ed. D. A. Russel and M. Winterbottom (Oxford: Oxford Univ. Press, 1989), 18.

30. Clifford Geertz, *The Interpretation of Cultures* (New York: Basic Books, 1973), 210.

31. Ahmad Karimi-Hakkak, *Recasting Persian Poetry: Scenarios of Poetic Modernity in Iran* (Salt Lake City: Univ. of Utah Press, 1995), 225. Even in the classical period, shifts in the meaning of a particular metaphor occurred. For Nizami, *shab* and *tiregi-e shab* (night and night's darkness) are often associated with misfortune and unpleasant situations. For Nasir Khusraw, *shab* at times signifies the disagreeable.

32. See Rivanne Sandler, "Literary Developments in Iran in the 1960s and the 1970s."

33. Mikhail Bakhtin, *Problems of Dostoevsky's Poetics.*

34. See Hélène Cixous, "The Laugh of the Medusa," in Marks and de Courtivron, *New French Feminisms,* 249.

35. Literary movements, to echo Voloshinov, generate an utterance that responds and anticipates other utterances. See V. N. Voloshinov, *Marxism and the Philosophy of Language* (Cambridge, Mass.: Harvard Univ. Press, 1986).

36. Mahmud Dawlatababi, *Ma Niz Mardumi Hastim,* 210.

37. See Nasir Muazin, *Dah Shab: Shabha-yi Shairan va Navisandigan dar Anjuman-i Farhangi-i Iran va Alman* (Ten Nights: Poets' and Writers' Evenings in the Irano-German Cultural Society) (Tehran: Amir Kabir, 1979).

2. Persianism: The Ideology of Literary Revolution in the Early Twentieth Century

1. Other traditionalists include Furughi Bastami, Azari Bigdili, and Nishat Isfahani.

2. Ann K. S. Lambton, *Qajar Persia: Eleven Studies* (London: I. B. Tauris, 1987).

3. Other factors also contributed to the rise of modernist ideas. First, some members of the ruling elite felt the need for strengthening the army in order to avoid another defeat like that they endured from Russia. Second, a substantial number of students and attachés were sent to Europe to study, and upon their

return, they translated a great number of books. Third, the establishment of the modern school, Dar al-Funun, in Tehran in 1852 was a practical implication of modernist ideas; the college offered a modern curriculum taught by Iranian and European teachers.

4. See Ervand Abrahamian, *Iran Between Two Revolutions* (Princeton. N.J.: Princeton Univ. Press, 1982); Janet Afary, *The Iranian Constitutional Revolution, 1906–11* (New York: Columbia Univ. Press, 1996); and Arthur Goldschmidt, *A Concise History of the Middle East* (Boulder, Colo.: Westview, 1983).

5. Goldschmidt, *Concise History of the Middle East.*

6. Hasan Taqizadih, Adib al-Mamalik Farahani, and Zayn al-Abidin Maraghi⁾i also show this tendency.

7. These journals were not alone. Others such as *Pars* (Persia), *Parvin* (Pleiades), *Paykar* (Figure), *Bamdad* (Morning), *Bahar* (Spring), *Tazih Bahar* (New Spring), *Chantih* (Satchel), *Pa Birahnih* (Bare Foot), *Chihrih Nama* (Mirror), and *Ganjinih* (The Treasure) also contributed to this development.

8. These data are available in Yahya Ariyanpur, *Az Saba Ta Nima: Tarikh-i Sad u Panjah Sal Adab-i Farsi* (From Saba to Nima: One Hundred Fifty Years History of Persian Literature)(Saarbrucken, Germany: Intisharat-i Nawid, 1988); and Muhammad Sadr Hashimi, *Tarikh-i jara⁾id va majallat-i Iran* (The History of Iranian Newspaper and Magazines) (Isfahan: Kamal, 1985).

9. These journals also published works of Bahar and Nasim-i Shumal on a regular basis.

10. Iraj Afshar, "Jariyanha-yi Adabi dar Majalat-i Farsi," (Literary Trends in Persian Magazines) in *Rahnama-yi Kitab* (A Guide to Books) 20, nos. 5–7 (summer 1977).

11. Other such journals included *Danishkadih* (College), *Zaban Azad* (Free Expression), *Tajadud* (Modernity), *Musiqi* (Music), *Kaveh, Armaghan* (Souvenir), *Ayandih* (The Future), *Yadgar* (For Remembrance), *Yaghma* (Plunder), *Taqadum* (Priority), *Mihr* (The Sun), *Payman* (Promise), and *Iranshahr* (Iran), which were all published in Tehran. *Farhang* (Culture) was published in Rasht, and *Dabistan* (School) in Mashhad. See Ariyanpur, *Az Saba Ta Nima,* and Muhammad Sadr Hashimi, *Tarikh-i jara⁾id va majallat-i Iran,* for more information. Of all the journals, *Sukhan* and its editor Parviz Khanlari played the most significant role in the systematic study of history of Persian language and in the promotion of a standard language. *Sukhan* also played a role in the later episode of Committed Literature.

12. *Namih-i Parsi,* n. 8.

13. Ibid., n. 9.

14. See *Ilm va Hunar* (Science and Art), July–Aug. 1928.

15. *Ibid.*, n. 8.

16. Ariyanpur, *Az Saba Ta Nima,* 459–64.

17. For more information and discussions of early modern poets, including Nima Yushij, see Ahmad Karimi-Hakkak, *Recasting Persian Poetry: Scenarios of Poetic Modernity in Iran* (Salt Lake City: Univ. of Utah Press, 1995), and Majid Naficy, *Modernism and Ideology in Persian Literature* (Lanham, Md.: Univ. Press of America, 1997).

18. Ahmad Karimi-Hakkak, *An Anthology of Modern Persian Poetry* (Boulder, Colo.: Westview, 1978), 3–5. For another theoretical and technical discussion of New Poetry, see Ismail Nuri-Ala, *Tiuri-i Shiᶜr: Az Muj i Naw ta Shi'r-i ᶜIshq* (The Theory of Poetry: From the New Wave to Love Poetry) (London: Ghazal Publications, 1994).

19. Fazl Allah Parvin, *Zibaʾi va Hunar* (Aesthetic and Art) (Tehran: n.p., 1966), 192.

20. Ahmad Kasravi, *Dar Piramun-i Adabiyat* (Bethesda, Md.: Kitabfurushi-i Iran, 1991).

21. See Jalal al-Din Mirza, *Namih-yi Khusrauvan* (The Book of the Greats) (Tehran: n.p., n.d.).

22. See A. H. Zarrinkub, *Du Qarn Sukut* (Two Centuries of Silence) (Tehran: Amir Kabir, 1958).

23. Shahrukh Miskub, *Huviyat-i Irani va Zaban-i Farsi* (The National Iranian Identity and the Persian Language) (Tehran: Intisharat-i Bagh-i Ainih, 1994), 177.

24. Iraj Pizishkzad in *Haji Mam Jafar dar Paris* (Haji Mohammad Ja'far in Paris)(Tehran: Safi ᶜAli Shah, 1954) and Jafar Shahribaf in *Haji dar Farang* (The Haji in Europe) (Tehran: Payam, 1965) render similar themes. They were clearly influenced by *Hajji Baba Isfahani,* the Persian translation (1905) of a book written by the English diplomat and writer James Morier that contributed to the development of the modern novel of social criticism.

25. Ehsan Yarshater, "The Development of Iranian Literatures" in *Persian Literature,* ed. Ehsan Yarshater (Albany, N.Y.: Bibliotheca Persica, 1988), 34.

26. Joya Saad, *The Image of Arabs in Modern Persian Literature* (Lanham, Md.: Univ. Press of America, 1996). Saad has keenly observed the anti-Arab, anti-Islamic, and at times racist rhetoric in the works of Jamalzadih, Hidayat, and others. The intention of these writers, Saad's observations notwithstanding, was not nation building, and the anti-Arab sentiment was in many ways a distant concern. Rather, it was the exigencies of modernity that drove them to modernize Persian language and literature through opposing anything of common practice at the time, including the use of Arabic words. Arabs and the Ara-

bic language were not derided for their own sake but because of their impact on Persian language and culture, an impact that in the modernists' minds stood in the way of progress. (Iranians and Iranian culture are also criticized and ridiculed in these works). Saad implies that this discourse was predominant until the 1979 Revolution, with Al-i Ahmad being the only anomaly. Contrary to Saad's expression, I believe that there are hardly any major works with racist rhetoric after the 1960s. Moreover, the major concerns of the women authors discussed in Saad's book are other social issues, such as justice and freedom (see chap. 3 of this volume). In fact, after the 1960s Iranian leftist activists and writers including women, were increasingly sympathetic to Islam, and sought unity with Arabs especially Palestinians and all other Middle Eastern revolutionary activists.

27. On a conceptual level, how can one define nationalism in such ethnically diverse society? Were not the socialists and the monarchists in a sense nationalists as well. As Benedict Anderson states, "Nation, nationality, nationalism— all have proved notoriously difficult to define, let alone to analyze." Indeed, Anderson emphasizes the ideological creation of the nation as the most significant issue in the study of nationalist movements and in doing so he pays special attention to language. Anderson, *Imagined Communities: Reflections on the Origin and Spread of Nationalism* (London: Verso, 1983), 12.

28. Gholam Ali Ra'di Azarakhshi, "Shi'r-i Farsi-yi Mu'asir" (Contemporary Persian Poetry), in *Sukhanraniha-yi Nakhustin Kungarih-i Shi'r Dar Iran* (Proceedings of the First Congress on Persian Poetry) (Tehran, 1968) (Tehran: Farhang va Hunar, 1960), 178.

29. Manoutchehr Mohandessi, "Hedayat and Rilke," in *Critical Perspectives on Modern Persian Literature,* ed. Thomas M. Ricks (Washington, D.C.: Three Continents, 1984), 259.

30. Nasrin Rahimieh provides insight on this topic in "A Systemic Approach to Modern Persian Prose Fiction," *World Literature Today* 63, no. 1 (winter 1989): 15–19, and "The Enigma of Persian Modernism," *New Comparison* 13 (spring 1992): 39–45.

31. Majid Naficy, in a recent scholarly work, *Modernism and Ideology* (Lanham, Md.: Univ. Press of America, 1997), has employed the expression "the catchword of nature (tabi'at)" (5) to explain the ideology of Nima Yushij and other pioneering Persian writers. It is true that the concepts of nature and naturalism abound in their works, but this "catchword" is far from being capable of conceptualizing the overall discourse of this period. Nature was not the overriding theme that tied these works together.

32. See A. A. Dastghayb, *Sayih Rushan-i Shi'r-i Farsi* (Light and Shade of Per-

sian Poetry) (Tehran: Farhang, 1969), 80; Siyavush Kasrai, "Dar Tamam-i Tul-i Shab," (All Night Long) in *Namah-i Shura-yi Navisandigan va Hunarmandan-i Iran* (Journal of the Association of Iranian Writers and Artists) 2 (winter 1980): 114–33; Sirus Tahbaz, *Hizar Sal Sh'r-i Farsi: Az Rudaki Ta Nima Yushij* (One Thousand Years of Persian Poetry: From Rudaki to Nima Yushij) (Tehran: Kanun-i Parvarish-i Fikri-i Kudakan Va Nujavanan, 1986), 382. Nima's suffering in this work is discussed later in this chapter.

33. Nasir Hariri, *Dar Barih-i Hunar va Adabiyat: Guft u Shanudi ba Ahmad Shamlu* (On Art and Literature: A Talk with Ahmad Shamlu) (Tehran: Avishan and Guharzad, 1993), 157.

34. Sadiq Hidayat, "Urashima," *Majallih-i Sukhan* (The Journal of Discourse) 92, no. 1 (Dec. 1944): 43–45.

35. Ahmad Karimi-Hakkak, "From Translation to Appropriation: Poetic Cross-Breeding in Early Twentieth-Century Iran," *Comparative Literature* 47 (winter 1995): 53.

36. Sirus Tahbaz, *Majmuah Kamil-i Ash'ar-i Nima Yushij: Farsi Va Tabari* (The Anthology of Nima Yushij) (Tehran: Intisharat-i Nigah, 1971), 350.

37. Keigo Seki, ed., *Folktales of Japan* (Chicago: Univ. of Chicago Press, 1963), 111. For more information, see Frederick Hadland Davis, *Myths and Legends of Japan* (London: George G. Harrap, 1912).

38. Hidayat's source is apparently identical to what the English version of Grace James used in *"Green Willow" and Other Japanese Fairy Tales* (London, MacMillan, 1910).

39. "Urashima" is also published in Sadiq Hidayat *Navishtahha-yi Parakandah* (Scattered Writings) (Stockholm: Arash, 1990), 250–56.

40. Nima Yushij, *Arzish-i Ihsasat va Panj Maqalih-i Digar* ("The Value of Feelings" and Five Other Articles on Literary Criticism) (Tehran: Zindigi, 1972), 103.

41. Manali states, "My toil has cost me my hair" (*mayih-yi zahmat-i man muyam bisiturdih zi sar*). See Tahbaz, *Majmuah Kamil-i Ash'ar-i Nima Yushij,* 359.

42. Exploring the title of a poem by Nima, "Murgh-i Amin" (The Amen Bird), Karimi-Hakkak states, "True to his habit of placing himself in his poem, often through the figure of a bird, Nima may have made up the bird's name by inverting the letters of his own pen name, thus: Nima → Amin." (Karimi-Hakkak, *Recasting Persian Poetry,* 262). Tufan argues that even the name Nima, which most probably is a variation of the Pahlavi *Neem-mah* (meaning "half-moon" or "half-month"), encodes a number (using ABJAD letter values) that represents his birth date. See Masud Tufan, "The Secret of the Name Nima," in *Takapu* 9 (Apr. 1994): 10–12.

43. Tahbaz, *Majmuah Kamil-i Ash'ar-i Nima Yushij,* 353.

44. Quoted in Janati ʿAtaʾi's book, *Nima Yushij: Zindagani va Asar-i U* (Nima Yushij: His Life and His Work) (Tehran: Safi Ali Shah, 1955), 12.

45. Shin Partaw, *Baziha-yi Masti* (Games of Drunkenness) (Tehran: Ilmi, 1946), 25.

46. Ibid., 25–26.

47. In a longer version of the tale, a tortoise takes him to the bottom of the sea.

48. For the views of Nima's opponents, see Hamdi Shirazi, in *Funun va Anvaʿi Shiʿr-i Farsi* (Tehran: Bita, 1972); Parviz Khanlari, "Jidal Ba Mudiʿi," *Sukhan* 21, no. 6 (Jan. 1971); and G. Raʿdi Azarakhshi, "Shiʿr-i Muaʿsir-i Iran," (Contemporary Iranian Poetry) *Yaghma* 21, no. 1 (Dec. 1967). Raʿdi Azarakhshi, in particular, discredited Nima, stating that Rafʿat, Kasaʾi, and Khaminahʾi had already started to experiment in new forms before 1921, and Nima simply imitated them. He also stated that Nima stopped writing in Khurasani style (a poetry characterized by lofty diction and highly literate language developed in classical period in eastern Iran and the province of Khurasan) because he was unsuccessful in it. To know more about Raʾdi Azarakhshi's views on poetry, see also his article "Shiʿir-i Muʿssir-i Farsi," in *Sukhanraniha-yi Nakhustine Kungirah-i Shiʿr Dar Iran* (Tehran: Farhang va Hunar, 1960), 179–81. Other opponents include Tundar Kiya, Abd al-Rahman Faramarzi, and Ali Dashti. For more information on their views, see A. Dastghayb, *Nima Yushij: Naqd va Barrasi* (Nima Yushij: Criticism and Analysis) (Tehran: Pazand, n.d.).

49. A. A. Dastghayb presents this view in *Sayih Rushan-i Shiʿr-i Farsi* (Light and Shade of Persian Poetry) (Tehran: Farhang, 1969), and Mahmud Falaki in *Nigahi Bih Nima* (A Look at Nima) (Tehran: Intisharat-i Murvarid, 1994).

50. Tahbaz, *Majmuah Kamil-i Ashʿar-i Nima Yushij*, 222–23.

51. I have traced the dates of these publications back to 1939 and 1969 when parts of these works were published in *Majallih-i Musiqi* (Journal of Music) 10 and *Faslha-yi Sabz* (Green Seasons) 2, respectively.

52. Nima Yushij, *Arzish-i Ihsasat va Panj Maqalih-i Digar*, (The Value of Feelings and Five Other Articles on Literary Criticism), 17.

53. Karimi-Hakkak has noticed this point about *Arzish-i Ihsasat va Panj Maqalih-i Digar* (The Value of Feelings and Five Other Articles on Literary Criticism): "The reader can see a young poet struggling to free himself from a slave-like dependence on time-honored but paralyzing rules of rhyme, rhythm, and the other precepts of poesy." See Ahmad Karimi-Hakkak, "Introduction to Modern Persian Poetry," in *Critical Perspectives on Modern Persian Literature*, ed. Thomas M. Ricks (Washington, D.C.: Three Continents Press, 1984), 215.

54. Nima Yushij, *Arzish-i Ihsasat va Panj Maqalih-i Digar*, 57.

55. Nima Yushij, *Harfha-yi Hamsayih* (The Neighbor's Word) (Tehran: Intisharat-i Dunya, 1984), 18.

56. Nima Yushij, *Arzish-i Ihsasat va Panj Maqalih-i Digar,* 73, 81–82.

57. Nima Yushij, *Harfha-yi Hamsayih,* 84–85.

58. Ibid., 96.

59. Ibid., 54.

60. Ibid., 120.

61. Ibid., 54.

62. Nima Yushij, *Barguzidah-i Ashʿar* (Selected Works) (Tehran: Kitabha-yi Jibi, 1963), quoted in Ehsan Yarshater, "The Modern Literary Idiom (1920s–1960)," in Ricks, *Critical Perspectives on Modern Persian Literature,* 42–62.

63. Nima Yushij, *Harfha-yi Hamsayih,* 54.

64. Ibid., 54–55. Although of a different genre, *Arzish-i Ihsasat va Panj Maqalih-i Digar* conveys the same ideas.

65. Nima Yushij, *Arzish-i Ihsasat va Panj Maqalih-i Digar,* 105.

66. Ibid., 104–5.

67. Nakhustin Kungirah-i Navisandigan-i Iran, (The First Iranian Writers' Congress) *Maqalat va Ashʿar-i Nakhustin Kungirah-i Navisandigan-i Iran* (Proceedings of the First Iranian Writers' Congress) (Tehran: Farabi Publishers, 1947), 63.

68. See, for example, Majid Rushangar, *Az Nima Ta Baʿd* (From Nima Onwards) (Tehran: Murvarid, 1984).

69. See Shahrukh Miskub, "Afsanah-i Tabiʿat" (Nature's Myth), in *Kilk* (Pen) 35–36 (Jan.–Feb. 1974): 22–51.

70. See A. Dastghayb, *Nima Yushij: Naqd Va Barrasi* (Tehran: Pazand, n.d.), 111.

71. A. A. Dastghayb, *Sayih Rushan-i Shiʿr-i Farsi* (Tehran: Farhang, 1969), 80.

72. See Mahmud Falaki, *Nigahi Bih Nima* (Tehran: Intisharat-i Murvarid, 1994).

73. Sirus Tahbaz, *Hizar Sal Shir-i Farsi: Az Rudaki Ta Nima Yushij* (Tehran: Kanun-i Parvarish-i Fikri-i Kudakan Va Nujavanan, 1986), 382.

74. See Siyavush Kasrai, "Dar Tamam-i Tul-i Shab," *Namah-i Shura-yi Navisandigan va Hunarmandan-i Iran* 2 (winter 1980): 114–33.

75. Nima Yushij, *Harfha-yi Hamsayih,* 63.

76. Quoted in A. Janati ʿAtai, *Nima Yushij: Zandigi Va Asar-i U* (Tehran: Safi Ali Shah, 1955), 23.

77. Quoted in ʿAta'i, *Nima Yushiji,* 23.

78. Partaw, *Baziha-yi Hasti,* 84.

79. Ibid., 81.

80. For more information on Jamalzadih, see Heshmat Moayyad and Paul Sprachman, introduction to *Once Upon a Time* (New York: Bibliotheca Persica, 1985). For more information about *Yiki Bud Yiki Nabud* (Once Upon a Time) in particular and Jamalzadih's life in general, see Christophe Balay and Michel Cuypers, *Sar Chesmihha-yi Dastan-i Kutah-i Farsi* (The Sources Persian Short Stories), trans. Ahmad Karimi-Hakkak (Tehran: Papirus, 1987); Haideh Daraghi, "The Shaping of the Modern Persian Short Story: Jamalzadeh's Preface *to Yiki Bud, Yiki Nabud*" in Ricks, *Critical Perspectives on Modern Persian Literature*, 104–23; and Saad, *The Image of Arabs in Modern Persian Literature*.

81. For an English translation of this book, see Jamalzadih [Jamalzadeh], *Once Upon a Time*, trans. Moayyad, Sprachaman, and Ricks, *Critical Perspectives on Modern Persian Literature*.

82. Muhammad Ali Jamalzadih [Jamalzadeh], "Farsi Shikkar Ast," in F. Kar, *Panj Shulih-i Javidan* (Five Eternal Flames) (Tehran: Gutanbirg, 1954), 281–90. This book has been translated into English. See the next note.

83. Jamalzadeh, *Once Upon a Time*, trans. Moayyad and Sprachman, (New York: Bibliotheca Persica, 1985), 35. The Latin words in the translation of this passage are "used to accommodate the shaikh's scholastic Persian into which learned Arabic expressions are inserted wholesale without regard for syntax or comprehensibility" (36).

84. Ibid., 36.

85. This short story is from Sadiq Hidayat's collection. *Sih Qatrah Khun* (Three Drops of Blood) (Tehran: Parastu, 1965), 74–88.

86. For more information on Karbala and Shiʿism see Juan Cole and Nikki Keddie, eds., *Shiʿism and Social Protest* (New Haven, Conn.: Yale Univ. Press, 1986), 18; and Moojan Momen, *An Introduction to Shiʿi Islam* (New Haven, Conn.: Yale Univ. Press, 1985), 28–33. I have previously discussed the treatment of this theme by modern authors in "The Changing Mode of Relationship Between Modern Persian Literature and Islam: Karbala in Fiction," in *The Postcolonial Crescent: Islam's Impact on Contemporary Literature*, ed. John Hawley (New York: Peter Lang, 1998), 249–66.

87. David Busby Edwards, in *Shiʿism and Social Protest*. Juan Cole and Nikki Keddie. eds. (New Haven, Conn.: Yale Univ. Press, 1986), 228.

88. This short story was first published in *Afsanih* 3. 31 (Aug., 1931).

89. Hidayat was a vegetarian, however, it is not clear if this may or may not have influenced his portrayal of this dog. In any event, his writings often portray animals with compassion.

90. Sadeq Hedayat, *Sadeq Hedayat: An Anthology*, ed. Ehasan Yarshater, (Boulder, Colo.: Westview, 1979), 334.

91. Sadeq Hedayat, "Sag-i Vilgard" (Stray Dog, 1942), *"Blind Owl" and Other Hedayat Stories* (Minneapolis, Minn.: Sorayya Publishers, 1984), 110.

92. For more information about Hidayat's work, see Michael Beard, "Sadeq Hedayat's Composite Landscapes: Western Exposure," in *Persian Literature*, ed. Ehsan Yarshater, (Albany, N.Y.: Bibliotheca Persica, 1988), 324–35; Ehasan Yarshater, ed., *Sadeq Hedayat: An Anthology* (Boulder, Colo.: Westview, 1979); Iraj Bashiri, *The Fiction of Sadeq Hedayat* (Lexington, Ky.: Mazda Publishers, 1984); and Homa Katouzian, *Sadeq Hedayat: The Life and Literature of an Iranian Writer* (New York: I. B. Tauris, 1991).

93. For a detailed analysis of this novel, see Michael C. Hillmann, *Hidayat's "The Blind Owl" Forty Years After* (Austin: Univ. of Texas Press, 1978), and Michael Beard, *Hedayat's "Blind Owl" as a Western Novel* (Princeton, N.J.: Princeton Univ. Press, 1990).

94. Nasrin Rahimieh, "A Systemic Approach to Modern Persian Prose Fiction," 16.

95. See the encyclopedic dictionaries *Farhang-i Muᶜin* (Moin Dictionary) and *Lughatnamah-i Dihkhuda*. (Dehkhoda Dictionary).

96. Sadiq Hidayat, *Buf-i kur* (Tehran: Sina, 1952), 88–89. For English translations of this novel and a selection of his short stories see *The Blind Owl, and Other Hedayat Stories*, comp. Carol L. Sayers, ed. Russell P. Christensen (Minneapolis, Minn.: Sorayya Publishers, 1984).

97. Sadiq Hidayat, *Afsanah-ʾi Afarinish: Khaymah Shab Bazi dar Sih Pardah* (The Myth of Creation: A Puppet Show in Three Acts) (Encino, Calif.: Ketab Corp, 1980). This book was also published in Paris in 1946: Sadiq Hidayat, *Afsanah-ʾi Afarinish: Khaymah Shab Bazi dar Sih Pardah*. Paris: Adrien-Maison neuve, 1946.

98. For more bibliographical and biographical information on Al-i Ahmad, see Jerome W. Clinton's article on Al-i Ahmad in *Encyclopedia Iranica*, ed. Ehsan Yarshater (London: Routledge and Kegan Paul, 1984); vol. 1: 745–47, and John Green, "The Modern Persian Short Story 1921–1981: A Bio-Bibliographic Survey" (Ph.D. diss., Univ. of Michigan, 1987).

99. Jalal Al-i Ahmad, *Sih Tar* (Tehran: Amir Kabir, 1971). The stories in this collection include "Bachah-i mardum," "Vasvas," "Lak-i surati," "Vadaᶜ," "Zindigi kih Gurikht," "Aftab-i Lab-i Bam," "Gunah, Nazdik-i MarzunᶜAbad," "Dahan-i Kaji, Arizu-yi Qudrat," "Ikhtilaf-i Hisab," and "al-Gumarak va al-Mukus."

100. Khusraw Shahani, "Murdah Kishi" (Pallbearing) *Adam-i Avazi: Majmuah-i Panzdah Dastan* (Tehran: Kitabha-yi Parastu, 1975).

101. Alavi, who met Sadiq Hidayat in the 1920s and was encouraged by him, wrote Persianist works as well. Later, of course, he became involved in

political activities in connection with the newly founded Communist Party, led by Dr. Erani. His works, include *Mirza* (Irvine, Calif.: Iranzamin, 1990, reprint), and *Chashmhayash* (Tehran: Muassasah-i Intisharat-i Amir Kabir, 1978). For more information on his works, see Donne Raffat, *The Prison Papers of Bozorg Alavi: A Literary Odyssey* (Syracuse, N.Y.: Syracuse Univ. Press, 1985).

102. Iraj Mirza, *Divan-i Kamil-i Iraj Mirza* (Complete Works of Iraj Mirza), ed. Muhammad Jafar Mahjub (Van Nuys, Calif.: Shirkat-i Kitab, 1989).

103. See Murtaza Mushfiq Kazimi, *Tehran-i Makhuf* (Frightening Tehran), 6th ed. (Tehran: Arghnun, 1968), Yahyah Dawlatabadi, *Shahrnaz* (Tehran: n.p., 1925). For a more detailed discussion of this topic, see Hassan Kamshad, *Modern Persian Prose Literature* (Bethesda, Md.: Iranbooks, 1996) and Hasan Abadzadih, *Sad Sal Datannivisi dar Iran* (One Hundred Years of Fiction Writing) (Tehran: Nashr-i Chashmih, 1998).

3. Revolutionary Literature: A Committed Literary Movement Before the 1979 Revolution

1. Misagh Parsa, *The Origins of the Iranian Revolution* (New Brunswick, N.J.: Rutgers Univ. Press, 1989), 44.

2. As the regime became intolerant of legal opposition, oppositional groups became more "integrated": that is, they sought fundamental socio-political changes.

3. Islamic fundamentalism gained prominence from the particular context of post–World War I conditions in several Middle Eastern societies and sought to establish the rule of Islam in all traditionally Muslim areas.

4. For more information and for discussion of other aspects of the concept of literary commitment in this period, see Hamid Dabashi, "The Poetics of Politics: Commitment in Modern Persian Literature," *Iranian Studies* 18, nos. 2–4 (spring–autumn 1985), 147–88; and Reza Baraheni, *Tala Dar Mis* (Gold in Copper) (Tehran: Nashr-i Zaman, 1968).

5. The proceedings of the First Iranian Writers' Congress are published in *Nakhustin Kungirah-i Navisandigan-i Iran. Maqalat va Ashʿar-i Nakhustin Kungirah-i Navisandigan-i Iran* (Articles and Poems Presented at the First Iranian Writers' Congress) (Tehran: Farabi Publishers, 1947).

6. *Nakhustin Kungirah-i Navisandigan-i Iran,* 113.

7. Ibid., 113–14.

8. See Ervand Abrahamian, *Iran Between Two Revolutions* (Princeton, N.J.: Princeton Univ. Press, 1982), 279–80. For more information on this topic see also Mansoor Moaddel, *Class, Politics, and Ideology in the Iranian Revolution*

(New York: Columbia Univ. Press, 1993); and Arthur Goldschmidt, *A Concise History of the Middle East* (Boulder, Colo.: Westview, 1983).

9. Goldschmidt, *A Concise History of the Middle East*, 333–34.

10. Terry Eagleton, *Marxism and Literary Criticism* (London: Methuen, 1976), 20. This view was especially common in the West before Lukacs and the Frankfurt School.

11. V. I. Lenin, *Collected Works* (English ed., Moscow: Foreign Languages Publishing House, 1962), vol. 10: 48–49, in Mao Tse-tung, *Talks at the Yenoan Forum on Literature and Art* (Peking, China: Peking Foreign Languages Press, 1967), 81–82.

12. Ibid.

13. Herbert Marcuse, *The Aesthetic Dimension* (Boston: Beacon Press, 1977), 2.

14. See Ernest Fisher, *Zarurat-i Hunar dar Ravand-i Takamul-i Ijtimaᶜi*, trans. Firuz Shirvanlu (Tehran: Intisharat-i Tus, 1969). The original English version was published in 1963: Ernest, Fischer *The Necessity of Art, a Marxist Approach* (Baltimore: Penguin Books, 1963).

15. Muhammad Ali Sipanlu, *Baz Afarini-i Vaqiiyat: Bist u Haft Qisah az Bist u Haft Nivisandah Muasir-i Iran* (The Interpretation of the Reality: Twenty-Seven Short Stories by Twenty-Seven Contemporary Iranian Writers) (Tehran: Nigah, 1988).

16. Sipanlu, "Introduction," in *Baz Afarini-i Vaqiiyat*, 17–18.

17. Hushang Gulshiri's short story, "Arusak-i Chini-i Man," is reprinted in *Hamyan-i Sitarigan*, eds. M. Khalili and M. Falah Gari (Tehran: Hush Va Ibtikar, 1992), 613–24.

18. Gulshiri, "Arusak-i Chini-i Man," 620.

19. Samad Bihrangi, *Mahi Siyah-i Kuchulu* (Tehran: Nahsr-i Azad, n.d.). This story has been translated by Mary and Eric Hooglund, *"The Little Black Fish" and Other Modern Persian Stories* (Washington, D.C.: Three Continents, 1976).

20. Masud Nuqrih Kar, "Chihrih-i Hirayt Angiz-i Taᶜahud" (The Astonishing Face of Commitment), *Arash* 57 (Aug.–Sept. 1996): 26–28.

21. Manuchir Hizarkhani's famous analysis of this short story confirms the point about philosophical messages. See Manuchir Hizarkhani, "Jahan Bini-i Mahi Siyah-i Kuchulu."

22. Masud Ahmadzadih, *Mubarizih-i Musalahanih; Ham Strategy, Ham Taktik* (Tehran: Sazman-i Chirikha-yi Fidaʾi-i Khalq-i Iran (OIPFG), 1969?).

23. Samad Behrangi, *Mahi Siyah-i Kuchulu*.

24. Sadiq Chubak, *Tangsir* (Los Angeles: Shirkat-i Kitab, 1990, reprint).

25. In his *Khaymih Shab Bazi* (The Puppet Show) (Tehran: Gutanbirg, 1955) and *Antari Kih Lutiyash Murdih Bud* (The Baboon Whose Buffoon Was

Dead)(Tehran: n.p., 1949), Chubak demonstrates how he shifts towards a more focused concern for the deprived classes.

26. *Klidar* was written in the prerevolutionary period, but the publication of some of its volumes was delayed until after the Revolution.

27. Moojan Momen, *An Introduction to Shi'i Islam* (New Haven, Conn.: Yale Univ. Press, 1985), 33.

28. Orayb Aref Najjar, "The Editorial Family of al-Kateb Bows in Respect: the Construction of Martyrdom Text Genre in One Palestinian Political and Literary Magazine," *Discourse and Society* 7, no. 4, (1996): 499.

29. M. R. Ghanoonparvar, *Prophets of Doom. Literature as a Socio-Political Phenomenon in Iran* (Lanham, Md.: Univ. Press of America, 1984), 27.

30. A volume of his work is available in English. See Ghulam Husayn Sa'idi, *Dandil: Stories from Iranian Life,* trans. Robert Campbell, Hasan Javadi, and Julie Scott Meisami (New York: Random House, 1981). See also Nithal Ramon, "Profile: Gholam Hoseyn Sa'idi," *Index on Censorship* 7, no. 1 (1978). For more biographical and bibliographical information, see John Green, "The Modern Persian Short Story 1921–1981: A Bio-Bibliographic Survey" (Ph.D. diss., Univ. of Michigan, 1987).

31. Ghulam Husayn Saidi, *Azadaran-i Bayal* (Bayal's Mourners) (Tehran: Intisharat-i Agah, 1978).

32. Dawlatabadi talks briefly about his arrest in *Ma Niz Mardumi Hastim* (Tehran: Nashr-i Parsi, 1989), 210.

33. See, for example, Jalal Al-i Ahmad's *Karnamah-i Sih Salih* (Tehran: Intisharat-i Ravaq, 1979) and *Gharbzadigi* (Tehran: Ravaq, 1978). In the former, he states that we should return both to purer Persian and Shiism to find an identity.

34. Jalal Al-i Ahmad, *Mudir-i Madrisih* (Tehran: Amir Kabir, 1971), 76.

35. Jalal Al-i Ahmad, *Arzyabi-i Shitabzadih* (Tehran: Ibn-i Sina, 1965).

36. Jalal Al-i Ahmad, *Dar Khidmat va Khiyanat-i Rushanfikran* (Concerning the Service and Betrayal of the Intellectuals) (Tehran: Intisharat-i Khavarazmi, 1978).

37. Reza Baraheni, *Junun-i Nivishtan* (The Madness of Writing) (Tehran: Risam, 1989), 454–55.

38. Sirus Tahbaz, *Majmuah Kamil-i Ash'ar-i Nima Yushij: Farsi Va Tabari* (Tehran: Intisharat-i Nigah, 1971), 301–2. For more information on a Committed reading of the poems, see chap. 2.

39. Tahbaz, *Majmuah Kamil-i Ash'ar-i Nima Yushij,* 301.

40. Dastghayb and Falaki, who represent such views, believe that Nima's portrayals are evidence of his commitment to the Revolution and leftist social-

ist ideology. See A.A. Dastghayb, *Sayih Rushan-i Shiʿr-i Farsi* (Tehran: Farhang, 1969), and Mahmud Falaki, *Nigahi Bih Nima* (Tehran: Intisharat-i Murvarid, 1994).

41. See my discussion of Nima's conception of form in chap. 2.

42. For a closer look at the transition in Nima's approach see Ahmad Karimi-Hakkak, *Recasting Persian Poetry: Scenarios of Poetic Modernity in Iran* (Salt Lake City: Univ. of Utah Press, 1995), 248.

43. Khusraw Gulsurkhi, *Siyasat-i Hunar, Siasat-i Shʿir* (The Politics of Art, the Politics of Poetics) (Tehran: Murvarid, 1965?).

44. For more information, see Terry Eagleton, *Marxism and Literary Criticism* (Los Angeles: Univ. of California Press, 1976), 20.

45. Every time a writer was imprisoned or executed, his or her book would be banned, and, as Reza Barahani mentions, "Every book which became banned would become more appealing and would have more readers." *Tarikh-i Muzakkar: Farhang-i Hakim va Farhang-i Mahkum* (A Male History: The Dominant Culture and the Doomed One) (Tehran: Nashr-i Avval, 1984), 202.

46. Khusraw Gulsurkhi, *Nawgiraʾi Va Haqiqat-i Khaki* (Modernity and the Earthly Reality) (Tehran: Murvarid, 1979).

47. Ibid., 1.

48. Said Sultanpur, *Nuʿi az Hunar, Nuʿi az Andishih* (A Kind of Art, A Kind of Thought) (Tehran: n.p., 1960), 5.

49. Ibid., 9.

50. Ahmad Shamlu, "Bagh-i Ainih" (The Garden of Mirrors) in *Sida-yi Shiʿr-i Imruz* (The Voice of Today's Poetry) (The Garden of Mirrors), ed. Bahman Mahabadi (Tabriz: Talash, 1989), 84–86.

51. Ahmad Shamlu, "Shiʿri Kih Zingist" (Poetry That is Live); Majid Rawshangar, *Az Nima Ta Baʿd* (From Nima Onward) (Tehran: Murvarid, 1968), 46–54.

52. See Hamdi Shirazi, *Funun va Anvaʿi Shiʿr-i Farsi* (Techniques and Types of Persian Poetry) (Tehran: Bita, 1972). See also chap. 2.

53. See Safar Fadainia, *Shʿir-i Junbish-i Nuvin: Inqilab dar Shiʿr-i Muasir* (The Poetry of the New Movement: Revolution in Contemporary Poetry) (Tehran: Intisharat-i Tus, n.d.).

54. See Fadainia, *Shiʿr-i Junbish-i Nuvin.*

55. Kadkani, "Zarurat" in *Shʿir-i Junbish-i Nuvin,* 11.

56. Hamid Musadiq, "Abi, khakistari, Siyah" (Blue, Gray, Black), in *Shiʿr-i Naw az Aghaz ta Imruz* (New Poetry from the Beginning to the Present), ed. Muhammad Huquqi (Tehran: Ravayat, 1992), 566.

57. Faridun Mushiri, "Yaghi," in *Barguzidih-i Ashʿar* (Selected Poems) (Tehran: Bamdad, 1987), 122.

58. Nakhustin Kungirah-i Navisandigan-i Iran, *Maqalat va Ashʿar-i Nakhustin Kungirah-i Navisandigan-i Iran* (The Proceedings of the First Iranian Writers' Congress) (Tehran: Farabi Publishers, 1947), 63.

59. Danishvar, quoted in Nasir Muʿazin, *Dah Shab: Shabha-yi Shairan va Navisandigan dar Anjuman-i Farhangi-i Iran va Alman* (Ten Nights) (Tehran: Amir Kabir, 1979), 13.

60. Gulshiri, quoted in Muʾazin, *Dah Shab*, 693.

61. See *Kayhan* and *Ittilaʿat* (July–Aug. 1977).

62. See Muʾazin, *Dah Shab*.

63. A shorter version of the comparison between the pre- and postrevolutionary women's writing appeared in my article in "Iranian Women's Literature: From Prerevolutionary Social Discourse to Postrevolutionary Feminism," *International Journal of Middle East Studies* 29, no. 4, (Nov. 1997): 53–58.

64. See Mary Beth Tierney-Tello, *Allegories of Transgression and Transformation: Experimental Fiction by Women Writing under Dictatorship* (New York: State Univ. of New York Press, 1996).

65. For an official view on the state's gender policy, see M. Reza Pahlavi, *Inqilab-i Safid* (The White Revolution) (Tehran: Kitabkhanih-i Saltanati, 1967), *Mamuriyyat Bara-yi Vatanam* (Tehran: Kitabkhanih-i Saltanati, 1962), and *Pasukh Bih Tarikh* (A Response to History) (Tehran: Kitabkhanih-i Saltanati, 1980). Farrkhru Parsay, a member of the cabinet, also represents a somewhat official view when she argues that since ancient times, Iranian women have not had any conflict with men but have always lived in peace and harmony with them; Farrkhru Parsay, H. Ahi, and M. Taliqani, *Zan Dar Iran-i Bastan* (Women in Ancient Iran) (Tehran: Jamiyat-i Zanan-i Danishgahi, 1967), 10.

66. For an overview of the status of women in Iranian society, see Guity Nashat, *Women and Revolution in Iran* (Boulder, Colo.: Westview, 1983); and Mahnaz Afkhami, "A Future in the Past: The Prerevolutionary Women's Movement in Iran," in *Sisterhood is Global: An International Women's Movement Anthology*, ed. Robin Morgan (New York: Doubleday, 1984).

67. Although the Pahlavi state made a separate feminist movement redundant, it should be noted that women's issues did not become a significant element of the state discourse as was the case with Kemalism in Turkey. Several scholars refer to Kemalism and women's emancipation as intimate elements of the same discourse; see Zehra Arat, "Turkish Women and the Republican Reconstruction," in *Reconstructing Gender in the Middle East*, ed. Fatma Muge Gocek and Shiva Balaghi (New York: Columbia Univ. Press, 1994), 57–81, and Kumari Jayawardena, *Feminism and Nationalism in the Third World* (London: Zed Books, 1986), 25–41. In fact, several scholars argue that even the rise of

feminism in 1980s in Turkey was a reaction to Kemalism and its "state femi-nism"; see Nukhet Sirman's well written and lucid article "Feminism in Turkey: A Short History," *New Perspectives on Turkey* 3 (fall 1989): 1–35, and Yesim Arat, "Women's Movement of the 1980s in Turkey: Radical Outcome of Liberal Kemalism?" in Gocek, *Reconstructing Genders*, 100–13.

68. See the discussion of Al-i Ahmad's *Gharbzadigi* earlier in this chapter. For general leftist views of the reform, see Sazman-i Chirikha-yi Fada'i Khalq-i Iran (Organization of Iranian People's Fada'i Guerrillas), *Islahat-i Arzi va Natayij-i Mustaqim-i An* (Land Reform and Its Direct Impact) (Tehran: OIPFG, 1974).

69. For a detailed study of the women's movement and the left in Iran, see Hammed Shahidian, "The Iranian Left and the 'Woman Question' in the Rev-olution of 1978–79," *International Journal of Middle East Studies* 26 (May 1994): 223–47, and Azar Tabari and N. Yaganeh, *In the Shadow of Islam: The Women's Movement in Iran* (London: Zed Press, 1982).

70. See, for example, the views of Nahzat-i Azadi on the granting of women's voting rights in 1962 in *Asnad-i Nahzat-i Azadi: Jariyan Tasis va Bayaniynaha* (The Documents of the Freedom Movement: Its Process of Estab-lishment and Its Announcements) (Tehran: Nahzat, 1982).

71. See M.R. Ghanoonparvar, *Prophets of Doom: Literature as a Socio-Political Phenomenon in Iran* (Lanham, Md.: Univ. Press of America, 1984).

72. Some of the women who joined the Left became top members of guer-rilla organizations. Of 341 guerrillas killed either in armed clashes or in prison, 39 were women (more than 11 percent). See Ervand Abrahamian, *Iran Between Two Revolutions* (Princeton, N.J.: Princeton Univ. Press, 1982), 480.

73. Concerning the favorable reaction to these short stories, see Maryam Mafi's afterword in *Simin Danishvar's "Playhouse"* (Washington, D.C.: Mage, 1989); H. Abidini in *Sad Sal Dastan Navisi* (One Hundred Years of Fiction Writ-ing) (Tehran: Tundar, 1980), 66, 76–82, 208; and M. Sipanlu in *Baz Afarini-i Vaqi'iyat* (Tehran: Nigah, 1989), 18, 76–82.

74. For similar analyses of this character, see Fereshteh Davaran, "Dar Talash-i Kasb-i Huviyat," *Nimeye Digar* 8 (fall 1987): 140–66; and Hamid Dabashi, "Hijab-i Chihrih-i Jan: Bih Justju-yi Zari dar Savushun-i Simin Dan-ishvar," *Nimeye Digar* 8 (fall 1987): 65–118.

75. Simin Danishvar, *Savushun* (Tehran: Kharazmi, 1978). For English trans-lations of this novel, see *Savushun: A Novel About Modern Iran*, trans. M. R. Ghanoonparvar; (Washington, D.C.: Mage, 1990), and *Savushun, A Persian Requiem: A Novel by Simin Daneshvar*, trans. Roxane Zand (London: P. Halban, 1991).

76. The title refers to the custom of celebrating the martyrdom of a mythi-

cal hero, Siyavush, from whose spilled blood a plant grows. The author implies that Yusof too was murdered innocently and that his death will cause trees to grow, i.e., his death will fuel a popular uprising.

77. Perhaps in this final scene, the author is inspired by Zaynab, Imam Husayn's sister, in the events of Karbala.

78. Later, on the eve of the Islamic Revolution, Danishvar became very sympathetic to the Islamic movement. In the short story "Kayd al-Khainin" (an Arabic-Islamic title meaning "Traitor's Intrigue"), her sympathies are shown in the portrayal of a clergyman who resists succumbing to the shah's secret police. Given the condition of the time, when the Islamic leaders promoted Arabic language as the country's second language and used a Persian filled with Arabic terms, the title of the short story promoted the Islamic movement.

79. Compare the two versions of this short story: the original, which appeared in *Alifba* (The Alphabet) 2 (Oct. 1973): 142–51, and the version, which was the title story of Danishvar's *Bih Ki Salam Kunam* (To Whom Can I Say Hello), 75–93.

80. This short story is also from the collection *Bih Ki Salam Kunam*, 53–74.

81. Simin Danishvar, *Danishvar's "Playhouse": A Collection of Stories*, trans. Maryam Mafi (Washington, D.C.: Mage, 1989), 32.

82. Published in her collection *Shahri Chun Bihisht* (A City Like Paradise), 1961.

83. See Maryam Mafi, *Simin Danishvar's "Playhouse"*.

84. One of her earlier works, a collection of short stories, *Atash-i Khamush* (The Quenched Fire) (1948), resembles a journalistic report on social conditions of the time.

85. See H. Abidini, *Sad Sal Dastan Navisi* (One Hundred Years of Fiction Writing), 24.

86. These two collections include poems that Farrukhzad wrote from 1959 to 1967.

87. Furugh Farrukhzad, *Asir* (Tehran: Amir Kabir, 1955), 75.

88. Ibid., 83.

89. Furugh Farrukhzad, *Divan-i Ashʿar* (Collected Poems) (Tehran: Murvarid, 1995), 305–6.

90. Furugh Farrukhzad (Forugh Farrokhzad), *Bride of Acacias: Selected Poems of Forugh Farrokhzad*, trans. Jascha Kessler, with Amin Banani (Delmar, N.Y.: Caravan Books, 1982), 22.

91. Furugh Farrukhzad, *Divan-i Ashʿar*, 456–62.

92. Furugh Farrukhzad, *Bride of Acacias*, 112–15.

93. See for example, her poem, "Delam Bara-ye Baghchih Misuzad." (I Pity

the Garden) in Muhammad Huquqi, *Furugh Farrukhzad Shiʿr-i Furugh Far-rukhzad az Aghaz ta Imruz* (Tehran: Intisharat-i Nigah, 1993).

94. Furugh Farrukhzad, *Furugh Farrukhzad: Shiʿr-i Furugh Farrukhzad az Aghaz ta Imruz*, ed. Muhammad Huquqi (Tehran: Intisharat-i Nigah, 1993), 280–86.

95. Iraj Gurgin, *Chahar Musahibih ba Furugh Farrukhzad* (Four Interviews with Furugh Farrukhzad) (Tehran: Intisharat-i Radio Iran, 1964), 23–24.

96. To use the terminology of Anne Herrmann in *The Dialogic and Difference: 'An/other Woman' in Virginia Woolf and Christa Wolf* (New York: Columbia Univ. Press, 1989), 6.

97. Muhammad Huquqi, *Shiʿr va Shaʿiran* (Poetry and Poets) (Tehran: Nigah, 1989), 396.

98. Farrukhzad herself confirms this by saying that her previous works *The Wall* and *Rebellion* are, in fact, "disappointing struggles between two stages of my life." Furugh Farrukhzad, *Guzinah-i Ashʿar* (A Selection of Poems) (Tehran: Murvarid, 1985), 47.

99. Farzaneh Milani's examination of these particular aspects has been the most successful.

100. Iraj Gurgin, *Chahar Musahibih ba Furugh Farrukhzad* (Four Interviews with Furugh Farrukhzad) (Tehran: Intisharat-i Radio Iran, 1964), 21. During these radio interviews with Farrukhzad, Gurgin states that there is no differ-ence between a poet and a poetess, yet he contends that one characteristic of Farrukhzad's poems is that they are womanish. Her response is an assertion of the social discourse of the intellectual elite in the 1960s and 1970s. Part of this interview is translated by Michael C. Hillmann in *A Lonely Woman: Furugh Farrukhzad and Her Poetry* (Washington, D.C.: Three Continents and Mage, 1987), 64:

> If . . . my poetry contains a degree of femininity, well it is quite natural owing to the fact that I am a woman. I am glad I am a woman. But if the criterion used is artistic value, then I do not think sex can be propounded (as a determining factor). Discussing this matter is not right in the first place. Naturally because of her physical, emotional and psychological qualities, a woman focuses on problems that are perhaps not apt to be scrutinized by a man, and a feminine "vision" relates to problems that differ from those of a man. I think that for those who choose artistic work as a means of expressing their existence, if they try to make sex a stan-dard for their artistic work, they will always remain on this same level, and this is really not good. If I think that because I am a woman, I should talk about my own womanhood all the time, this would indicate a kind

of stagnation and lack of growth, not just as a poet but as a human being. Because the consideration is that a person nurtures the positive aspects of his or her own existence in some way so he or she can attain a certain level of human values. The essential thing is being a person. Being a man or woman is not the issue.

The truth is that her poetry engaged in a nontraditional view of human beings, whether male or female. She derives her artistic values from a humanistic notion of life and literature freed from the bindings of gender conditioning. This can at best correspond to Elaine Showalter's definition of the feminine stage in Western women's writings. See Showalter, "A Literature of Their Own," in *Feminist Literary Theory: A Reader*, ed. Mary Eagleton (Oxford: Basil Blackwell, 1986), 11–15.

101. For detailed information on Bihbahani's biography and works, see Farzaneh Milani, ed., *Nimeye Digar* 2, Special issue on Simin Bihbahani (autumn 1993), and the special issue of *Daftar-i Hunar: Bizhan Assadipour* (Bizhan Asadipur, Bidjan Assadipour), *Daftar-i Hunar* 2, no. 4 (Sept. 1995).

102. *Chilchiragh* (Chandelier) 5th ed. (Tehran: Zavvar, 1991) (it was first published in 1966); *Marmar* (Marble) (Tehran: Kitabfurushi Zavvar, 1967); *Rastakhiz* (Resurrection) (Tehran: Kitabfurushi-i Zavvar, 1983). Second edition of the poems written in the years between 1963 to 1973; *Jay-i pa* (The Footstep) (Tehran: Zavvar, 1991). This is the fourth edition and the poems were written in the years between 1946 to 1956; *Sih tar i Shikastih* (Broken Seh Tar) (Tehran: Kitabfurushi Ilmi, 1951).

103. Simin Bihbahani, *Ja-yi Pa* (Tehran: Ma'rafat, 1956).

104. Simin Bihbahani, "Jibbur" (Pickpocket); *Guzinah-i Ash'ar* (A Selection of Poems) (Tehran: Intisharat-i Murvarid, 1988), 80–83.

105. Bihbahani, "Ruspi" (Prostitute) in *Jay-i Pa*, 27.

106. Bihbahani, Raqasih" (Dancer) in *Jay-i Pa*, 45.

107. Victimized men and sick children appear in poems such as "Dandan-i Murdih" and "Raqib" from the collection *Chilchiragh*.

108. Bihbahani, "Az Butah-i Khushbu-i Gulpar" (From the Good Smelling Marjoram), *Guzinah-i Ash'ar* (A Selection of Poems) (Tehran: Intisharat-i Murvarid, 1988), 127.

109. This period is, in a way, less radical than even the end of the nineteenth century, when works such as Bibi Khanum's *Ma'ayib al-Rijal* (Vices of Men) were appearing and Zaynab Pasha's group was carrying on an armed struggle in Tabriz for women's rights. For more information about Bibi Kahnum's book, see Afsaneh Najmabadi, ed., *Women's Autobiographies in Contemporary Iran* (Cambridge: Harvard Univ. Press, 1990), 20.

4. Revolution and Literature: The Rise of the Islamic Literary Movement after the 1979 Revolution

1. See Mansoor Moaddel and Kamran Talattof in the introduction to *Contemporary Debates in Islam: An Anthology of Modernist and Fundamentalist Thought*. (New York: St. Martin's Press, 1999). They write that "while Islamic modernism had a predominantly social orientation, a distinctive feature of the fundamentalist movement was a high level of political activism aiming to seize state power. In fundamentalism, the political reorganization of society is the necessary step in its overall Islamization project."

2. Iranian literary critics and some of the secular authors themselves have characterized Persian literary works produced in the first few years after the Revolution as critical, regressive, repetitive, or inconspicuous. See the series of interviews with literary activists on this topic in *Dunya-yi Sukhan* (The World of Speech) 48 (Feb. 1992): 16–33.

3. Asghar Abdulahi, "A Dust Laden Room," trans. Afshin Nassiri, *Barasi-i Kitab* (1994). First published in Persian in Gardun 1. 3. (December 1990), 24–29.

4. Ali Khudayi, *Az Miyan-i Shishh, az Miyan-i Mih: Majmuah-i Dastan* (Through the Glass, Through the Fog: A Short Story Collection) (Tehran: Khudayi, 1991); Abbas Ma'rufi, *Sanfuni-i Murdagan* (Tehran: Nashr-i Gardun, 1989); Riza Farkhal, in *Ah Istanbul, va Shish Dastan-i Digar* (Oh Istanbul and Six Other Short Stories) (Tehran: Intisharat-i Isparak, 1989); Riza Jula'i, *Shab-i Zulmani Yalda va Hadis-i Durd Kishan* (The Dark Long Winter Night and the Tale of the Dregs of Wine Drinkers) (Tehran: Nashr-i Alburz, 1970).

5. Riza Farkhal, "Ah Istanbul," in *Ah Istanbul*, 155.

6. F. Mizani and A. Muhit *Shir bih Daqiqih-i Aknun* (Poetry in this Minute) (Tehran: Nuqrih, 1988).

7. Shams Lnagrudi, *Qasidih-i Labkhand-Chak Chak* (Ode of the Ruptured Smile) (Tehran: Nashr-i Markaz, 1990), 23–25.

8. Ahmad Karimi-Hakkak, "Censorship," in *Encyclopaedia Iranica* vol. 5, 135–42. Costa Mesa, Calif.: Mazda Publishers.

9. In the prerevolutionary period, there were religious collections such as Murtiza Mutahari's *Dastan-i Rastan* (The Story of the Virtuous) and Ali Davani's *Dastanha-yi Islam* (Islamic Stories) that echoed Quranic stories, and there were poetry works that revolved around the lives of the Prophet and Imams and their families. These works resembled classical literature in their form, but never attained sufficient literary significance to constitute a literary movement. Murtiza Mutahari's *Dastan-i Rastan* (Tehran: Muhammadi, 1963) is a collection of fables extracted from the Hadith or historical texts about the life of Muhammad, and Ali Davani's *Dastanha-yi Islami* (Tehran: Intishar, 1960)

consists solely of maxims, anecdotes, and accounts of historical incidents in the lives of religious leaders.

10. Other authors, such as Davari, Surush, Khuram Shahi, Mirshakak, and Ibrahimi, directly represent and promote the state discourse in their works.

11. After all the universities across the country were closed, this council came into existence in order to accomplish several tasks, which included the eradication of leftist academics, the "reform" of the curriculum, and the general Islamization of academic environments.

12. Jalal Rafi, "Tarha va Musavabat-i Farhangi" (Cultural Projects and Bylaws), *Adabistan* 54 (June 1994): 34–36.

13. See Musa Mimudarris, "Risalat-i Hunar" (The Mission of Art) in *Mahnamah-i Pasdar-i Islam* (The Guardian of Islam, a Monthly Journal) 164 (Aug. 1995): 16–20.

14. Shi'ism has historically been a political faction; it began with a political movement to support the legitimacy of Ali, Mohammad's son-in-law and the fourth caliph, who was murdered in 661 by his opponents. After Ali, Muawiyah and later his son Yazid became caliphs. Husayn, the younger son of Ali rejected the legitimacy of Yazid as kaliph. Yazid and the governor of Iraq attacked Husayn and his supporters in Iraq, where he had hoped to establish his caliphate. For more information on this topic, see Moojan Momen, *An Introduction to Shi'i Islam* (New Haven, Conn.: Yale Univ. Press, 1985), 33.

15. Orayb Aref Najjar, "'The Editorial Family of al-Kateb Bows in Respect': The Construction of Martyrdom Text Genre in One Palestinian Political and Literary Magazine." *Discourse and Society* 7, no. 4. (Oct. 1996): 499–530.

16. Among these new authors are Qasim Farasat, Muhammad Nurizad, Muhsin Makhmalbaf, Akbar Khalili, Hasan Ahmadi, Vahid Amiri, Mustafa Rahmaddust, Qasimali Farasat, Habib Ghanipur, Mihdi Shujai, Kambiz Malik, and M. Khushdil.

17. This short story appeared in a collection by the same title: Muhammad Nurizad, *Mard Va Karbala* (The Man and Karbala) (Tehran: Ministry of Islamic Culture and Guidance, 1990), 9.

18. Nusrat Allah Muhmudzadih, *Marsiah Halabchih* (The Elegy of Halabja) (Tehran: Raja, 1989).

19. Samad Bihrangi, *Mahi Siyah-i Kuchulu* (Tehran: Nahsr-i Azad, c. 1960).

20. Mihdi Shujai, "Zarih-i Chishmha-yi Tu" (The Shrine of Your Eyes), in *Majmuah Qisah* (A Collecton of Short Stories) (Tehran: Surush, 1985).

21. Here the story deals, even in a short and forced way, with the concept of nation. Y. Miyanduabi, "Maqtal," (Place of Slaughter), in *Khanvadah-i Ma* (Tehran: Kitab-i Javanih, 1989), 9–41.

22. Muhsin Makhmalbaf, "Mara Bibus" (Kiss Me), in *Gung-i Khvabdidah*

(The Sleeping Mute), vol. 1 (Tehran: Nashr-i Nay, 1994), 20. This is a multivolume collection of works that includes the selcted short stories, plays, screen plays, and critical essays.

23. See, for example, Ashraf Dihqani, *Hamasih-i Muqavamat* (The Epic of Resistance) (Tehran: Junbish, 1978).

24. Muhsin Makhmalbaf, "Mara Bibus" (Kiss Me), in *Gung-i Khvabdidih*, 24.

25. Gulnaraqi, a prerevolutionary singer, sang this song, whose lyrics were written by H. Raqabi. The Tudah Party claimed that the song was composed in memory of Colonel Mubashiri, a member of the party executed by the shah's regime.

26. For more information on Marziyeh Ahmadi Osku'i's life and poetry, see Marziyeh Ahmadi Osku'i, *Khatirati az Yik Rafiq* (A Comrade's Memoir) (Tehran: OIPFG, n.d).

27. See, for example, M. Muhammadi, *Tahlili bar Inqilab-i Islami* (An Analysis of the Islamic Revolution) (Tehran: Amir Kabir, 1986).

28. Makhmalbaf, *Bagh-i Blur* (Crystal Garden) a novel included in *Gung-i Khvabdidih*, 336.

29. Mahmud Shahrukhi and Mushfiq Kashani, introduction to *Sugnamih-'i Imam* (An Elegy for Imam Khomeini)(Tehran: Surush, 1980).

30. Mahmud Shahrukhi and Mushfiq Kashani, introduction to *Majmu'ah-i Shi'r-i Jang* (An Anthology of Poems on War) (Tehran: Amir Kabir, 1987).

31. Amiri, "Su'al" (Question), in Shahrukhi and Kashani, *Majmu'ah-i Shi'r-i Jang*, 24–25.

32. Taymur Gurgin, "Ru-yi Telex," in *Farhang-i Shairan-i Jang va Muqavimat* (An Anthology of War and Resistance Poetry), ed. Muhamad Baqir Najafzadih Barfurush (Tehran: Kayhan, 1993), 265.

33. Ali Musavi Garmarudi, "Man Shi'r-i Shi'iam" ("I Am Shiite Poetry"), in *Inqilab-i Islami dar Shi'r-i Sha'iran* (Poetry of the Islamic Revolution), trans. Ali Khaza'i, (Mashad: Astan-i Quds-i Razavi, 1986), 11–13. This is a dual language anthology on the Islamic revolution in which the Persian poems are translated by the editor of the book.

34. This is a slightly modified version of the translation of the poem as presented in *Inqilab-i Islami dar Shi'r-i Sha'iran* (Poetry of the Islamic Revolution).

35. Pishtaz (literally, the one who moves to the front in a battle) referred to those revolutionary intellectuals who were temporarily fighting without the support of the masses.

36. Tahirih Saffarzadih, "Chahar Rah i Shahadat," 62–67.

37. Tahirih Saffarzadih, "The Roads of Martyrdom." This is a slightly modified version of the translation of this poem by Ali Khazifar in the dual lan-

guage anthology of poetry on the Islamic revolution, *Inqilab-i Islami dar Shiᶜr-i Sha'ᶜiran* (Poetry of The Islamic Revolution), trans. Ali Khazifar, (Mashad: Astan-i Quds-i Razavi, 1986), 62–67.

38. Taherih Saffarzadih, "Introduction" to *Selected Poems.* bilingual ed. trans. M. H. Kamyabee and N. Mirkiani (Shiraz, Iran: Navid, 1987), 3 and xv respectively.

39. Taherih Saffarzadih, "Fath Kamil Nist," (Victory Is Not Complete) *Selected Poems,* bilingual ed. trans. M. H. Kamyabee and N. Mirkiani (Shiraz, Iran: Navid, 1987), 34, 36.

40. This is a slightly modified version of the English translation of the "Fath Kamil Nist" (Victory Is Not Complete), 35, 37.

5. Feminist Discourse in Postrevolutionary Women's Literature

1. The attitude of the oppositional forces, including women, towards Islam changed once again as religious tenets became established state ideology.

2. The shah's Family Protection Law (introduced in 1967) resulted in an increase in women's social participation and in a decrease in men's privileges.

3. For information about the Islamic Punishment Codes, see "Qanun-i Mujazat-i Islami, Majmuah-i Qavanin-i Sal-i 1370" (Islamic Criminal Law, Listing of the Laws for the Year 1991), *Ruznamah-i Rasmi* (The Official Newsletter of Government of the Islamic Republic of Iran) (summer 1992), 593–654.

4. It was not the first time the image of woman offered such symbolic significance in the development of a revolution; it was also used in the shah's White Revolution. Much earlier it was an important symbol in the French Revolution; see Claire Goldberg Moses, *French Feminism in the Nineteenth Century* (Albany, N.Y.: State Univ. of New York Press, 1984).

5. Farzaneh Milani, *Veils and Words: The Emerging Voices of Iranian Women Writers* (Syracuse, N.Y.: Syracuse Univ. Press, 1992), 5.

6. This Islamic law requires women to be veiled in the presence of strangers (men not related through marriage or blood); however, it imposes certain rules of conduct as well.

7. See the journals *Ayandigan* (Mar. 11, 12, 14, 18 and 19, 1979) and *Ittilaᶜat* (Mar. 8–12, 1979).

8. *Ayandigan,* Mar. 8, 1979.

9. Ibid.

10. *Ittilaᶜat,* Mar. 8, 1979.

11. *Ayandigan,* Mar. 1979.

12. Ibid., Mar. 10, 1979.

13. Ibid., Mar. 10, 1979.

14. Ibid., Mar. 11, 1979.

15. Ibid., Mar. 10, 1979.

16. For a detailed account of these incidents see *Ittila'at* (Mar. 8, 1979) and *Ayandigan* (Mar. 11, 12, 14, 18, and 19, 1979).

17. The latter slogan has since become the major refrain of groups who have continued to regularly attack women on the streets. Slogans such as "Death to the unveiled" or "If unveiling is civilization then animals are more civilized" persistently appear on city walls.

18. *Ayandigan,* Mar. 12, 1979, 1.

19. For a more detailed study of the women's movement and the Left in Iran, see Hammed Shahidian, "The Iranian Left and the 'Woman Question' in the Revolution of 1978–79," *International Journal of Middle East Studies* 2, no. 26 (May 1994): 223–47.

20. The first of these reports appeared in journals such as *Haftih Namih-i Susiyalisti-i Kargar* (Socialist Workers' Weekly) and *Fasli Dar Gul-i Surkh* (A Season of Roses).

21. These works, which include the historical, contemporary, and theoretical treatment of women's concerns, attempt to find a "proper" form of feminist assertion to avoid obstacles such as censorship. The works of Banafshih Hijazi and Mihrangiz Kar exemplify such efforts.

22. See Fatamah Givihchiyan, "Sang-i Zirin-i Asiyab: Zan Ya Mard?" (The Milestone: Woman or Man?), *Falsnamah-i Ilami-Pazhuhishi Mutali'at-i Barnamih Rizi* (Studies and Research in Planning Quarterly) 3 (spring 1995).

23. Women's journals *Zanan* (Women) and *Zan-i Ruz* (Today's Woman) follow these debates. *Payam-i Hajar,* (Hagar's Message), ed. Azam Taliqani, publishes articles concerning women's rights from a religious point of view.

24. See the interview with Guli Taraqi in *Adinih: Vizhah-i Guft-i Gu* (Friday: Special Interview Issue) (Aug. 1993): 61–66. It has also become common for *Zan-i Ruz* (Today's Woman), a women's magazine under Islamic influence, to discuss "urgent women's issues" and to publish articles on feminism; see, for example, *Zan-i Ruz* 13 (Aug. 1993), 14–17.

25. Women after the Revolution have compiled volumes of bibliographical indexes that provide subject guides to printed material in the fields of women's studies and include thousands of titles of articles written before 1986 about women. See Maryam Ra'yat et al., *Maqalih Namih-i Zan* (Women's Article Index) (Tehran: Pazhuhishha-yi Farhangi, 1989); V. Khavhiran, *Fihrist-i Mawzu'i-i Kutub va Maqalat dar Barih-i Zan* (A Subject Index for Books and Articles about Women) (Tehran: Idarah-i Kull-i Intisharat, 1984); and Daftar-i San-

duq-i Kudikan (Office of the Children's Fund), *Fihrist-i Mushtarak-i Kitabha* (A Common Bibliography) (Tehran: Sanduq-i Kudikan-i, 1994). In the first volume alone, there are entries for 2,757 titles of articles written about women after the Revolution.

26. See Milani, *Veils and Words*, 232, 234.

27. Cited in *Gender and Text in Modern Hebrew and Yiddish Literature*, ed. Naomi B. Sokoloff, Anne Lapidus Lerner, and Anita Norich (New York and Jerusalem: Jewish Theological Seminary, 1991).

28. Lists of women authors' names, titles of their publications, and the names of journals in which they publish are extensive, and they all demonstrate a concern for women's issues. To examine the extent of such lists, see various bibliographical indexes by women, such as the one by Maryam Ra'yat et al., cited in n. 25, above as well as Siddiqah Sultanifar, *Kitab Namah-i Zan*, Shahrzad Khashi, *Kitab Shinasi Naqd*, and Zahra Chihrih Khand, *Kitab Namah-i Zan*. Each one of these four bibliographical indexes contain hundreds of entries from various periods. More information on women's publications is available in women's journals such as, *Payam-i Zan* (Women's Message), *Zanan* (Women), *Zan-i Ruz* (Today's Woman), *Farzanih* (Learned, also a female name), *Payam-i Hajar* (Hagar's Message), *Mahjubih* (Modest), *Bultan-i Zanan* (Women's Bulletin), *Sunbulih* (Hyacinth), *Khanvadih* (Family), *Fazilat-i Khanvadah* (Family Virtue), *Payk-i Mama* (Mother's Messenger), *Vizhih Namah-i Daftar-i Umur-i Zanan* (Special Journal of the Office of Women's Affairs), *Sal Namah-i Zan*, (Women's Annual), *Nida* (Voice), and *Takapu-yi Banuvan* (Women's Search). More specifically, look at *Zan-i Ruz*, nos. 1435 and 1436 (1972) and no. 1467 (1994), for detailed bibliographies of works on women's issues and women's literature. These bibliographies exclude male writers who write on women's issues in Iran and women writers who live and write abroad. Iranian women living abroad have written a great deal of literature in which they express their concern for the situation of women in Iran from a feminist point of view; they have also published influential periodicals, such as *Nimeye Digar* (A Persian Language Journal of Feminist Studies), which is published in the United States.

29. Today's Iran is probably the only country in which a woman's daily newspaper, *Zan*, can hit the stands and be immediately, voraciously consumed.

30. See Reza Barahani, "Tarikh Ulaviyatha-yi Adabi Ra Ja Bi Ja Kardah," (History has Replaced Literary Priorities), *Adinih* (Friday) 42–43 (Mar. 1, 1992), 80; Nasrin Takhayuri, "Mukhataban Jiditar va 'Amiqtar az Intizar" *Adinah* 44 (Mar. 20, 1992); Karim Imami, "Bazar-i Garm-i Ruman va Khanumha-yi Ruman Khan," *Adinih* 44 (Mar. 20, 1992), 70.

31. Many works, such as Ravanipur's *Sangha-yi Shaytan* (Satan's Stones),

were reprinted within a month, and many others' works, such as Simin Bih-bahani's new collections of poetry and Fatanih Haj Sayyid Javadi's novel *Bamdad-i Khumar* (Half-drunk Morning) 3rd ed. (Tehran: Nashr-i Alburz, 1992), have been reprinted several times. Readers also play a role in determining the candidates for an award given by *Gardun* literary magazine. Nasrin Samani's *Guli dar Shurih zar* (A Flower in a Salt-marsh) (Tehran: Kitab-i Afarin, 1992) was reprinted fourteen times within a short time after its first publication. Nahid A. Pazhvak's *Shab-i Sarab* (The Night of the Mirage) (Rasht: Hidayat, 1998) has also been reprinted several times. Muniru Ravanipur, Guli Taraqi, Farkhundih Aqai were at the top of *Gardun* literary magazine's list of best authors for 1993–94, and Farkhundih Aqai won the first prize for her collection of short stories, *Raz-i Kuchak* (The Little Secret). For the complete coverage of this competition, see *Gardun* 4, nos. 35–36 (winter 1994), 15; and *Gardun* 5, no. 41 (summer 1994), 27.

32. For discussion of both these works, see my introduction to *Women Without Men: A Novella* by Shahrnush Parsipur, trans. Kamran Talattof and Jocelyn Sharlet (Syracuse, N.Y.: Syracuse Univ. Press, 1998).

33. Shahrnush Parsipur, *Tuba va Ma'na-yi Shab* (Tuba and the Meaning of the Night) (Tehran: Isparak, 1989), 483.

34. Parsipur's only prerevolutionary novel, *Sag va Zimistan-i Buland* (The Dog and the Long Winter) (Tehran: Amir Kabir, 1976), has a female protagonist who supports revolutionary activities because of loyalty to her brother rather than because of opposition to patriarchy.

35. Shahrnush Parsipur, *Zanan Bidun-i Mardan* (Women Without Men) (Tehran: Nuqrah, 1990), 79. For the English version of this novel, see Shahrnush Parsipur, *Women Without Men*.

36. Quoted in Janet Lazariyan, "Musahibih Ba Muniru Ravanipur" (An Interview with Muniru Ravanipur), *Adinih* 35 (Oct. 1990): 4.

37. Lazariyan, "Musahibih Ba Muniru Ravanipur," 47.

38. Muniru Ravanipur, "The Sad Story of Love," trans. Kamran Talattof, in *Persian Heritage* 3, no. 9 (spring, 1998), 36–37. This short story is the translation of Muniru Ravanipur, "Qisah-i Ghamangiz-i Ishq," in *Sangha-yi Shaytan* (Satan's Stone) (Tehran: Markaz, 1990): 29–34. This story and the collection is translated into English: "Love's Tragic Tale" in *Satan's Stones* by Moniru Ravanipur, ed., with an introduction by M. R. Ghanoonparvar and trans. Persis Karim, Atoosha Kourosh, Parichehr Moin, Dylan Oehler-Stricklin, Reza Shirazi, and Catherine Williamson (Austin: Univ. of Texas Press, 1996), 19–25.

39. Shahrnush Parsipur, *Zanan Bidun Mardan*, the book's second section on Mahdokht.

40. Parsipur, *Zanan Bidun Mardan*, 129.

41. Ravanipur, "The Sad Story of Love".

42. For more information, see Ja'far Sajadi, *Farhang-i Mua'rif-i Islami* (Dictionary of Islamic Sciences) (Tehran: Shirkat-i Mu'allifan va Mutarjiman, 1984).

43. For the story of Hallaj, see Farid al-Din Attar, *Mantiq al-Tayr. The Conference of the Birds*, trans., with an introduction, by Afkham Darbandi and Dick Davis (Harmondsworth, England: Penguin, 1984), or Farid al-Din 'Atar, *Tazkirat al-Awliya*, ed. Muhammad Isti'lami (Tehran: Zuvvar, 1967).

44. For more information, see M. R. Ghanoonparvar's introduction to Moniru Ravanipur's *Satan's Stones*, trans. by Karim et al.

45. Ahamad Karimi-Hakkak presented an analysis of the connection between this Woolfian metaphor and the theme of the novel in "The Alterity in the Subaltern: Two Recent Works by Two Iranian Woman Writers," presented at the annual meeting of the Middle Eastern Studies Association, 1994.

46. Ravanipur spent twenty months convincing the authorities to permit this book's third printing after it was discovered that it had violated "some" censorship restrictions. See Lazariyan, "Interview with Muniru Ravanipur," *Adinih*, 35 (Oct. 1990): 4, 47.

47. Both "Kanizu" and "A Long Night" are from this collection: Muniru Ravanipur, *Kanizu* (Tehran: Nilufar, 1991).

48. Ravanipur, Muniru. *Ahl-i Gharq* (Tehran: Khanah-i Aftab, 1989). *Ahl-i Gharq*, especially, draws upon the beliefs of the inhabitants of the southern coastal area. For an analysis of this work, see Nasrin Rahimieh, "Magical Realism in Moniru Ravanipur's *Ahl-e Gharq*," *Iranian Studies* 23, nos. 1–4, (1990): 61–75.

49. Faraj Sarkuhi, a male literary critic, believes that Ravanipur's *Ahl-i Gharq* is not a great success, yet he confesses that in it, "Women have principal roles. The portrayals are lively"; see Faraj Sarkuhi, "Dar Barih-i Ahl-i Gharq," *Adinih* 48 (Aug. 1970): 30–32.

50. In Western countries, however, feminism had existed as an articulated force since the nineteenth century. In some Middle Eastern countries such as Egypt and Turkey, the women's movement was part of the social fabric long before the 1980s. See Margot Badran, *Feminists, Islam, and Nation: Gender and the Making of Modern Egypt* (Princeton, N.J.: Princeton Univ. Press, 1995), and Nukhet Sirman, "Feminism in Turkey: A Short History," *New Perspectives on Turkey* 3, no. 1 (fall 1989): 1–35.

51. Nasir Hariri, *Hunar va Adabiyat-i Imruz* (Contemporary Art and Literature) (Babul: Kitabsara-yi Babul, 1987), 66.

52. Simin Danishvar, "A Letter to Readers," in *Danishvar's "Playhouse": A Collection of Stories*, trans. Maryam Mafi (Washington, D.C.: Mage, 1989), 154–70.

53. Danishvar, "A Letter to Readers," 156.

54. Ibid., 159.

55. Simin Danishvar, *Ghurub-i Jalal* (Tehran: Hadis-i Nafs, 1981), 13–19. The first section of the book was written before the Revolution but was not published until 1982. Thereafter, it has also been published by other publishers: Intisharat-i Ravaq, 1982 and Kitab-i Sadi, 1990.

56. Simin Danishvar, "Bih Ki Salam Kunam" (To Whom Can I Say Hello) in *Bih Ki Salam Kunam* (Tehran: Kharazmi, 1986), 82.

57. Compare the two versions of this short story in *Alifba* 2 (Oct. 1973): 142–51, and Simin Danishvar, *Bih Ki Salam Kunam,* 75–93, 84.

58. This poem was published in an anthology of women's poetry, *Zanan Surayandih* (Women Poets) (Washington, D.C.: Par Publishers, 1991), 28.

59. Simin Bihbahani, *An Mard, Mard-i Hamraham* (That Man, My Fellow Companion) (Tehran: Zavvar, 1990), 34.

60. Simin Bihbahani, "Finjan-i Shikastih," in *Dunya-yi Sukhan* (The World of Speech) 64 (June–July 1995): 72. For the English translation of this story, see Kamran Talattof "Bihbahani's 'The Broken Cup': A Window to the Past and Future," in *Iranian Studies* 30, nos. 3–4 (summer–fall 1997): 249–54.

61. Simin Bihbahani, *Guzinah-i Ashʿar* (A Selection of Poems) (Tehran: Intisharat-i Murvarid, 1988), 29.

62. Simin Bihbahani, *Yik Darichih-i Azadi* (A Window for Freedom) (Tehran: Intisharat-i Sukhan, 1995).

63. For information about this genre, see *Women's Autobiographies in Contemporary Iran,* ed. Afsanah Najmabadi (Cambridge, Mass.: Harvard Univ. Press, 1990). In one of the articles included in this book, William Hanaway states that the reason women did not write autobiographies even in the open decades of 1960s and 1970s was they never ceased to maintain their sense of boundaries, the dividing line between the public and the private. . . ." See William Hanaway, "Half-Voices: Persian Women's Lives and Letters" in Najmabadi, ed., *Women's Autobiographies,* 55–63.

64. Shahin Hannanih, *Pusht-i Darichah-ha: Guft Gu Ba Hamsaran-i Hunarmandan* (Behind the Windows: A Conversation with Artists' Spouses) (Tehran: Dunya-yi Madar, 1992).

65. Ibid., 6.

66. "Naqd-i Kitab Az *Pusht-i Panjiriha*" (A Book Review of Behind the Windows) *Adinih* 75 (Oct. 1992): 38.

67. Layla Gulistan, *Rabitih-i Shoma ba Mader Shoharetan Chetor Ast?* (How Are Your Relations with Your Mother-in-law?) *Adinih* 75 (Oct. 1992): 38–39.

68. "Zanan-i Hunarmandan" (Artists' Wives) *Adinih* 74 (Sept. 1992).

69. Faridih Gulbu's new best-selling novels include *Ba'd az Ishq* (After Love) (Tehran: Kitabsara, 1998); *Khusraw va Shirin: Dastani Bar Asas-i Manzumah-'i Nizami Ganjavi* (Khusraw and Shirin: A Story Based on Nizami Ganjavi's Poem) (Tehran: Kitabsara, 1997); *Hikayat-i Ruzgar* (The Story of Life) (Tehran: Rawshangaran, 1994); and Nasrin Samani's novels include *Arus-i Siyah Push* (A Bride in Black) (Tehran: Shirkat-i Nashr-i, 1986); *Ahang-i Judayi* (The Song of Separation) (Tehran: Intisharat Arghavan, 1995); *Akhirin Didar* (The Last Visit) (Tehran: Nashr-i Parya, 1994); *Asir-i Gham* (Captive of Sorrow) (Tehran: Arghavan, 1994); *Bazi-i Sarnivisht* (Games of Fate) (Tehran: Nashr-i Kitab, 1994); *Dar Justju-yi Ishq* (In Search of Love) (Tehran: Parya, 1994); *Dunya-yi Pur Umid* (A World Filled with Hope) (Tehran: Nashr-i Kitab, 1993); *Ghurub-i Arizu: 'Isyan* (The Sunset of Wishes: Rebellion) (Tehran: Intisharat-i Par, 1993); *Tandis-i Ishq* (Love's Image) (Tehran: Urdibihisht, 1993); *Shiftagan-i Mahabbat* (Infatuated with Compassion) (Tehran: Nazm, 1992).

70. Zahra Kadkhudaiyan, *Dukhtar-i Haji Agha* (Tehran: the author, 1991), 183.

71. Tahirih Aybud, "Bih Rang-i Khakistar" (In the Color of Ashes), in *Kitab-i Surush,* ed. Fraydun A. Khalili, Sayyd E. Nabavi, and Hassan Ahmadi (Surush's Book: A Collection of Short Stories) (Tehran: Surush, 1989), 84.

72. This severe economic crisis and high unemployment have given rise to polygamy and temporary marriages *(sighih)*.

73. Khatirah Hijazi, *Anduh-i Zan Budan* (Tehran: Rushangaran, 1992), 12.

74. Firishtah Sari, *Pizhvak-i Sukut* (The Echo of Silence) (Tehran: Bahman, 1989), 7.

75. Nizami Ganjavi, in *Haft Paykar* (Seven Beauties), ed. H. Vahid Dastgirdi (Tehran: Ibn-i Sina, 1955) and Abd al-Rahman Jami, in *Masnavi Haft Awrang* (Jami's Haft Awrang), ed. Mudarris Gilani (Tehran: Sa'di, 1958) especially employ this image in their poetry. For example, in Nizami's *Haft Paykar,* the story told by the Slavic princess "gah rokh buseh dad u gah labash / gah nārash gazid o gah rotabash" (Now he kissed her cheek, at times her lips; some times he tasted / her pomegranates [her breasts], and sometimes her dates [her lips]): Nizami, *Haft Paykar,* 233.

76. For information about these publications, see Hammed Shahidian, "Dushvariha-yi Nigarish-i Tarikh-i Zanan Dar Iran" (Difficulties with Women's Historiography in Iran), *Iran Nameh: A Persian Journal of Iranian Studies* 12; no. 1 (winter 1994): 81–128.

77. Banafshah Hijazi, *Zan Bih Zann-i Tarikh: Jaygah-i Zan dar Iran-i Bastan* (Women According to History: The Place of Women in Ancient Iran) (Tehran: Nashr-i Shahr-i Ab, 1991).

78. See, for example, the historian and researcher Mihrangiz Kar, *Firishtih-i Adalat va Parihha-yi Duzakh* (The Angel of Justice and Hell's Wings) (Tehran: Rushangaran, 1991), 7.

79. *Payam-i Zan* (Women's Message), *Zanan* (Women), *Zan-i Ruz* (Today's Woman), *Farzanah* (Learned, also a female name), *Payam-i Hajar* (Hagar's Message), *Mahjubih* (Modest), *Bultan-i Zanan* (Women's Bulletin), *Sunbulih* (Hyacinth), *Khanvadih* (Family), *Fazilat-i Khanvadah* (Family Virtue), *Payk-i Mama* (Mother's Messenger), *Vizhih Namah-i Daftar-i Umur-i Zanan* (Special Journal of the Office of Women's Affairs), *Sal Namah-i Zan* (Women's Annual), *Nida* (Voice), *Takapu-yi Banuvan* (Women's Search), and *Zan* (Women) are some of these journals. Iranian women also publish a daily newspaper that deals with women's issues. *Zan* wants to pursue a feminine perspective toward "women's problems" in an attempt to promote "women's social rights and to fill a vacuum" (*Zan*, Aug. 7, 1998).

80. In addition to self-expression through literature, women also resist the veil by such dangerous yet incredibly effective methods as wearing their scarves loosely, displaying stray locks, violating the conventional use of color, participating in the social arena, attending classes in higher education, and even holding clandestine fashion shows. For a report on the latter, see *Payam-i Imruz*, no. 6 (May-June 1995): 100.

6. Conclusion: Applicability of Episodic Literary Movement in Arabic and Turkish Literature

1. Mikhail Bakhtin, *Problems of Dostoevsky's Poetics*, ed. and trans. Caryl Emerson, with an introduction by Wayne Booth (Minneapolis: Univ. of Minnesota Press, 1984).

2. Identifying a dominant trend in each episode does not mean all works represent the dominant ideology. In both of these literatures, there are works that can be considered romantic, symbolic, social realistic, and even postmodern at different times. Moreover, some of the prominent writers, such as Najib Mahfuz, wrote in more than one episode and in an array of styles and modes.

3. For more information on the history of Arab modernity, see the works of Albert Hourani, especially *A History of the Arab Peoples* (Cambridge, Mass: Harvard Univ. Press, 1991), and the works of Bashru'i and Michael Naimah.

4. See Sabry Hafez, *The Genesis of Arabic Narrative Discourse: A Study in the Sociology of Modern Arabic Literature* (London: Saqi Books, 1993), 157–89.

5. Muhammad Husayn Haykal, *Zaynab* (Cairo: Dar al-Hilal, 1953).

6. For a general discussion of the rise of modern Arabic literature, see Edwar Kharrat, "The Mashriq," in *Modern Literature in the Near and Middle East, 1850–1970,* ed. Robin Ostle (London: Routledge, 1991), 181–92.

7. For more information on the development of modern Turkish literature, see Feyyaz Kayacan Fergar and Richard McKane, *Modern Turkish Poetry* (Ware, U.K.: Rockingham, 1992); Kemal Silay, *An Anthology of Turkish Literature* (Bloomington, Ind.: Indiana Univ. Press, 1996); Talat Sait Halman, *Contemporary Turkish Literature: Fiction and Poetry* (Rutherford, N.J.: Fairleigh Dickinson Univ. Press, 1982); Ahmet Omur Evin, *Origins and Development of the Turkish Novel* (Minneapolis, Minn.: Bibliotheca Islamica, 1983); and the works of Fahir Iz.

8. Sabry Hafez, *The Genesis of Arabic Narrative Discourse,* 85. For more information about the background of contemporary Arabic literature, see Roger Allen, *The Arabic Novel: An Historical and Critical Introduction* (Syracuse, N.Y.: Syracuse Univ. Press, 1982).

9. See Yashar Kemal, *Murder in the Ironsmiths Market* (The Lords of Akchasaz), trans. Thilda Kemal (London: Collins, 1979), and *Seagull,* trans. Thilda Kemal (New York: Pantheon, 1981).

10. Quoted in Emmanuel Sivan, *Radical Islam: Medieval Theology and Modern Politics* (New Haven, Conn.: Yale Univ. Press, 1990).

11. For more information on Arab women writers, see Joseph T. Zeidan, *Arab Women Novelists: The Formative Years and Beyond* (Albany: State Univ. of New York Press, 1995); and *Opening the Gates: A Century of Arab Feminist Writing,* ed. Margot Badran and Miriam Cooke (Bloomington: Indiana Univ. Press, 1990).

12. Abubaker Bagader, Ava M. Heinrichsdorff, and Deborah S. Akers, eds and trans. in their introduction to *Voices of Change: Short Stories by Saudi Arabian Women Writers.* (Boulder, Colo.: Lynne Rienner, 1998), 4.

13. *Twenty Stories by Turkish Women Writers* (Indiana University Turkish Studies joint series with the Ministry of Culture of the Turkish Republic, v. 8.), trans. Nilufer Reddy Mizanoglu (Bloomington, Ind.: Indiana Univ. Turkish Studies, 1988).

14. Nukhet Sirman, "Feminism in Turkey: A Short History," *New Perspectives on Turkey* 3, no. 1 (fall 1989): 1–35.

15. See Zehra Arat, "Turkish Women and the Republican Reconstruction," in *Reconstructing Gender in the Middle East,* ed. Fatma Muge Gocek and S. Balaghi (New York: Columbia Univ. Press, 1994), 57–81, and Kumari Jayawardena, *Feminism and Nationalism in the Third World* (London: Zed, 1986), 25–41.

16. See Sirman, "Feminism in Turkey," and Yesim Arat, "Women's Movement of the 1980s in Turkey: Radical Outcome of Liberal Kemalism?" in Gocek and Balaghi, *Reconstructing Gender*, 100–13.

17. Latife Tekin, *Berji Kristin: Tales from the Garbage Hills* (London and New York: Marion Boyars, 1993).

18. Nilufer Reddy Mizanoglu, *Twenty Stories by Turkish Women Writers.*

19. For more information on Turkish poetry, see Feyyaz Kayacan Fergar, *Modern Turkish Poetry* (Ware, U.K.: Rockingham Press, 1992).

Bibliography

Abidini, Hasan. *Sad Sal Dastan Navisi* (One Hundred Years of Fiction Writing). Tehran: Tundar, 1980.

Abrahamian, Ervand. *Iran Between Two Revolutions*. Princeton, N.J.: Princeton Univ. Press, 1982.

Afary, Janet. *The Iranian Constitutional Revolution, 1906–11*. New York: Columbia Univ. Press, 1996.

Afkhami, Mahnaz. "A Future in the Past: The Prerevolutionary Women's Movement in Iran," In *Sisterhood is Global: An International Women's Movement Anthology* edited by Robin Morgan. New York: Doubleday, 1984.

Afshar, Iraj. "Jariyanha-yi Adabi dar Majalat-i Farsi" (Literary Currents in Persian Journals). *Rahnama-yi Kitab* (A Guide to Books) 20, nos. 5–7 (summer 1977).

Ahmadi Oskuʾi, Marziyeh. *Khatirati az Yik Rafiq* (A Comrade's Memoir). Tehran: Sazman-e Chirikha-ye Fedai-e Khalq-e Iran (Organization of Iranian People's Fadaʾi Guerrillas) [OIPFG], n.d.

Ahmadzadih, Masud. *Mubarizih-i Musalahanih; Ham Stratigi, Ham Taktik* (Armed Struggle; Both Strategy and Tactic). Tehran: (OIPFG), 1969?

Al-i Ahmad, Jalal. *Arzyabi-i Shitabzadih* (A Quick Assessment). Tehran: Ibn-i Sina, 1965.

———. *Dar Khidmat va Khiyanat-i Rushanfikran*. (Concerning the Service and Betrayal of the Intellectuals). Tehran: Intisharat-i Khavarazmi, 1978.

———. *Gharbzadigi* (Plagued by the West). Tehran: Ravaq, 1978.

———. *Karnamah-i Sih Salih*. Tehran: Intisharat-i Ravaq, 1979.

———. *Mudir-i Madrisih*. (School Principle). Tehran: Amir Kabir, 1971.

———. *Sih Tar* (Seh Tar: Collection of Short Stories). Tehran: Amir Kabir, 1971.

Allen, Roger. *The Arabic Novel: An Historical and Critical Introduction*. Syracuse, N.Y.: Syracuse Univ. Press, 1982.

Anderson, Benedict. *Imagined Communities: Reflections on the Origin and Spread of Nationalism*. London: Verso, 1983.

Arat, Yesim. "Women's Movement of the 1980s in Turkey: Radical Outcome of Liberal Kemalism?" In Gocek, *Reconstructing Gender*, 100–13.

Arat, Zehra. "Turkish Women and the Republican Reconstruction." In *Recon-*

structing Gender in the Middle East, edited by Fatma Muge Gocek and S. Balaghi, 57–81. New York: Columbia Univ. Press, 1994.

Ariyanpur, Yahya. *Az Saba Ta Nima: Tarikh-i Sad u Panjah Sal Adab-i Farsi* (From Saba to Nima: One Hunderd Fifty Years History of Persian Literature). Saarbrucken, Germany: Intisharat-i Navid, 1988.

Assadipour, Bijan. (Bizhan Asadipur, Bidjan Assadipour). Editor of Special Issue of *Daftar-i Hunar* 2, no. 4 (Sept. 1995).

ʿAtaʿi, Janati. *Nima: Zindagani va Asar-i U* (Nima: His Life and His Work). Tehran: Safi Ali Shah, 1955.

ʿAttar, Farid al-Din. *Tazkirat al-Awliya* (Biography of Muslim Saints), edited by Muhammad Istiʿlami. Tehran: Zuvvar, 1967.

———. *Mantiq al-Tayr. The Conference of the Birds*. Translated, with an introduction, by Afkham Darbandi and Dick Davis. Harmondsworth, England: Penguin, 1984.

Aybud, Tahirah. "Bih Rang-i Khakistar" (In the Color of Ashes). In *Kitab-i Surush* (Surush's Book: A Collection of Short Stories), 81–82. Sayyd E. Navavi, and Hassan Ahmadi eds. Tehran: Surush, 1989.

Badran, Margot, and Miriam Cooke, eds. *Opening the Gates: A Century of Arab Feminist Writing*. Bloomington: Indiana Univ. Press, 1990.

———. *Feminists, Islam, and Nation: Gender and the Making of Modern Egypt*. Princeton, N.J.: Princeton Univ. Press, 1995.

Bagader, Abubaker, Ava M. Heinrichsdorff, and Deborah S. Akers, ed. and trans. *Voices of Change: Short Stories by Saudi Arabian Women Writers*. Boulder, Colo.: Lynne Rienner Publishers, 1998.

Bakhtin, Mikhail. *Problems of Dostoevsky's Poetics*. edited and translated by Caryl Emerson, with an introduction by Wayne Booth. Minneapolis, Minn.: Univ. of Minnesota Press, 1984.

———. "Toward a Methodology for the Human Sciences." In *Speech Genres and Other Late Essays*, translated by V. McGee and edited by Caryl Emerson and Michael Holquist. Austin: Univ. of Texas Press, 1986.

Balay, Christopher, and Michel Cuypers. *Sar Chesmihha-yi Dastan-i Kutah-i Farsi* (The Sources Persian Short Stories). Translated by Ahmad Karimi-Hakkak. Tehran: Papirus, 1987.

Barahani, Reza. *Junun-i Nivishtan* (The Madness of Writing) Tehran: Risam, 1989.

———. *Tala Dar Mis* (Gold in Copper). Tehran: Nashr-i Zaman, 1968.

———. "Tarikh Ulaviyatha-yi Adabi Ra Ja Bi Ja Kardah" (History Has Replaced Literary Priorities). *Adinih* (Friday) 42–43 (Mar. 1, 1992): 80.

———. *Tarikh-i Muzakkar: Farhang-i Hakim va Farhang-i Mahkum* (A Male History: The Dominant Culture and the Doomed One). Tehran: Nashr-i Avval, 1984.

Bashiri, Iraj. *The Fiction of Sadeq Hedayat*. Lexington, Ky.: Mazda Publishers, 1984.

Beard, Michael. *Hedayat's "Blind Owl" as a Western Novel*. Princeton, N.J.: Princeton Univ. Press, 1990.

———. "Sadeq Hedayat's "Composite Landscapes: Western Exposure." In *Persian Literature*, edited by Ehsan Yarshater. Albany, N.Y.: Bibliotheca Persica, 1988.

Bihbahani, Simin. *An Mard Mard-i Hamraham* (That Man, My Fellow Companion). Tehran: Zuvvar, 1990.

———. "Az Butih-i Khushbu-i Gulpar" (From the Good Smelling Marjoram). *Guzinah-i Ash'ar* (A Selection of Poems). Tehran: Intisharat-i Murvarid, 1988, 127.

———. "Finjan-i Shikastih" (Broken Cup). In *Dunya-yi Sukhan* (The World of Speech) 64 (June-July 1995): 72.

———. *Guzinah-i Ash'ar* (A Selection of Poems). Tehran: Intisharat-i Murvarid, 1988.

———. *Chilchiragh* (Chandelier) Fifth edition. Tehran: Zavvar, 1991.

———. *Jay-i pa* (The Footstep). Tehran: Zavvar, 1991.

———. *Marmar* (Marble). Tehran: Kitabfurushi Zavvar, 1967.

———. *Rastakhiz* (Resurrection). Tehran: Kitabfurushi-i Zavvar, 1983. Second edition of the poems written in the years between 1963 to 1973.

———. *Sih tar i Shikastih* (Broken Seh Tar). Tehran: Kitabfurushi Ilmi, 1951.

———. *Yik Darichih-i Azadi* (A Window to Freedom). Tehran: Intisharat-i Sukhan, 1995.

Bihrangi, Samad. *Mahi Siyah-i Kuchulu* (The Little Black Fish). Tehran: Nahsr-i Azad, n.d.

Bono, James. "Science, Discourse, and Literature: The Role/Rule of Metaphor in Science," edited by Stuart Peterfreund. In *Literature and Science*, 61–62. Boston: Northeastern Univ. Press, 1990.

Browne, Edward G. *The Press and Poetry of Modern Persia*. Los Angeles: Kalimat, 1983.

Chubak, Sadiq. *Tangsir*. Lus Anjilis, Amrika: Shirkat-i Kitab, 1990.

Cixous, Hélène. "The Laugh of the Medusa." In *New French Feminisms*, edited by Elaine Marks and Isabelle de Courtivron. New York: Schocken, 1981.

Clinton, Jerome W. "Al-i Ahmad." In *Encyclopedia Iranica*, edited by Ehsan Yarshater, vol. 1, 745–47. London: Routledge and Kegan Paul, 1984.

Cole, Juan and Nikki Keddie, eds. *Shi'ism and Social Protest*. New Haven, Conn.: Yale Univ. Press, 1986.

Dabashi, Hamid. "Hijab-i Chihrih-i Jan: Bih Justju-yi Zari dar Savushun-i Simin Danishvar." *Nimeye Digar* 8 (fall 1987): 65–118.

———. "The Poetics of Politics: Commitment in Modern Persian Literature." *Iranian Studies* 18, nos. 2–4, (spring–autumn 1985): 147–88.

Daftar-i Sanduq-i Kudakan (Office of the Children's Fund). *Fihrist-i Mushtarak-i Kitabha* (A Common Bibliography). Tehran: Sanduq-i Kudikan-i, 1994.

Danishvar, Simin. *Atash-i Khamush* (The Quenched Fire). Tehran: n.p., 1948.

———. *Bih Ki Salam Kunam* (To Whom Can I Say Hello). Tehran: Kharazmi, 1986.

————. "Bih Ki Salam Kunam." (To Whom Can I Say Hello) *Alifba* 2 (Oct. 1973): 142–51.

————. *Danishvar's "Playhouse": A Collection of Stories*. Translated by Maryam Mafi, Washington, D.C.: Mage Publishers, 1989.

————. *Ghurub-i Jalal*. Tehran: Hadis-i Nafs, 1981.

————. *Savushun*. Tehran: Kharazmi, 1978.

————. *Savushun: A Novel About Modern Iran*. Translated from the Persian by M. R. Ghanoonparvar, with an introduction by Brian Spooner. Washington, D.C.: Mage Publishers, 1990.

————. *Savushun, A Persian Requiem: A Novel by Simin Daneshvar*. Translated by Roxane Zand. London: P. Halban, 1991.

Daraghi, Haideh. "The Shaping of the Modern Persian Short Story: Jamlzadih's [Jamalzadeh's] Preface to *Yiki Bud, Yiki Nabud*." In *Critical Perspectives on Modern Persian Literature*, edited by Thomas Ricks. 104–23. Washington D.C.: Three Continents Press, 1984.

Dastghayb, A. A. *Nima Yushij: Naqd va Barrasi* (Nima Yushij: Criticism and Analysis). Tehran: Pazand, n.d.

————. *Sayih Rushan-i Shiʿr-i Farsi* (Light and Shade of Persian Poetry). Tehran: Farhang, 1969.

Davani, Ali. *Dastanha-yi Islami* (Islamic Stories). Tehran: Intishar, 1960.

Davaran, Fereshteh. "Dar Talash-i Kasb-i Huviyat." *Nimeye Digar* 8 (fall 1987), 140–166.

Davis, Frederick Hadland. *Myths and Legends of Japan*. London: George G. Harrap, 1912.

Dawlatabadi, Mahmud. *Ma Niz Mardumi Hastim* (We Are People Too). Tehran: Nashr-i Parsi, 1989.

Dawlatabadi, Yahyah. *Shahrnaz*. Tehran: n.p. 1925.

Derrida, Jacques. *Grammatology*. Translated by G. Spivak. Baltimore: Johns Hopkins Univ. Press, 1976.

Dihqani, Ashraf. *Hamasih-i Muqavamat* (The Epic of Resistance). Tehran: Junbish, 1978.

Eagleton, Terry. *Ideology: An Introduction*. London: Verso, 1991.

————. *The Ideology of the Aesthetic*. Oxford, England: Basil Blackwell, 1991.

————. *Marxism and Literary Criticism*. Los Angeles: Univ. of California Press, 1976.

Emerson, Caryl. Introduction to *Bakhtin in Contexts: Across the Disciplines*, edited by Amy Mandelker. Evanston, Ill.: Northwestern Univ. Press, 1995.

Evin, Ahmet Omur. *Origins and Development of the Turkish Novel*. Minneapolis, Minn.: Bibliotheca Islamica, 1983.

Fadainia, Safar. *Shir-i Junbish-i Nuvin: Inqilab dar Shir-i Muasir* (The Poetry of the New Movement: Revolution in Contemporary Poetry). Tehran: Intisharat-i Tus, n.d.

Falaki, Mahmud. *Nigahi Bih Nima* (A Look at Nima). Tehran: Intisharat-i Murvarid, 1994.

Farkhal, Riza. *Ah Istanbul va Shish Dastan-i Digar* (Oh Istanbul and Six Other Short Stories). Tehran: Intisharat-i Isparak, 1989.

Farrukhzad, Furugh. *Asir* (Captive). Tehran: Amir Kabir, 1955.

———. (Forugh Farrokhzad) *Bride of Acacias: Selected Poems of Forugh Farrokhzad.* Translated by Jascha Kessler, with Amin Banani. Delmar, N.Y.: Caravan Books, 1982.

———. "Delam Baray-e Baghcheh Misuzad" (I Pity the Garden). In *Furugh Farrukhzad: Shiʿr-i Furugh Farrukhzad,* edited by Muhammadd Huquqi, 280–86. Tehran: Intisharat-i Nigah, 1993.

———. *Divan-i Ashʿar* (Collected Poems). Tehran: Murvarid, 1995.

———. *Guzinah-i Ashʿar* (A Selection of Poems). Tehran: Murvarid, 1985.

Fergar, Feyyaz Kayacan, and Richard McKane. *Modern Turkish Poetry.* Ware, U.K.: Rockingham Press, 1992.

Field, Claude. *Persian Literature.* London: Herbert & Daniel, 1912.

Fischer, Ernest. *Zarurat-i Hunar dar Ravand-i Takamul-i Ijtimaʿi* (The Necessity of Art, a Marxist Approach). Translated by Firuz Shirvanlu. Tehran: Intisharat-i Tus, 1969.

Foucault, Michel. *The Order of Things; An Archeology of the Human Sciences.* New York: Vintage, 1973.

Garcia Marquez, Gabriel. *One Hundred Years of Solitude.* Translated from the Spanish by Gregory Rabassa. London: J. Cape, 1991.

Geertz, Clifford. *The Interpretation of Cultures.* New York: Basic Books, 1973.

Ghanoonparvar, M. R. *Prophets of Doom: Literature as a Socio-Political Phenomenon in Iran.* Lanham, Md.: Univ. Press of America, 1984.

Gheissari, Ali. "Naqd-i Adab-i Idiulugik" (A Review of Ideological Literature). *Iran Nameh: A Persian Journal of Iranian Studies* 12 (spring 1994): 233–58.

Givihchiyan, Fatamah. "Sang-i Zirin-i Asiyab: Zan Ya Mard?" (The Milestone: Woman or Man?). *Falsnamah-i Ilami-Pazhuhishi Mutaliʿat-i Barnamah Rizi*s (Studies and Research in Planning Quarterly) 3 (spring 1995).

Goldschmidt, Arthur. *A Concise History of the Middle East.* Boulder, Colo.: Westview, 1983.

Green, John. "The Modern Persian Short Story 1921–1981: A Bio-Bibliographic Survey." Ph.D. diss., University of Michigan, 1987.

Gulistan, Layla. "Rabitih-i Shuma ba Madar Buzurgitan Chetur Ast?" (How Are Your Relations with Your Mother-in-law?). *Adinih* (Friday) 75 (Oct. 1992): 38–39.

Gulshiri, Hushang. "Arusak-i Chini-i Man" (My China Doll). In *Hamyan-i Sitarigan,* edited by M. Khalili and M. Falah Gari. 613–24. Tehran: Hush Va Ibtikar, 1992.

Gulsurkhi, Khusraw. *Nawgaraʾi Va Haqiqat-i Khaki* (Modernity and the Earthly Reality). Tehran: Murvarid, 1979.

———. *Siyasat-i hunar, Siasat-i Sh^cir* (The Politics of Art, the Politics of Poetics). Tehran: Murvarid, 1965?

Gurgin, Iraj. *Chahar Musahibih Ba Furugh Farrukhzad* (Four Interviews with Furugh Farrukhzad). Tehran: Intisharat-i Radio Iran, 1964.

Gurgin, Taymur. "Ru-yi Telex." In *Farhang-i Shairan-i Jang va Muqavimat* (An Anthology of War and Resistance Poetry), edited by Muhamad Baqir Najafzadih Barfurush, 265. Tehran: Kayhan, 1993.

Ha'iri, Ali. *Zihniyat Va Zaviyih-i Did Dar Naqd Va Naqd-i Adabiyat-i Dastani: Naqdi Bar, Sad Sal Dastan Nivisi-i Iran* (Mentality and Points of View in the Criticism and Analysis of Fiction: A Review of One Hundred Years of Fiction Writing). Tehran: Kubah, 1990.

Hafez, Sabry. *The Genesis of Arabic Narrative Discourse: A Study in the Sociology of Modern Arabic Literature.* London: Saqi Books, 1993.

Hajj Sayyid Jaradi, Fattanih. *Bamdad-i Khumar* (Half-drunk Morning) Tehran: Nashr-i Alburz, 1992 .

Hakimi, Muhammad Riza. *Adabiyat va Ta^cahud dar Islam.* (Literature and Commitment in Islam). Tehran: Daftar-i Nashr-i Farhang-i Islami (Office of Publications of Islamic Culture), 1979.

Halman, Talat Sait. *Contemporary Turkish Literature: Fiction and Poetry.* Rutherford, N.J.: Fairleigh Dickinson University Press, 1982.

Hanaway, William. "Half-Voices: Persian Women's Lives and Letters." In *Women's Autobiographies in Contemporary Iran,* edited by Afsaneh Najmabadi. Cambridge, Mass.: Harvard Univ. Press, 1990: 55–63.

Hannanih, Shahin. *Pusht-i Darichah-ha: Guft Gu Ba Hamsaran-i Hunarmandan* (Behind the Windows: A Conversation with Artists' Spouses). Tehran: Dunya-yi Madar, 1992.

Hariri, Nasir. *Dar Barih-i Hunar va Adabiyat: Guft u Shanudi ba Ahmad Shamlu* (On Art and Literature: A Talk with Ahmad Shamlu). Tehran: Avishan and Guharzad, 1993.

———. *Hunar va Adabiyat-i Imruz* (Contemporary Art and Literature). Babul: Kitabsara-yi Babul, 1987.

Herrmann, Anne. *The Dialogic and Difference: "An/other Woman" in Virginia Woolf and Christa Wolf.* New York: Columbia Univ. Press, 1989.

Hidayat, Sadiq. [Hedayat, Sadeq]. *Afsanah-i Afarinish: Khaymah Shab Bazi dar Sih Pardah* (The Myth of Creation: A Puppet Show in Three Acts). Encino, Calif.: Ketab Corp., 1980.

———. *"Blind Owl" and Other Hedayat Stories.* Compiled by Carol L. Sayers. Edited by Russell P. Christensen. Minneapolis, Minn.: Sorayya Publishers, 1984.

———. *Buf-i kur* (Blind Owl). Tehran: Sina, 1952?

———. *Navishtahha-yi Parakandah.* (Scattered Writings) Stockholm: Arash, 1990.

———. *Sih Qatrah Khun* (Three Drops of Blood). Tehran: Parastu, 1965.

———. "Urashima." *Majallah-i Sukhan* (The Journal of Discourse) 92, no. 1 (Dec. 1994): 43–45.

Hijazi, Banafshah. *Zan Bih Zann-i Tarikh: Jaygah-i Zan dar Iran-i Bastan* (Women According to History: The Place of Women in Ancient Iran). Tehran: Nashr-i Shahr-i Ab, 1991.

Hijazi, Khatirah. *Anduh-i Zan Budan* (The Sorrow of Being a Woman). Tehran: Rushangiran, 1992.

Hillmann, Michael C. *Hidayat's "The Blind Owl" Forty Years After*. Austin: Univ. of Texas Press, 1978.

———. *A Lonely Woman: Furugh Farrukhzad and Her Poetry*. Washington, D.C.: Three Continents and Mage Publishers, 1987.

Hizar Khani, Manuchinr. "Jahan Bini-i Mahi Siyah-i Kuchulu." Tehran: n.p., n.d.

Holquist, Michael. Introduction to *The Dialogic Imagination: Four Essays by M. M. Bakhtin*. Austin: Univ. of Texas Press, 1992.

Hooglund, Eric and Mary Hooglund. *"The Little Black Fish" and Other Modern Persian Stories*. Washington, D.C.: Three Continents, 1976.

Hourani, Albert. *A History of the Arab Peoples*. Cambridge, Mass.: Harvard Univ. Press, 1991.

Huquqi, Muhammad. *Shiᶜr va Shaᶜiran* (Poetry and Poets). Tehran: Nigah, 1989.

———, ed. *Shiᶜr-i Naw az Aghaz ta Imruz* (New Poetry from Beginning to Present). Tehran: Ravayat, 1992.

Imami, Karim. "Bazar-i Garm-i Ruman va Khanumha-yi Ruman Khan." *Adinih* (Friday) 44 (Mar. 20, 1992), 70.

Islamic Republic of Iran. "Qanun-i Mujazat-i Islami, Majmuah-i Qavanin-i Sal-i 1370" (Islamic Criminal Law, Listing of the Laws for the Year 1991). *Ruznamah-i Rasmi* (The Government's Official Newsletter) (summer 1992), 593–654.

Jaᶜfari, Muhammad Taqi. *Nigahi Bih Falsafah-ʾi Hunar Az Didgah-i Islami* (A Look at Art Philosophy From the Islamic Viewpoint). Tehran: Intisharat-i Nur, 1982.

Jaffe, Audrey. "Spectacular Sympathy: Visuality and Ideology in Dickens's *A Christmas Carol*." *PMLA* 109, no. 2 (Mar. 1994): 254–65.

Jakobson, Roman, and Morris Halle. *Fundamentals of Language, Two Aspects of Language and Two Types of Aphasic Disturbances*. The Hague: Mouton, 1956.

Jamalzadih [Jamalzadeh], Muhammad Ali. "Farsi Shikkar Ast" (Persian Is Sugar), In *Panj Shulih-i Javidan* (Five Eternal Flames), edited by F. Kar. 281–90. Tehran: Gutanbirg, 1954.

———. *Once Upon a Time*. Translated by Heshmat Moayyad and Paul Sprachman. New York: Bibliotheca Persica, 1985.

James, Grace. *"Green Willow" and Other Japanese Fairy Tales*. London: MacMillan, 1910.

Jami, Abd al-Rahman. *Masnavi Haft Awrang* (Jami's Haft Awrang). Edited by
    Mudarris Gilani. Tehran: Sa'di, 1958.
Janati Atai, A. *Nima Yushij: Zandigi Va Asar-i U* (Nima Yushij: His Life and His
    Poetry). Tehran: Safi Ali Shah, 1955.
Jayawardena, Kumari. *Feminism and Nationalism in the Third World*. London:
    Zed Books, 1986.
Jeffreys, Mark. "Ideologies of Lyric: A Problem of Genre in Contemporary
    Anglophone Poetics." *PMLA* 110, no. 2 (Mar. 1995): 196–205.
Jula'i, Riza. *Shab-i Zulmani Yalda va Hadis-i Durd Kishan* (The Dark Long Win-
    ter Night and the Tale of the Dregs of Wine Drinkers). Tehran: Nashr-i
    Alburz, 1970.
Kadkhudaiyan, Zahra. *Dukhtar-i Haji Agha* (Haji Agha's Daughter). Tehran: the
    author, 1991.
Kamshad, Hassan. *Modern Persian Prose Literature*. Bethesda, Md.: Iranbooks,
    1996.
Kar, Mihrangiz. *Firishtih-i Adalat va Parihha-yi Duzakh* (The Angel of Justice and
    Hell's Wings). Tehran: Rushangran, 1991.
Karimi-Hakkak, Ahmad. "The Alterity in the Subaltern: Two Recent Works by
    Two Iranian Woman Writers." Paper presented at the annual meeting of
    the Middle Eastern Studies Association, Phoenix, Arizona, November
    19–22, 1994.
———. *An Anthology of Modern Persian Poetry*. Boulder, Colo.: Westview, 1978.
———. "Censorship." In *Encyclopaedia Iranica*, vol. 5, ed. Ehasan Yarshater,
    135–142. Costa Mesa, Calif.: Mazda Publishers.
———. "From Translation to Appropriation: Poetic Cross-Breeding in Early
    Twentieth-Century Iran." *Comparative Literature* 47 (winter 1995): 53–78.
———. "Introduction to Modern Persian Poetry." In *Critical Perspectives on
    Modern Persian Literature*, edited by Thomas M. Ricks. Washington, D.C.:
    Three Continents, 1984.
———. "Poetry Against Piety: The Literary Response to the Iranian Revolu-
    tion." *World Literature Today* 60, no. 2 (spring 1986): 251–56.
———. *Recasting Persian Poetry: Scenarios of Poetic Modernity in Iran*. Salt Lake
    City: Univ. of Utah Press, 1995.
Kashani, Mushfiq. *Majmuʿah-i Shiʿr-i Jang* (An Anthology of Poems on War).
    Tehran: Amir Kabir, 1987.
———. *Sugnamah-'i Imam*. Tehran: Surush, 1980.
Kasrai, Siyavush. "Dar Tamam-i Tul-i Shab." In *Namah-i Shura-yi Navisandigan
    va Hunarmandan-i Iran* 2 (winter 1980): 114–33.
Kasravi, Ahmad. *Dar Piramun-i Adabiyat*. Bethesda, Md.: Kitabfurushi-i Iran, 1991.
Katouzian, Homa. *Sadeq Hedayat: The Life and Literature of an Iranian Writer*. New
    York: I.B. Tauris, 1991.

Kemal, Yashar. *Murder in the Ironsmiths Market* (The Lords of Akchasaz). Translated by Thilda Kemal. London: Collins, 1979.

———. *Seagull*. Translated by Thilda Kemal. New York: Pantheon, 1981.

Khanlari, Parviz. "Jidal Ba Muda'i." *Sukhan* 21, no. 6 (Jan. 1971).

Kharrat, Edwar. "The Mashriq." In *Modern Literature in the Near and Middle East, 1850–1970*, edited by Robin Ostle, 180–92. London: Routledge, 1991.

Khavhiran, V. *Fihrist-i Mawzu'i-i Kutub va Maqalat dar Barih-i Zan* (A Subject Index for Books and Articles about Women). Tehran: Idarah-i Kull-i Intisharat, 1984.

Khaza'ifar, Ali, trans. *Inqilab-i Islami dar Shi'r-i Sha'iran.* / *Poetry of the Islamic Revolution*. Mashad: Astan-i Quds-i Razavi, 1986.

Khudayi, Ali. *Az Miyan-i Shishih, az Miyan-i Mih: Majmuah-i Dastan* (Through the Glass, Through the Fog: A Short Story Collection). Tehran: Khudayi, 1991.

Kritzeck, James. *Anthology of Islamic Literature*. New York: Holt, Rinehart & Winston, 1964.

———. *Modern Islamic Literature*. New York: Holt, Rinehart & Winston, 1970.

Lambton, Ann K. S. *Qajar Persia: Eleven Studies*. London: I. B. Tauris, 1987.

Lazariyan, Janet. "Musahibih Ba Muniru Ravanipur" (An Interview with Muniru Ravanipur). *Adinih* (Friday) 35, no. 4 (Oct. 1990): 4, 47.

Lenin, V. I. *Collected Works*. Vol. 10, [English edition.] Moscow: Foreign Languages Publishing House, 1962.

Lnagrudi, Shams. *Qasidih-i Labkhand-Chak Chak.* (Ode of the Ruptured Smile). Tehran: Nashr-i Markaz, 1990.

Ma'rufi, Abbas. *Sanfuni-i Murdagan.* (Symphony of the Dead). Tehran: Nashr-i Gardun, 1989.

Makhmalbaf, Muhsin. *Gung-i Khvabdidih* (The Sleeping Mute). Vol. 1. Tehran: Nashr-i Nay, 1994.

Mao Tse-tung. *Talks at the Yenoan Forum on Literature and Art*. Peking, China: Peking Foreign Languages Press, 1967.

Marcuse, Herbert. *The Aesthetic Dimension*. Boston: Beacon Press, 1977.

Milani, Farzaneh. *Veils and Words: The Emerging Voices of Iranian Women Writers*. Syracuse, N.Y.: Syracuse Univ. Press, 1992.

———, ed. Special issue on Simin Bihbahani. *Nimeye Digar* 2 (autumn 1993).

Mirmudarris, Musa. "Risalat-i Hunar" (The Mission of Art). *Mahnamah-i Pasdar-i Islam* (The Guardian of Islam, a Monthly Journal) 164 (Aug.–Sep. 1995): 16–20.

Mirza, Iraj. *Divan-i Kamil-i Iraj Mirza* (Complete Works of Iraj Mirza). Edited by Muhammad Jafar Mahjub. Van Nuys, Calif.: Shirkat-i Kitab, 1989.

Mirza, Jalal al-Din. *Namih-yi Khusrauvan* (The Book of the Greats). Tehran: n.p., n.d.

Miskub, Shahrukh. "Afsanah-i Tabiat" (Nature's Myth). *Kilk* (Pen) 35–36 (Jan.–Feb. 1974): 22–51.

———. *Huviyat-i Irani va Zaban-i Farsi* (The National Iranian Identity and the Persian Language). Tehran: Intisharat-i Bagh-i Ainih, 1994.

Miyanduabi, Y. "Maqtal" (A Place of Slaughter). In *Khanvadah-i Ma,* 9–41. Tehran: Kitab-i Javanan, 1989.

Mizani, F., and A. Muhit. *Shir bih Daqiqih-i Aknun* (Poetry in This Minute). Tehran: Nuqrih, 1988.

Moaddel, Mansoor. *Class, Politics, and Ideology in the Iranian Revolution.* New York: Columbia Univ. Press, 1993.

———. "Ideology as Episodic Discourse: The Case of The Iranian Revolution." *American Sociological Review* 57 (June. 1992): 353–79.

———. "The Social Bases and Discursive Context of the Rise of Islamic Fundamentalism: The Case of Iran and Syria." *Sociological Inquiry* 66 (Aug. 1996).

———. and Kamran Talattof. *Contemporary Debates in Islam: An Anthology of Modernist and Fundamentalist Thought.* New York: St. Martin's, 1999.

Moayyad, Heshmat, and Paul Sprachaman, trans. *Mohammad Ali Jamalzadih: Once Upon a Time.* New York: Bibliotheca Persica, 1985.

Mohandessi, Manoutchehr. "Hedayat and Rilke." In *Critical Perspectives on Modern Persian Literature.* Edited by Thomas M. Ricks. 258–65. Washington, D.C.: Three Continents, 1984.

Momen, Moojan. *An Introduction to Shiʿi Islam.* New Haven, Conn.: Yale Univ. Press, 1985.

Moses, C. *French Feminism in the Nineteenth Century.* Albany: State Univ. of New York Press, 1984.

Muʿazin, Nasir. *Dah Shab: Shabha-yi Shairan va Navisandigan dar Anjuman-i Farhangi-i Iran va Alman* (Ten Nights: Poets' and Writers' Evenings in the Irano-German Cultural Society). Tehran: Amir Kabir, 1979.

Muhammadi, M. *Tahlili ba Inqilab-i Islami* (An Analysis of the Islamic Revolution). Tehran: Amir Kabir, 1986.

Muhmudzadih, Nusrat Allah. *Marsiah Halabchih* (The Elegy of Halabchih). Tehran: Raja, 1989.

Musadiq, Hamid. "Abi, Khakistari, Siyah" (Blue, Gray, Black). In *Shi'r-i Naw az Aghaz ta Imruz,* edited by Muhammad Huquqi. Tehran: Ravayat, 1992.

Musavi Garmarudi, Ali. "Man Shiʿr-i Shiʿiam" ("I Am Shiite Poetry"). In *Inqilab-i Islami dar Shi'r-i Sha'iran* (Poetry of the Islamic Revolution), translated by Ali Khazaʾi, 11–13. Mashad: Astan-i Quds-i Razavi, 1986.

Mushfiq Kazimi, Murtaza. *Tehran-i Makhuf* (Frightening Tehran). 6th ed. Tehran: Arghnun, 1968.

Mushiri, Faridun. *Barguzidih-i Ashʿar* (Selected Poems). Tehran: Bamdad, 1987.

Mutahari, Murtiza. *Dastan-i Rastan* (The Story of the Virtuous). Tehran: Muhammadi, 1963.

Naficy, Majid. *Modernism and Ideology in Persian Literature*. Lanham, Md.: Univ. Press of America, 1997.

Nahzat-i Azadi. *Asnad-i Nahzat-i Azadi: Jariyan Tasis va Bayaniyaha* (The Documents of the Freedom Movement: Its Process of Establishment and Its Announcements). Tehran: Nahzat, 1982.

Najjar, Orayb Aref. "The Editorial Family of al-Kateb Bows in Respect: The Construction of Martyrdom Text Genre in One Palestinian Political and Literary Magazine." *Discourse and Society* 7, no. 4 (Oct. 1996): 499–530.

Najmabadi, Afsaneh, ed. *Women's Autobiographies in Contemporary Iran*. Cambridge, Mass.: Harvard Univ. Press, 1990.

Nakhustin Kungirih-i Navisandigan-i Iran (The First Iranian Writers' Congress). *Maqalat va Ashᶜar-i Nakhustin Kungirah-i Navisandigan-i Iran* (Proceedings of the First Iranian Writers' Congress). Tehran: Farabi Publishers, 1947.

Nashat, Guity. *Women and Revolution in Iran*. Boulder, Colo.: Westview, 1983.

Nizami Ganjavi, Iliyas Yusuf. *Haft Paykar* (Seven Beauties). Edited by Vahid Dastgirdi (Tehran: Ibn-i Sina, 1955).

Nuqrih Kar, Masud. "Chihrih-i Hirayt Angiz-i Taᶜahud" (The Astonishing Face of Commitment). *Arash* 57 (Aug.–Sept. 1996): 26–28.

Nuri-Ala, Ismail. *Tiuri-i Shiᶜr: Az Muj i Naw ta Shiᶜr-i Ishq* (The Theory of Poetry: From the New Wave to Love Poetry). London: Ghazal Publications, 1994.

Nurizad, Muhammad. *Mard Va Karbala* (The Man and Karbala). Tehran: Ministry of Islamic Culture and Guidance, 1990.

Pahlavi, M. Reza. *Inqilab-i Safid* (The White Revolution) Tehran: Kitabkhanih-i Saltanati, 1967.

———. *Mamuriyyat Bara-yi Vatanam* (A Mission For My Country). Tehran: Kitabkhanih-i Saltanati, 1962.

———. *Pasukh Bih Tarikh* (A Response to History). Tehran: Kitabkhanih-i Saltanati, 1980.

Parsa, Misagh. *Social Origins of the Iranian Revolution*. New Brunswick, N.J.: Rutgers Univ. Press, 1989.

Parsay, Farrkhru, H. Ahi, and M. Taliqani. *Zan Dar Iran-i Bastan* (Women in Ancient Iran). Tehran: Jamiyat-i Zanan-i Danishgahi, 1967.

Parsipur, Shahrnush. *Adab-i Chai dar Huzur-i Gurg* (Tea Ceremony in the Presence of a Wolf). San Diego, Calif.: Nashr-i Zamanih; Los Angeles: Tasvir, 1993.

———. *Khatirat-i Zindan* (Prison Memoirs). Sponga, Sweden: Baran, 1996.

———. *Sag va Zimistan-i Buland* (The Dog and the Long Winter). Tehran: Amir Kabir, 1976.

———. *Tuba va Maᶜna-yi Shab* (Tuba and the Meaning of the Night). Tehran: Isparak, 1989.

———. *Women Without Men*. Translated by Kamran Talattof and Jocelyn Sharlet. New York: Syracuse Univ. Press, 1998.

————. *Zanan Bidun-i Mardan* (Women Without Men). Tehran: Nuqrah, 1990.

Partaw, Shin. *Baziha-yi Masti* (Games of Drunkenness). Tehran: Ilmi, 1946.

Parvin, Fazl Allah. *Ziba⁀i va Hunar* (Aesthetic and Art). Tehran: n.p., 1966.

Pazhvak, Nahid A. *Shab-i Sarab* (The Night of the Mirage) Rasht: Hidayat, 1998.

Ra⁀di Azarakhshi, Gholam Ali. "Shi⁀r-i Mua⁀sir-i Iran" (Contemporary Iranian Poetry). In *Yaghma* 21, no. 1 Dec. 1967.

————. "Shi⁀r-i Farsi-yi Mu⁀asir" (Contemporary Persian Poetry). In *Sukhan-raniha-yi Nakhustin Kungarih-i Shi⁀r Dar Iran* (Proceedings of the First Congress on Persian Poetry—Tehran, 1968). Tehran: Farhang va Hunar, 1960.

Raffat, Donne. *The Prison Papers of Bozorg Alavi: A Literary Odyssey*. Syracuse, N.Y.: Syracuse Univ. Press, 1985.

Rafi, Jalal. "Tarha va Musavabat-i Farhangi" (Cultural Projects and Bylaws). *Adabistan* 54 (June 1994): 34–36.

Rahimieh, Nasrin. "A Systemic Approach to Modern Persian Prose Fiction." *World Literature Today* 63, no. 1, (winter 1989): 15–19.

————. "The Enigma of Persian Modernism." *New Comparison* 13 (spring 1992): 39–45.

————. "Magical Realism in Moniru Ravanipur's *Ahl-e Gharq*." *Iranian Studies* 23, nos.1–4, (1990): 61–75.

Ramon, Nithal. "Profile: Gholam Hoseyn Sa⁀idi." *Index on Censorship* 7, no. 1 (1978).

Ravanipur, Muniru. *Ahl-i gharq*. Tehran: Khanah-i Aftab, 1989.

————. *Kanizu*. Tehran: Nilufar, 1991.

————. *Sangha-yi Shaytan*, 29–34. Tehran: Markaz, 1990.

————. (Ravanipur, Moniru). *Satan's Stones*. Edited with an introduction by M. R. Ghanoonparvar. Translated by Persis Karim, Atoosha Kourosh, Parichehr Moin, Dylan Oehler-Stricklin, Reza Shirazi, and Catherine Williamson. Austin: Univ. of Texas Press, 1996.

————. "The Sad Story of Love." Translated by Kamran Talattof, *Persian Heritage* 3, no. 9 (spring 1998): 36–37.

Rawshangar, Majid. *Az Nima Ta Ba⁀d*. Tehran: Murvarid, 1984.

Ra⁀yat, Maryam, et al. *Maqalah Namah-i Zan* (Women's Article Index) Tehran: Pazhuhishha-yi Farhangi, 1989.

Reddy, Nilufer Mizanoglu, trans. *Twenty stories by Turkish Women Writers*. (Indiana University Turkish Studies joint series with the Ministry of Culture of the Turkish Republic, v. 8). Bloomington, Ind.: Indiana Univ. Turkish Studies, 1988.

Ricks, Thomas M. ed. *Critical Perspectives on Modern Persian Literature*. Washington, D.C.: Three Continents, 1984.

Robinson, Forrest G. "The New Historicism and the Old West." *Western American Literature* 25, no. 2, (Aug. 1990): 103–23.

Russel, D. A., and M. Winterbottom, eds. *Classical Literary Criticism*. Oxford: Oxford Univ. Press, 1989.

Saad, Joya. *The Image of Arabs in Modern Persian Literature.* Lanham, Md.: Univ. Press of America, 1996.

Sadr Hashimi, Muhammad. *Tarikh-i jaraʾid va majallat-i Iran* (The History of Iranian Newspaper and Magazines). Isfahan: Kamal, 1985.

Saffarzadih, Tahirih. "Chahar Rah i Shahadat" (The Roads of Martyrdom). In *Inqilab-i Islami dar Shiʾr-i Shaʾiran* (Poetry of The Islamic Revolution), tranlated by Ali Khazifar, 62–67. Mashad: Astan-i Quds-i Razavi,1986.

———. (Tahereh Saffarzadeh). "Fath Kamil Nist" (Victory Is Not Complete). In *Selected Poems,* a bilingual edition translated by M. H. Kamyabee and N. Mirkiani. Shiraz, Iran: Navid, 1987.

Said, Edward W. "Opponents, Audiences, Constituencies, and Communities." *Critical Inquiry* 9 (Sept. 1982): 1–26.

Saʿidi, Ghulam Husayn. *Azadaran-i Bayal* (Bayal's Mourners). Tehran: Intisharat-i Agah, 1978.

———. *Dandil: Stories from Iranian Life.* Translated by Robert Campbell, Hasan Javadi, and Julie Scott Meisami. New York: Random House, 1981.

Sajadi, Jaʿfar. *Farhang-i Muaʿrif-i Islami* (Dictionary of Islamic Sciences). Tehran: Shirkat-i Muʿallifan va Mutarjiman, 1984.

Samani, Nasrin. *Guli dar Shurihzari* (A Flower in a Salt-marsh). Tehran: Kitab-i Afarin, 1992.

Sandler, Rivanne. "Literary Developments in Iran in the 1960s and the 1970s Prior to the 1979 Revolution." *World Literature Today* 60, no. 2 (spring 1986): 246–51.

Sari, Firishtah. *Pizhvak-i Sukut* (The Echo of Silence). Tehran: Bahman, 1989.

Sarkuhi, Faraj. "Dar Barih-i Ahl-i Gharq." *Adinih* (Friday) 48 (Aug. 1970): 30–32.

Sartre, Jean-Paul. *Quʾest-ce que la litterature?* Paris: Gallimard, 1948.

———. *What Is Literature?* London: Methuen, 1950.

Saussure, Ferdinand de. *Course in General Linguistics.* New York: McGraw-Hill, 1964.

Sazman-i Chirikha-yi Fadaʾi Khalq-i Iran. *Islahat-i Arzi va Natayij-i Mustaqim-i An* (Land Reform and Its Direct Impact). Tehran: OIPFG, 1974.

Seki, Keigo, ed. *Folktales of Japan.* Chicago: Univ. of Chicago Press, 1963.

Shahani, Khusraw. "Murdih Kishi" (Pallbearing). *Adam-i Avazi: Majmuah-i Panzdah Dastan.* Tehran: Kitabha-yi Parastu, 1975.

Shahidian, Hammed. "Dushvariha-yi Nigarish-i Tarikh-i Zanan Dar Iran" (Difficulties with Women's Historiography in Iran). *Iran Nameh: A Persian Journal of Iranian Studies* 12, no. 1 (winter 1994): 81–128.

———. "The Iranian Left and the 'Woman Question' in the Revolution of 1978–79." *International Journal of Middle East Studies* 2, no. 26 (May 1994): 223–47.

Shamlu, Ahmad. "Bagh-i Ainah" (The Garden of Mirrors). In *Sida-yi Shiʿr-i Imruz* (The Voice of Today's Poetry), edited by Bahman Mahabadi, 84–86. Tabriz: Talash, 1989.

————. "Shi'ri Kih Zingist" (Poetry That Is Live). Majid Rawshangar, *Az Nima Ta Ba'd* (From Nima Onward), 46–54. Tehran: Murvarid, 1968.

Shirazi, Hamdi. *Funun va Anvaᶜi Shiᶜr-i Farsi.* (Techniques and Types of Persian Poetry). Tehran: Bita, 1972.

Showalter, Elaine. "A Literature of Their Own." In *Feminist Literary Theory: A Reader,* edited by Mary Eagleton. Oxford: Basil Blackwell, 1986.

Shujai, Mihdi. "Zarih-i Cheshmha-yi Tu" (The Shrine of Your Eyes). In *Majmuah Qisah* (A Collection of Short Stories). Tehran: Surush, 1985.

Silay, Kemal. *An Anthology of Turkish Literature.* Bloomington, Ind.: Indiana Univ. Press, 1996.

Sinfield, Alan. *Faultlines: Cultural Materialism and the Politics of Dissident Reading.* Berkeley: Univ. of California Press, 1992.

Sipanlu, Muhammad Ali, ed. *Baz Afarini-i Vaqiᶜiyat: Bist u Haft Qisah az Bist u Haft Nivisandah Muᶜasir-i Iran* (The Interpretation of the Reality: Twenty Seven Short Stories by Twenty-Seven Contemporary Iranian Writers). Tehran: Nigah, 1988.

Sirman, Nukhet. "Feminism in Turkey: A Short History." *New Perspectives on Turkey* 3, no. 1 (fall 1989): 1–35.

Sivan, Emmanuel. *Radical Islam: Medieval Theology and Modern Politics.* New Haven, Conn.: Yale Univ. Press, 1990.

Sokoloff, Naomi B., Anne Lapidus Lerner, and Anita Norich, eds. *Gender and Text in Modern Hebrew and Yiddish Literature.* New York: Jewish Theological Seminary, 1991.

Spivak, Gayatri Chakravorty. "The Politics of Interpretations." *Critical Inquiry* 9 (Sept. 1982): 259–78.

Sultanpur, Said. *Nuᶜi az Hunar, Nuᶜi az Andishih* (A Type of Art, a Type of Thinking). Tehran: n.p., 1960.

Tabari, Azar, and N. Yaganeh. *In the Shadow of Islam: The Women's Movement in Iran.* London: Zed Press, 1982.

Tahbaz, Sirus. *Hizar Sal Shᶜir-i Farsi: Az Rudaki Ta Nima Yushij* (One Thousand Years of Persian Poetry: From Rudaki to Nima Yushij). Tehran: Kanun-i Parvarish-i Fikri-i Kudakan Va Nujavanan, 1986.

————. *Majmuah Kamil-i Ashᶜar-i Nima Yushij: Farsi Va Tabari* (The Anthology of Nima Yushij). Tehran: Intisharat-i Nigah, 1971.

Takhayuri, Nasrin. "Mukhataban Jiditar va ᶜAmiqtar az Intizar." *Adinih* (Friday) 44 (Mar. 20, 1992).

Talattof, Kamran. "Bihbahani's 'The Broken Cup': A Window to the Past and Future." *Iranian Studies* 30, nos. 3–4 (summer–fall 1997): 249–54.

————. "The Changing Mode of Relationship Between Modern Persian Literature and Islam: Karbala in Fiction." In *The Postcolonial Crescent: Islam's Impact on Contemporary Literature,* edited by John Hawley. New York: Peter Lang, 1998: 249–66.

———. Introduction to *Women Without Men: A Novella,* by Shahrnush Parsipur, translated by Kamran Talattof and Jocelyn Sharlet. New York: Syracuse Univ. Press, 1998.

———. "Iranian Women's Literature: From Pre-revolutionary Social Discourse to Postrevolutionary Feminism." *International Journal of Middle East Studies* 29, no. 4 (Nov. 1997): 531–58.

Taraqi, Guli. Interview in *Adinih: Vizhah-i Guft-i Gu,* (Friday: A Special Interview Issue). (Aug. 1993): 61–66.

Tekin, Latife. *Berji Kristin: Tales from the Garbage Hills.* London: Marion Boyars, 1993.

Tierney-Tello, Mary Beth. *Allegories of Transgression and Transformation: Experimental Fiction by Women Writing Under Dictatorship* (New York: State Univ. of New York Press, 1996).

Tufan, Masud. "The Secret of the Name Nima." *Takapu* 9 (Apr. 1994): 10–12.

Voloshinov, V. N. *Marxism and the Philosophy of Language.* Cambridge, Mass.: Harvard Univ. Press, 1986.

Yarshater, Ehsan. "The Development of Iranian Literatures." In *Persian Literature,* edited by Ehsan Yarshater. Albany, N.Y.: Bibliotheca Persica, 1988: 3–37.

———. "The Modern Literary Idiom (1920s-1960)." In Ricks, *Critical Perspectives on Modern Persian Literature,* 42–62.

———. ed. *Persian Literature.* Albany, N.Y.: Bibliotheca Persica, 1988.

———. ed. *Sadeq Hedayat: An Anthology.* Boulder, Colo.: Westview, 1979.

Yushij, Nima. *Arzish-i Ihsasat va Panj Maqalih-i Digar* ("The Value of Feelings" and Five Other Articles on Literary Criticism). Tehran: Zindigi, 1972.

———. *Barguzidih-i Ash'ar* (Selected Works). Tehran: Kitabha-yi Jibi, 1963.

———. *Harfha-yi Hamsayih* (The Neighbor's Word). Tehran: Intisharat-i Dunya, 1984.

Zarrinkub, A. H. *Du Qarn Sukut* (Two Centuries of Silence). Tehran: Amir Kabir, 1958.

Zeidan, Joseph T. *Arab Women Novelists: The Formative Years and Beyond.* Albany: State Univ. of New York Press, 1995.

Index